A PHILOSOPHY OF MIZVOT

A PHILOSOPHY OF MIZVOT

The Religious-Ethical Concepts Of Judaism,
Their Roots In Biblical Law
And The Oral Tradition

by

GERSION APPEL

Ktav Publishing House, Inc.
NEW YORK

Library of Congress Cataloging in Publication Data

Appel, Gersion.
A philosophy of mizvot: the religious-ethical concepts
of Judaism.

Includes bibliographical references.
1. Commandments (Judaism) 2. Ethics, Jewish.
3. Aaron, ha-Levi, of Barcelona, 13th cent. Sefer ha-hinukh.
I. Title.
BM520.7.A65   296.3   75-1226
ISBN 0-87068-250-4

MANUFACTURED IN THE UNITED STATES OF AMERICA

CONTENTS

אשת חיל עטרת בעלה

TO

MIRIAM

Acknowledgment

The author gratefully acknowledges permission to reprint his article entitled "A Rational Conception of Mitzvot" from the *Samuel K. Mirsky Memorial Volume: Studies in Jewish Law, Philosophy and Literature,* Gersion Appel, editor; published by Sura Institute for Research, Jerusalem, and Yeshiva University, New York 1970.

PREFACE

The *Sefer ha-Hinnuk* has long been recognized as one of the principal, medieval works in Jewish ethical and halakic literature, and as a primary source for an investigation of the meaning and the purpose of the mizvot. Notwithstanding this, there has been no systematic study, either in Hebrew or in English, of the Hinnuk's ethical and religious philosophy, nor has there been a definitive evaluation of his contribution to the search for *ta'amei ha-mizvot,* the reasons for the commandments, to which Jewish philosophers have been committed in every age.

This book seeks to fill this need, and also to relate the Hinnuk to the philosophical schools and the intellectual currents of Jewish thought which preceded him. In this respect, it is devoted not only to a study of the Hinnuk, but to a broader exploration of the main concepts of Jewish ethical and religious philosophy.

The Hinnuk emerges from this study as a towering figure in Jewish scholarship and, more significantly, as a great educator and moral and religious guide. His classic work is revealed as a treasure-trove of Jewish knowledge, moral insights, religious inspiration, and brilliant perceptions in the molding of human character.

This book is arranged as follows:

The Introduction attempts concisely to define the nature of mizvot and to indicate the necessary relationship between the mizvot, the Halakah and Jewish philosophy. Chapter I is a brief, historical survey of the subject of *ta'amei ha-mizvot,* and serves as an introduction to the Hinnuk's work in this field. Chapters II through X are a study of the Hinnuk's exposition of the mizvot and his views in the areas of Jewish ethics and Jewish religious philosophy. Chapters XI and XII are an evaluation of the Hinnuk's thesis, and include, as well, a discourse on new perspectives and directions that may prove productive in a further investigation of the subject. The Excursus concerns itself with the Hinnuk's sources and the problem of authorship.

Notes have been placed at the end of the book to allow for continuity of presentation, and are designed to provide documentation and references to relevant sources, as well as additional pertinent information and discussion. They are intended not only for the scholar, but also for the general reader who desires to follow the discourse on a deeper level. The appended index of biblical, talmudic and rabbinic references, the index of mizvot and the index of subjects are intended to serve a similar purpose.

The mizvot are numbered according to the standard, printed editions of the *Sefer ha-Hinnuk,* which follow the scriptural sequence. Quotations from the *Sefer ha-Hinnuk* have been translated by me from the Hebrew original. Translations of other Hebrew texts, while also mine, generally conform to the standard translations.

The central thesis of this book was first developed as a doctoral dissertation, submitted to Harvard University, under the sponsorship of the late Professor Harry Austryn Wolfson, to whom I am greatly indebted for direction and guidance in the preparation of the dissertation.

I am especially grateful to Professor Isadore Twersky, Professor of Hebrew Literature and Philosophy at Harvard University, for his critical evaluations and for his numerous suggestions regarding both the substance and the structure of the manuscript.

I wish to express to Dr. Samuel Belkin, President of Yeshiva University, my sincere and deepfelt appreciation of his abiding friendship and encouragement of my scholarly endeavors while at Yeshiva. To Professor David Mirsky, Dean of Stern College, I extend my warm thanks for his valued advice and kind assistance and for his intellectual companionship over the years.

To my dear wife, Miriam, to whom this volume is dedicated, my gratitude is boundless for her love and devotion, and her understanding and cheerful help in the course of my work on this and other scholarly pursuits. I pray that we may be blessed "to see our children and children's children occupied with Torah and mizvot."

I write these concluding lines in the *sheloshim* period of mourning, following the untimely passing of my beloved sister, Ruth, on the ninth of Elul, 5734. May the memory of her good life and righteous deeds be a consolation to her family and an everlasting blessing.

Gersion Appel

September 5, 1974

A PHILOSOPHY OF MIZVOT

INTRODUCTION

THE MIZVOT: THEIR NATURE AND IMPORT
IN JEWISH PHILOSOPHY

THE NATURE OF THE MIZVOT

The basic elements of Jewish law, covering the full range of human experience, are the mizvot, the commandments of God. Ethical norms and religious concepts are, in Judaism, given concrete expression through the mizvot of the Torah, by means of which the Jewish ideal of morality and its commitment of faith are translated into the reality of life.

As formulated by the Halakah, the commandments are the divine blueprint for the ideal life. They constitute a divinely-ordered discipline for man's existence, cultivating his ethical concerns for his fellowman and directing his spiritual life in the service of God. Whether of a positive nature, decreeing action, or of a negative nature, prohibiting certain acts or enjoining self-control, they encompass every aspect of life, both the sacred and the secular, the private interests of the individual and the public interests of society.

The mizvah has validity, essentially, as a divinely revealed command, its sanction and ultimate origin traceable to a transcendent Being. An apprehension of its fundamentally theonomous nature is reflected in the maxim which accords the highest value to the mizvah performed *lishmah,* that is, for the love of God, because it is God's commandment.[1]

The revealed laws, both written and oral, form the basis of the eternal covenant. Thus, the Bible states, "These are the statutes and ordinances and laws which the Lord made between Him and the children of Israel in Mount Sinai by the hand of Moses" (Leviticus

3

26:46).[2] In its response to the divine command, which is in essence God's call to man, Israel is drawn into an intimate relationship with God in a community of existence which, in the biblical tradition, may be characterized as the "covenanted faith community."[3]

The mizvot thus impart a religious dimension to life. By performing the mizvot in obedience to divine command, man is able to relate to God and to serve Him. Through the involvement of the whole of his physical and intellectual being, of his material and spiritual nature, they afford him the means of attaining an awareness of living continually in the presence of God.

THE ROLE OF MIZVOT IN A PHILOSOPHY OF JUDAISM

Viewed conceptually, in their elemental sense as defined above, the mizvot are fundamental constructs in building an ideology or a philosophy of Judaism. Whether we deal with mizvot which address themselves to man's spiritual needs, determining the bounds of faith and the nature of his relationship with God, or with mizvot oriented toward the attainment of *kedushah* and designed to concretize the ethical ideals of justice and righteousness, they embody the decisive expression of Judaism on the level of religious commitment and human endeavor. Viewed nomistically within their halakic frame, a view presaged by the Hinnuk, the mizvot are the key to a true conception of Judaism, both as regards its religious tenets and its ethical norms.

An ethical and religious philosophy of Judaism cannot be developed independent of the commandments as set forth in the Torah and subsequently structured in the Halakah. It is not at all possible to approach the world of Jewish ideas without first entering into the pulsating world of Jewish life, which is the domain of the mizvot and of Jewish Law. The failure to recognize the essential link between Jewish philosophy and the Halakah which has directed and molded Jewish life and Jewish thought through the ages has been a prime factor in the inadequacy of philosophies formulated in the past.[4]

An authentic philosophy of Judaism must be grounded in the

mizvot and in Jewish Law. For a full and proper comprehension of the teachings of Judaism as they bear upon its theology and its philosophical view of man and the world, such a philosophy must be as conversant with Halakah as with Aggadah, drawing upon the traditional sources as represented in biblical, midrashic, talmudic and rabbinical literature.[5]

When viewed from this perspective, the Hinnuk's exposition of the mizvot constitutes a unique contribution to Jewish thought. By establishing an integral relationship between the halakic and the conceptual elements of the mizvot, and by revealing their ethical, religious and philosophical meaning, the Hinnuk has delineated a philosophy of mizvot, an essential component in a philosophy of Halakah, as the basis for the development of a truly indigenous philosophy of Judaism.

In investigating the reasons of the commandments, to assure their observance by demonstrating that there is purpose to the divine laws, the Hinnuk was in the classic, traditional mold, yet responsive as well to the religious needs and intellectual concerns that recurrently manifest themselves in Jewish life. His approach to *ta'amei ha-mizvot* is distinctive and of profound importance in charting new directions and foretokening broader dimensions to this vital, yet controversial, area of inquiry.

Finally, the Halakah, as a system of law, is predicated upon a chain of authority that is ultimately derived from the Torah. In this respect, the mizvah is the focal point of contact between the Oral Law and the Written Law in the continuum of the halakic process. In tracing the mizvot to their scriptural origin and further outlining the law as determined in Halakah, the Hinnuk affirms the continuity and the structural integrity of the halakic process, preserving in form and in substance the organic unity represented by the Halakah.

CHAPTER ONE

THE QUEST FOR THE MEANING OF MIZVOT

THE RABBINIC TRADITION

Hukim and Mishpatim

The biblical designation of the commandments as *hukim*, statutes, and *mishpatim*, ordinances, is presumed by rabbinic tradition to indicate a distinction between statutory laws divinely revealed to Israel, and laws that commend themselves to reason and are universally recognized as just and righteous. This classification of mizvot is already evident in the very first commandments given to Israel following the departure from Egypt. Referring to Israel's sojourn at Marah on their way to Mount Sinai, Scripture states, "There He made for them a statute (*hok*) and an ordinance (*mishpat*)" (Exodus 15:25).[1] The Rabbis believed that at Marah the people were given certain fundamental laws corresponding essentially to the distinction indicated. According to the opinions expressed in the Mekilta[2] *hok* refers either to the Sabbath or to forbidden relations,[3] while *mishpat* refers either to honoring parents or to laws of damages and fines.[4]

A more definitive characterization is given by the Rabbis in the Talmud[5] in their exposition of the verse "Mine ordinances shall ye do and my statutes shall ye keep, to walk therein; I am the Lord your God" (Leviticus 18:4). They expound the verse as follows: " 'Mine ordinances shall ye do'—things which were they not written, it would be necessary to write them, such as, the prohibition of idolatry, forbidden relations, murder, robbery, and blasphemy. 'My statutes shall ye keep' —things which Satan repudiates,[6] such as, the prohibition of eating swine, the prohibition of wearing a mixture of wool and linen, the

7

rite of *halizah* in the case of a *yebamah,* i.e. the widow of a brother who died without offspring (Deuteronomy 25:5-10), purification of the leper, and the rite of the scapegoat.[7] Lest you say that the latter are worthless observances, Scripture states, 'I am the Lord'—I the Lord have decreed and you are not permitted to criticize them."[8]

The rabbinic characterization of *hukim* and *mishpatim* is generally followed by the biblical exegetes. Thus Rashi[9] defines *mishpatim* as precepts "prescribed in the Torah which are in conformity with justice, such as ought to be ordained if they had not already been ordained by the Torah." *Hukim* are "decrees of the King against which the evil inclination raises objections: 'why should we observe them?' and against which also the nations of the world raise objections."

Theonomous Character of Mizvot

The distinction drawn by the Sages between *hukim* and *mishpatim* intimates the tension between the seeming irrationality of the former to man, who must nonetheless submit to the yoke of the commandments, and their rationality from the standpoint of the divine lawgiver. The mizvot were nevertheless given for the benefit of man, as indicated in the Bible[10] and attested by the Rabbis.[11] Although some of them, such as the *hukim,* may prove to be inexplicable and incomprehensible to man, their reasons are certainly known to God. Thus, while the tenor of certain rabbinic statements would appear to emphasize the irrational character of the commandments, we yet perceive a recognition by the Sages of the essential rationality of the *mishpatim,* from the perspective of man, and the presumed supra-rational nature of those designated as *hukim,* from the standpoint of God.

Judaism perceives the prime significance of the commandments to stem from their essentially theonomous character. This is to be seen from the statement of the Rabbis, "Greater is the one who performs the mizvah when he is commanded, than the one who performs it though he is not commanded."[12] The Rabbis thus stress the need for man's observance of the commandments, especially the *hukim,* in conscious submission to divine authority, rather than in response to an intuitive, autonomous sense of duty or inclination. Noteworthy in this connection is the rabbinic directive that a man should not say, "I have no desire to eat swine's flesh, I have no desire to enter into a forbidden marriage," but he should say, "I do indeed want to, but what can I do since my Father in heaven has imposed these decrees upon me." [13] The commandments are thus theonomous, all of them having been divinely ordained.

Rabbinic Exposition of Biblical Laws

Rabbinical literature contains a number of statements in which the Sages apparently ascribe motives and reasons for the commandments.[14] Some of these ascriptions are in essence symbolic interpretations of the precepts, such as the allegorical treatment of the four species on Sukkot recorded in the Midrash.[15] Some point up the practical benefits which derive from the mizvot, as in the law requiring abstention from marital relations during the menstrual period, where the stated motive is, "so that she be as beloved to her husband as at the time that she entered under the bridal canopy." [16] Others are of a religious-historical significance, such as the commandments commemorating the Sabbath and the Holy Days. We may note in particular the reasons given by Rabban Gamliel for the Passover sacrifice, the *mazah,* and the *maror.*[17]

There are mizvot which the Rabbis view from an ethical perspective. A striking example of this is the moral lesson on the evil of slander which they draw from the biblical characterization of the leper.[18] Especially illustrative are the moral reflections of R. Yohanan ben Zakkai on the slave whose ear is bored as a mark of servitude. "What is the reason that the ear had to be pierced rather than any other limb? The ear which heard on Mount Sinai, 'Thou shalt not steal,' and yet its owner went and stole and was therefore sold as a slave, let it be pierced. Or, in the case of him who sold himself the reason is: the ear which heard on Mount Sinai, 'For unto Me the children of Israel are servants' and he went and procured for himself another master, let it be pierced." [19] Rabbi Simeon, who is often said to have expounded the reasons of the scriptural texts, is similarly quoted as having given the law an ethical signification.[20] The laws regarding multiple restitution in certain instances of theft are the occasion for ethical reflections in the same vein by R. Meir and by R. Yohanan ben Zakkai.[21]

Notwithstanding the above, the Rabbis were at pains to emphasize that any inquiry as to the reason for a mizvah dare not overlook its fundamental, mandatory character. Thus, to the question posed in the Talmud, "Why do we blow the *shofar* on Rosh Hashanah?", the initial, incisive response is, "Why do we blow it? Because God commanded 'Blow the *shofar*'." [22] The Rabbis did not endeavor to develop a systematic rationale of the mizvot. They focused upon a select number, highlighting certain of their aspects, in order to impart some moral lesson or spiritual concept. Their objective was clearly educational; their method, an exposition of scriptural laws and texts, rather than a deliberate inquiry into the rational basis of mizvot. Basically, however, the Rabbis took a pragmatic view of the commandments. Not the *midrash*, the conceptualization of the mizvah, was of the essence, but the deed, the practical observance. This was manifestly in accord with their overall educational philosophy. Moreover, and more importantly, it was in consonance with their ultimate conception of mizvot as expressions of the divine will.

TA'AMEI HA-MIZVOT

The characterization of the mizvot, thus generally outlined in Scripture and further delineated by the Sages, was reflected subsequently in Jewish religious philosophy, consequent upon a continuing search for the meaning and the purpose of the mizvot.[23]

Allegorical Interpretation of the Laws

The first of the Jewish philosophers to expound the meaning and moral significance of the scriptural laws was Philo Judaeus of Alexandria.[24] Philo interprets many of the laws allegorically in accordance with his general assumption that biblical texts have both a literal or obvious meaning and an underlying or symbolic meaning. Apart from their intrinsic value and importance as divine ordinances, the biblical laws, Philo believes, have an intellectual or moral purpose.

Philo was evidently prompted by a desire to reveal Judaism to the world as possessing an ideal law capable of implanting the highest standard of virtue among the Jewish people. He therefore classifies the laws according to the cardinal virtues which they impart. These are, first, intellectual or contemplative virtues, which foster correct opinions concerning God and promote the service of God, and, second, moral virtues, such as justice and philanthropy, which he also characterizes as the virtue of humanity. Among the practical moral laws he includes those which he regards as a divine discipline designed to teach moderation and self-restraint.

The Law of Moses, Philo maintained, is the ideal law sought after by the philosophers, since the laws of the Torah are in perfect accord with nature and inculcate the highest virtues upon which the ideal law must be based.

Rational and Revealed Laws

Saadiah Gaon was the first of the medieval Jewish philosophers to classify the mizvot as rational and revealed laws, a distinction basically similar to the biblical designation of *hukim* and *mishpatim* as understood by the Rabbis.[25] The rational laws are essentially ethical commandments recognized and approved by reason. Though the approval or disapproval of these laws is implanted in the mind, they are nonetheless part of the scriptural revelation because reason would suggest only general principles; revelation provided detailed instruction and practical guidance. The revealed laws are traditional commandments of a ritualistic and ceremonial nature imposed by divine command and made manifest to man solely through revelation. Saadiah describes the revealed laws as consisting of acts which, from the standpoint of reason, would be optional, but which have been enjoined by the Law and thus demonstrate submissiveness to God.

All of the commandments, rational and revealed alike, become intelligible when they are examined in the light of knowledge drawn from the three bases of our religion, namely Scripture, reason, and tradition. The revealed laws are not merely arbitrary but have a rational basis. Though the chief reason for the observance of these precepts is that they represent the will of God, most of them can be shown to have some purpose, although the wisdom and the view that the Creator had in mind in decreeing them is beyond the grasp of men. Significantly, although he legitimates an allegorical interpretation when it is designed to bring Scripture into harmony with either reason or tradition, Saadiah pointedly takes note of the limits to be imposed upon the allegorical method relative to the mizvot.[26]

While Saadiah underscores the theonomous nature of the commandments, his characterization of a portion of them as rational and his endeavor to ascertain a utilitarian basis even for the revealed laws would indicate a desire to impart to them an autonomous character as well, insofar as the mizvot find their substantiation in reason by which man is fully capable of apprehending ultimate truth.

Saadiah's distinction between rational and revealed laws was generally accepted, with some modifications, by succeeding Jewish philosophers, such as Bahya Ibn Pakuda, Judah Halevi, Abraham Ibn Ezra, Abraham Ibn Daud and Maimonides, even as his conception of the fundamental relationship between reason and revelation dominated medieval Jewish as well as scholastic philosophy.

The Rationalist View

The clearest enunciation of the rationalist view of the mizvot is made by Maimonides in his philosophical work, *The Guide of the Perplexed.*[27] "All of us," Maimonides states, "the common people as well as the scholars, believe that there is a reason for every precept, although there are commandments the reason of which is unknown to us, and in which the ways of God's wisdom are incomprehensible."[28]

Maimonides explains that the apparently irrational nature of the latter precepts is only from the perspective of man. "Our Sages generally do not think that such precepts have no cause whatever and serve no purpose; for this would lead us to assume that God's actions are purposeless. On the contrary, they hold that even these precepts have a cause and are certainly intended for some use, although it is not known to us, owing either to the deficiency of our knowledge or the weakness of our intellect. Consequently there is a cause for every commandment; every positive or negative precept serves a useful object."[29]

From the perspective of the divine lawgiver, then, all of the miz-vot are rational. This view is, in the opinion of Maimonides, dis-tinctly expressed in Scripture, when it speaks of "righteous statutes and judgments" (Deuteronomy 4:8). The rational character of the mizvot, he points out, nevertheless does not render them autonomous. To contend that they are purposeful is not to say that they originated in human reason. They are heteronomous laws of divine origin, ful-filling a divinely ordained purpose.[30]

Following the traditional classification of the mizvot, Maimonides defines *mishpatim* as commandments whose object and reason are generally known and whose beneficial effects are evident, while *hukim* are those whose object and reason are not generally known. Were the latter not enjoined by God, human reason would not dic-tate their observance.[31] In his *Shemonah Perakim*[32] he further dis-tinguishes between the rational and the revealed laws. Among the former he includes laws against murder, theft, fraud and the like. Of the revealed laws he cites the prohibitions of boiling meat and milk together, wearing garments of wool and linen, forbidden rela-tions,[33] and the rites of the red heifer and the scapegoat.[34]

A significant ethical distinction is drawn by Maimonides between these two kinds of laws in respect of the motives involved in their observance. An inclination to transgress the rational laws, which are in accord with a universal human conception of right and wrong, is certainly contemptible. One who is free of such evil inclination, but is rather moved by an innate moral consciousness, is deemed by all, both the philosophers and the Sages, to be superior. With regard to the revealed laws, on the other hand, the exercise of self-restraint and control of one's personal desires in complying with them, as the Sages point out, is indicative of the higher virtue. For Maimonides, then, the *hukim* exemplify most clearly the divine imperative and truly reflect the submission of man's own will and inclination to the will of God.[35]

Comprehension of the purpose of the commandments, of the di-vine wisdom and goodness underlying them, by means of rational reflection and investigation, is a major task which man, possessed of the intellectual capacity for apprehension of the ways of God, must set for himself. "For those who observe the nature of the universe and the commandments of the Law, and know their purpose, see clearly God's mercy and truth in everything; they seek therefore that which the Creator intended to be the aim of man, namely, comprehension." [36]

The Twofold Objective of the Torah

The final purpose of the divine law, as Maimonides conceives it, is the establishment of a social order based upon justice and righteousness, which will make possible the ethical, spiritual, and intellectual perfection of man. The scriptural laws, along with the narrative portions of the Bible, are to be viewed teleologically as serving a general objective. This object of the Torah is of a twofold nature, namely, the well-being or perfection of the soul and the well-being or perfection of the body. The latter, while "anterior in nature and time" and a pre-condition for attaining the former, is yet secondary to perfection of the soul which is "superior in kind and is alone the source of eternal life." [37]

The well-being of the body is achieved by fostering good morals and peaceful relations among men, and by establishing a just society. The well-being of the soul is attained by training in faith and by imparting true opinions. Maimonides will be seen as basically in agreement with the philosophical tradition regarding moral and intellectual virtue, and the asserted superiority of intellectual perfection.[38] Moreover, the laws, which are of divine origin and designed for man's well-being in a well-ordered society, are equally in consonance with nature, as they are in accord with reason.[39] Indeed the ideal condition for man in human society is achieved through the divine law, precisely because it manifests divine wisdom and is concerned not alone with his material, but also his intellectual and spiritual well-being.

Maimonides concludes his remarks preliminary to his exposition of the mizvot by stating, "I am prepared to tell you my explanation of all these commandments and to assign for them a true reason supported by proof, with the exception of some minor rules and of a few commandments." [40] Accordingly, he groups the divine commandments into fourteen classes for the purpose of philosophical inquiry.[41] In his investigation of the mizvot and explanation of their meanings, he advances varied reasons. Some laws are plainly of a moral nature, while others, in keeping with the general objective of the Law, namely a just society, are of an ethical, social character. He also takes into consideration the utility and the beneficial physical and spiritual effects of certain laws. Many of the commandments are of a historical, religious import, designed to invoke a constant awareness of God.

Maimonides endeavors to show that certain of the precepts, especially of the *hukim,* are intended to prevent idolatry, to guard against its false doctrines, and to uproot its heathen practices. In a summary of his views on these laws, he states, "Most of the statutes (*hukim*), the reason of which is unknown to us, serve as a fence against idolatry." [42] Even the sacrifices offered in the course of the divine service were instituted to serve this objective as well, that is to keep the Israelites from idolatrous worship and to establish the true faith.[43]

It would appear from Maimonides' exposition of the mizvot that, while his methodology is essentially a rationalistic one, which he readily applies to rational laws, he is reluctant to apply it to revealed laws unless he has either internal scriptural evidence or convincing external evidence to support it. This may explain his admission of his inability to offer reasons for several of the commandments.[44] It is noteworthy that Maimonides, likewise, does not accord universal acceptance to the aggadic and midrashic explanations advanced by the Rabbis in connection with certain mizvot. He views such interpretations as being generally of a metaphorical, moralistic, or pedagogical nature; instructive, to be sure, but not necessarily reflective of the essential reasons.[45] For Maimonides the reasons for the commandments must be scripturally or historically validated, and ultimately they must accord with reason itself.

The Fundamentalist View

The endeavor to probe for *ta'amei ha-mizvot,* although given such great impetus by Maimonides, and consistently pursued by the most authoritative figures in Jewish religious philosophy, did not however meet with universal acceptance and approval. It was initially in halakic circles, generally unsympathetic to the incursion of philosophy into matters of religion, that resistance arose.

While the opposition regarding the quest for *ta'amei ha-mizvot* encompassed the whole range of commandments, it was primarily in respect of ascribing reasons for the *hukim,* whatever their precise connotation,[46] that the lines were sharply drawn. The fundamentalist view was clearly articulated by Rashi, who firmly maintained that *hukim* are laws "for which there are no apparent reasons, but which are the King's decrees and enactments imposed on His subjects." [47]

Rashi is most explicit as to the theonomous nature of these laws, as can be seen particularly in his commentary on a verse in Proverbs, where it is clearly evident that he is stating his own view. In his exegesis of the verse, "It is the glory of God to conceal a thing; but the glory of kings is to search out a matter" (Proverbs 25:2), Rashi comments: "When you expound regarding the honor of kings or the honor of Sages, who have made hedges for the Torah and promulgated decrees, you are to investigate and inquire and seek reasons. However, when you will expound on matters of theosophy or cosmogony, and on the statutes that are written in the Torah, namely *hukim,* things which Satan denounces and repudiates, such as the prohibition of eating swine, of mixing diverse kinds, and of wearing a mixture of wool and linen, you must not investigate but you should rather conceal and say it is a decree of the King." An equally consistent and perspicuous representation of his view is made by Rashi in his commentary on the Talmud. On the explanation advanced by the Sages for the ruling in the Mishnah that one is silenced if he prays for God's mercies upon a bird's nest, "because he makes the ordinances of God to be acts of mercy, whereas they are injunctions," Rashi notes: "These are God's commandments which were not given for compassion, but only to impose upon Israel His statutes and injunctions, to make known that they are His servants, keeping His commandments, injunctions and statutes, even in such things that Satan and the idolatrous nations seek to repudiate." [48]

Rashi's view is shared by some of the Tosafists as is evident from the commentary of Tosafot on the above discussion in the Talmud.[49]

Tosafot cites a *piyut* by R. Eleazar Kalir in which the poet infers that the command not to slaughter an animal and its young on the same day is due to God's compassion.[50] Tosafot rejects Kalir's assumption that it is an indication of divine mercy, maintaining that it is rather to be taken as simply a divine decree.[51]

The Meta-Rational View

The fundamentalist viewpoint is vigorously challenged by Nahmanides, who asserts that "each commandment has a reason and a purpose, as well as a benefit for man, quite apart from the reward which God grants for its observance."[52] The Sages did not mean to convey the notion that certain mizvot are merely sovereign decrees, to be regarded as arbitrary and devoid of any reason. They are, he believes, divine commands whose object, while known to God, is not revealed to the people. The *hukim* are "God's secrets in the Torah" which the people cannot fathom by their reason as they do the *mishpatim;* but all of them have a proper reason and a sound purpose.[53] Furthermore, while the reason and beneficial purpose are not known to the common people, they are made manifest to the wise. "God knows the need and object of the mizvah which He commands, though He does not relate this to the people, except to the wise among His counselors."[54] In corroboration of the latter assertion, Nahmanides notes that the patriarch Abraham, as intimated by the Sages, learned the reasons for the commandments through divine inspiration.[55] The *hukim* are thus viewed by Nahmanides as meta-rational precepts of a wholly esoteric nature.

Nahmanides differs basically from Rashi in the distinction to be drawn between the two classes of mizvot.[56] The *mishpatim,* he agrees, are laws intended to preserve the life of man in society and to maintain peaceful relations among men. People readily recognize their need, knowing that human society cannot exist without just laws. The *hukim,* he insists however, are not divine decrees without reason. They are laws whose reasons were not revealed and, admittedly, some foolish people may be inclined to reject them.[57] They are indeed "royal decrees," but in the same sense that a king who is wise in the conduct of his realm knows the need and the benefit of a law which he promulgates, yet he deems it best not to make the facts known to the people, with the exception of his sage advisers.[58]

Nahmanides' critique notwithstanding, it should be pointed out that though Rashi appears to have taken a strictly literalist position regarding the mizvot, upon closer scrutiny it is a more equivocal stand than is at first apparent. Although he maintains that the commandments ought to be accepted as tokens of submission to the sovereignty of God, he does not expressly deny that reasons known at least to God do in fact exist. Even the *hukim* then would be conceived of, not as irrational, but rather as supra-rational, precepts.[59] It would seem, moreover, that the stricture against inquiring after reasons is directed primarily to the *hukim;* he does not specifically forbid reflective speculation as to the reasons for the other commandments.[60] Indeed, any more adamant position would be at variance with the tenor of rabbinical statements to the contrary.[61]

Although Nahmanides accepts the characterization of the mizvot essentially as given by the Sages,[62] he is, generally, not as restrictive in his definition of the term *hok,* believing that its meaning is determined by the scriptural context.[63] Thus, diverging from the rabbinic view, he offers his own interpretation of the verse, "There He made for them a statute (*hok*) and an ordinance." Contending that prior to revelation of the Law at Sinai the Israelites had not received any laws, he maintains that at Marah they were given guidance as to the customs which they were to follow and the proper manner in which they should conduct themselves under the trying conditions of life in the wilderness. They were taught to trust in God, to heed the counsel of elders, the love of fellowman, modesty, peaceful relations, and general ethical conduct.[64]

Mizvot Are of Intrinsic Worth

On the whole, Nahmanides tends to reject the historical approach in his explanation of the mizvot, as is amply demonstrated in his discussion of the meaning of sacrifices, where he takes issue with Maimonides.[65] The mizvot are possessed of intrinsic worth and imbued with inherent sanctity. They reflect divine concern for man in the preservation of his physical well-being, as in the prohibition of certain foods which are detrimental to his health,[66] and they aim at the development of his moral and spiritual character by educating him in ethical and religious principles and by helping him to be ever mindful of his commitment to his faith. Thus the mizvah *of tefillin,* which directs that a scroll bearing the account of the exodus from Egypt be placed next to one's heart and mind, serves as a constant reminder of the unity of God, which is the root of faith, and of the divine commands and divine retribution.[67] Similarly, one who places a *mezuzah* upon his doorpost acknowledges thereby God's creation of the world, His omniscience, providence, and loving-kindness, and professes belief in prophecy and in the principles of the Torah.[68] The Ten Commandments, Nahmanides notes, are comprised of five devoted to the honor of God and five which provide for man's personal needs and social welfare, the latter enabling the maintenance of a peaceful, well-ordered society.[69]

Apart from their significance as social laws or as testimonies to the manifold manifestations of divinity, Nahmanides takes many of the commandments to be possessed of mystical, kabbalistic meanings, as he intimates for example in the case of sacrifices[70] and the laws of *Shemitah* and the jubilee year.[71] Whatever their apparent or deeper meaning, it is through the mizvot that the Jew is bidden to hallow the name of God and, if need be, to accept martyrdom on their account in the supreme act of *kiddush ha-shem.*[72]

TOWARD A PHILOSOPHY OF MIZVOT

Philosophical Perspectives

There is evident in the philosophical literature on the commandments a tendency of considerable import in foreshadowing an approach to a philosophy of mizvot. The search for the purpose of the commandments by the medieval Jewish philosophers reflects their analytical and rational approach to religious doctrine, as well as a teleological concern characteristic of their philosophic tradition. The reasons given by the philosophers are, on the whole, designed to make the Torah laws comprehensible within their respective philosophic modes of thought, and to give them relevance in terms of a distinctive value structure.

Thus, Saadiah tends to view the commandments eudaemonistically, while imparting to the rational precepts a somewhat autonomous character, in consonance with a marked utilitarian bent in his ethical philosophy, and his bold contention that man by employing his reason is capable of apprehending ultimate truth.

Bahya ibn Pakuda, although influenced by Saadiah's methodology, and affirming the essential unity of all knowledge, stemming as it does from one divine source of truth, and acknowledging man's duty to use his divinely endowed reason, on the other hand, disregards the social and historical meanings of the commandments. He stresses rather the inner devotion of the heart in observance of the mizvot, whose purpose he conceives to be the perfection of the individual soul in the service of God, preparing it for eternal bliss in the world to come.

Judah Halevi offers historical, even psychological and physiological, reasons for the commandments, but primarily underscores their distinctively Jewish character. Viewing them from the perspective of the preservation of Israel's elect status, Halevi focuses upon the religio-nationalistic aspects of the mizvot. Their object, he believes, is to enable the Jew not only to attain human perfection, but to develop his uniquely innate spiritual essence, and to varying degrees, achieve communion with God.

A Teleological Conception

In keeping with his general philosophy, Maimonides proceeds along rationalistic lines in his conception of the mizvot. Man's reason, while it affords him the capacity to exercise freedom of will and judgment, also renders him subject to divine command.[73] While we cannot, even with our divinely endowed intellect, grasp the purpose of creation, since it is the product of God's unfathomable will, we may, nevertheless, discern the purpose of the varied elements of its inner structure, which clearly reflect His incomparable wisdom. The divine wisdom that manifests itself in the world created by God is likewise inherent in the commands ordained by God. They are, therefore, rational and purposeful, for God's will is essentially identical with His reason.[74] Through the medium of his intellect, which is man's channel for rational communication with the cosmic Intelligence,[75] he may endeavor to ascertain the purpose of the divine commands within the scope of human knowledge and experience, which are the limits of the world intelligibly accessible to man.

Maimonides' declared intent in discussing the reasons of the commandments is, in part, to show "the justice and wisdom of the Law," which is perfect because it alone is divine law.[76] Indeed, the endeavor to understand the reason and meaning of a mizvah is integral to its observance.[77]

The commandments are to be perceived, as we have noted, in accord with a teleological conception of the world and man's place in it, as designed to achieve the perfection of man, which is the ultimate objective of the Torah. "Every one of the six hundred and thirteen precepts," Maimonides states, "serves to inculcate some truth, to remove some erroneous opinion, to establish proper relations in society, to diminish evil, to train in good manners, or to warn against bad habits." [78] The mizvot thus enable every man to acquire exemplary moral and intellectual qualities, each according to his ability, by directing him in the improvement of his ways and by teaching him principles of justice and fundamental truths.[79]

By means of the Torah's directives for ethical self-discipline and the perfection of the soul through true knowledge, in particular the knowledge of God which leads to the love of God, man can attain his highest goal in life, namely, communion with God. If, therefore, one could only fathom the inner intent of the law, he would realize that its essence, and that of the divine religion that it ordains, lies in the deeper meaning of its commands.[80]

A Rational-Historical Perspective

Maimonides evidently thought the converse to be an equally valid assumption, namely, that a knowledge of the nature of man and an understanding of the conditioning of his environment, in its physical, social and political aspects, should enable us to ascertain some of the reasons for the mizvot. In further taking account of the religious and historical factors which occasioned some of the precepts, particularly those intended to guard against heathen cults, Maimonides thereby introduced a rational-historical perspective in his evaluation of the commandments.

We may discern an additional requisite in Maimonides' approach to a philosophy of mizvot. As in his general philosophy, he proceeded here, as well, deductively from a structured frame of reference. This would, parenthetically, further explain his admitted inability to offer reasons for some of the revealed mizvot,[81] such as the table and the show bread in the Temple;[82] the offering of wine as a libation;[83] and the prescribed objects that were to be used in the purification of the leper, in the sacrifice of the red heifer and in the sprinkling of the blood of the Passover lamb.[84] Maimonides in effect acknowledges this when, in rejecting the meaning assigned by the Midrash to the prescribed rites in purification of the leper, he writes, "The explanation does not agree with our theory. I do not know at present the reason for any of these things . . . I cannot find any principle upon which to found an explanation why these particular things have been chosen." [85]

It is significant, moreover, that Maimonides confines his discourse on the purpose of the commandments exclusively to his philosophical work, *The Guide of the Perplexed.* With few exceptions, he does not propound reasons in his other, predominantly halakic, works. While this may indicate a desire to keep his own rationale of the mizvot distinct from their halakic validation, it nevertheless points to the fact that he intended his discourse to be viewed within the broader framework of his philosophy as a whole.

THE POLEMIC ON TA'AMEI HA-MIZVOT

The Fear of Allegorism

The quest for *ta'amei ha-mizvot* continued to encounter considerable opposition of varying degree and intensity. The reluctance to ascribe reasons for the commandments on the part of the Sages of the Talmud and some of the scholars in the post-Talmudic era reflected a general concern regarding the ever-present danger of an allegorical interpretation of the laws. A critical evaluation of the commandments, whether predicated upon rationalistic or symbolic formulations, presumably challenged their very grounding as divinely revealed laws. It was feared that this would eventually tend to divest the mizvot of their binding character. For, having ascertained to one's own satisfaction the purpose, and the moral or spiritual significance of the mizvot, one might be misled into believing that a commitment to their underlying principles and truths exempted one from literal compliance with the prohibitions or actual observance of the positive precepts of the Torah.

Indeed Philo, who was the first Jewish philosopher to introduce the allegorical method, already found such a misconception prevalent and expressed his concern regarding it. "There are some who, understanding the letter of the laws to be a symbol of intellectual things, are very particular about the latter but readily neglect the former. I, for my part, should blame such unscrupulousness." [86] Similar reservations are voiced by Saadiah, lest extreme allegorical interpretation of revealed laws result in their losing their literal meaning, with the consequence that "all revealed laws would be abolished." [87]

Hence, the fundamentalist position on ta'amei ha-mizvot may be seen primarily as a defense against an excessive rationalism and an immoderate allegorization of the commandments. While rooted, no doubt, in an ingenuous, unquestioning belief in a divinely revealed Law, it gave rise, in its extreme form, to a school of thought which maintained that the mizvot are arbitrary, purposeless commands, expressive only of the unfathomable will of God. The latter is precisely the view which Maimonides rejects at the outset of his investigation of the reasons for the commandments. [88]

Significantly, the fundamentalist position received increasingly greater articulation following Maimonides' venture into this area of speculative inquiry, especially on the part of later halakic authorities. This, evidently, was one of the pivotal issues in the bitter controversy that enveloped the Jewish communities of Spain and France at the turn of the thirteenth century. In the historic ban proscribing the study of philosophy issued in 1305 by R. Solomon ben Adret (Rashba) and his colleagues in Barcelona, and concurred in by

R. Abba Mari of Lunel and the scholars of Montpellier, Rashba specifically decries the allegorization of the narratives and the commandments in the Bible, and points to the destructive effects of an allegorical exposition of mizvot upon the literal observance of the biblical laws.[89]

Maimonides continued to be the epicenter of the polemic on *ta'amei ha-mizvot,* assailed by those who believed that his rationalistic explanations of the commandments weakened their mandatory character and diminished their value. Typical of the developing opposition is the opinion expressed by Rabbi Jacob ben Asher, the fourteenth-century author of the *Turim.* In opposing Maimonides' contention that certain biblical prohibitions were intended to prevent idolatrous practices, he writes, "We need not seek reasons for the mizvot. We must accept them as commands of the King, even if we do not know their reasons." [90]

The Defense of Maimonides

The position on the question of *ta'amei ha-mizvot* maintained by the classical expositors of Jewish religious thought, one responsive both to the demands of reason and the dictates of faith, while sensitive to the constant tension between them, found adherents among some of the leading halakic authorities of a later age. Thus, a spirited defense of Maimonides, directed against Rabbi Jacob ben Asher's stricture cited above, is made by Rabbi Joseph Karo, the sixteenth-century author of the *Shulhan 'Aruk.*

Rabbi Karo notes that it is apparent that the criticism of Maimonides stems from the implication drawn by these critics that should a satisfactory reason not be found for a given commandment, one would not be obliged to observe it. "God forbid that the words of Maimonides should be so construed," he writes. "Indeed, who is more careful than he of the honor to be accorded the Torah and the commandments." He proceeds to explain Maimonides' view as follows. "Even though all of the laws of the Torah are to be regarded as royal commands, nevertheless for whatever commandment we can find a reason we should do so, in the manner of R. Simeon, who explained the reasons for certain laws in the Torah. Wherever we can find no reason, we should ascribe it to our limited comprehension. In the latter case, we are nonetheless obliged to observe the laws, just as in the case of the commandments whose reasons we know, because they are all the commands of the King." [91]

The Age of Inquiry

This polemic notwithstanding, the end of the thirteenth and the beginning of the fourteenth centuries saw Jewish scholars fully embarked upon the investigation of the reasons for the scriptural commandments. That this development was a result of the initiative of Maimonides is pointed up in a remark by a contemporary of the Hinnuk, who writes: "In regard to the reasons for the commandments, he [Maimonides] opened up the rock and there flowed forth water from the nether regions, to draw therewith the living, faithful waters from the upper regions." [92]

However, it was in all likelihood the influence of Nahmanides which not only gave impetus to this development, but more important, determined its character and direction. This is not to minimize the profound impact of Maimonides. A few scholars, to be sure, such as Ralbag and Ibn Caspi, continued to espouse the rationalism of Maimonides, often venturing beyond the master himself. Others, for the most part, while still in awe of Maimonidean authority, tended, nevertheless, toward the mystical, meta-rational approach of Nahmanides. [93]

Significantly characteristic of this period, however, is the prevailing mood of inquiry into the reasons for the commandments. This was the intellectual climate in which the author of the *Sefer ha-Hinnuk* embarked upon his own inquiry into the meaning of the mizvot.

CHAPTER TWO

THE TARYAG MIZVOT

The tradition of *taryag mizvot*,[1] which teaches that the commandments of the Torah total six hundred and thirteen, is recorded in
the Talmud by Rabbi Simlai, who states: "Six hundred and thirteen
commandments were communicated to Moses; three hundred and
sixty-five negative commandments, corresponding to the number of
days in the solar year, and two hundred and forty-eight positive
commandments, corresponding to the number of the members of
the human body."[2] This tradition, which is apparently of long standing since it is also found in the earlier Tannaitic literature,[3] was
generally accepted as the legal frame for the codification of Jewish
law.[4]

The actual enumeration of the six hundred and thirteen commandments first appears in the *Halakot Gedolot,* a halakic compendium of the gaonic period.[5] The *Halakot Gedolot,* however, departs from the numerical division as given by Rabbi Simlai, and also
includes in the total number several rabbinic laws.[6] Maimonides
likewise structures the *Sefer ha-Mizvot,* his basic work on the commandments, on the system of *taryag mizvot,*[7] though he differs sharply
with the *Halakot Gedolot,* maintaining in particular that rabbinic
laws are not to be reckoned.[8] The early codes, while at variance as to
certain of the commandments that are to be included,[9] generally follow the principles and guidelines established by Maimonides.[10]

THE SEFER HA-HINNUK

Among the foremost of this class of codes which groups the laws
under the *taryag mizvot* is the *Sefer ha-Hinnuk,* the *Book of Edu-*

26

cation, attributed to Rabbi Aaron ha-Levi of Barcelona, a leading talmudic scholar of the thirteenth century.[11]

Maimonides greatly influenced the Hinnuk,[12] as he did the other codifiers of the commandments.[13] Indeed, the *Sefer ha-Hinnuk* follows throughout the reckoning of the mizvot as given in the *Sefer ha-Mizvot.*[14] However, while the latter served the Hinnuk as a primary source for an exposition of the commandments, the two works nonetheless differ fundamentally in scope as well as in their basic objectives. Maimonides' *Sefer ha-Mizvot* treats exclusively of the halakic aspects of the commandments, since the work was intended to be an introduction to his great code of Jewish law, the *Mishneh Torah.*[15] Maimonides, therefore, does not assign therein any reasons for the observance of the mizvot nor discuss their moral or religious significance. The *Sefer ha-Hinnuk,* on the other hand, while it deals with the halakic aspects of the commandments, also sets as its prime objective an understanding of the religious and ethical roots of the commandments. By virtue of its distinctive halakic and philosophical exposition of the mizvot, the *Sefer ha-Hinnuk* remains a primary, essential source for a study of Jewish law and the philosophy of Judaism.

CLASSIFICATION OF THE MIZVOT

The dictum of Rabbi Simlai, quoted above, refers to a division of the *taryag mizvot* into positive, affirmative commandments and negative, prohibitive commandments.[16] This division, which is adhered to in the codes, particularly in the *Sefer ha-Mizvot* of Maimonides and in the *Sefer Mizvot Gadol* of Rabbi Moses of Coucy, is retained by the *Sefer ha-Hinnuk,*[17] except that the division is within each scriptural portion. This arrangement was altered in the later editions of the *Sefer ha-Hinnuk,* and the commandments were placed in the order of their appearance in the Torah.[18]

General Categories

The Hinnuk indicates that the *taryag mizvot* fall into several general categories.[19] With regard to their application, they may be grouped as follows:[20]

a. Commandments that are obligatory upon all Israel, both men and women, everywhere and in all times.
b. Commandments that are obligatory everywhere and in all times, but only upon Israelites, and not upon priests or levites.
c. Commandments that are obligatory upon levites only.
d. Commandments that are obligatory upon priests only, everywhere and in all times.
e. Commandments that are obligatory upon the king of Israel only.
f. Commandments that are obligatory upon the whole community, and not upon the individual alone.
g. Commandments that are obligatory only in a specified place and in a specified time, namely in the land of Israel, and in the time that the majority of the people of Israel is there.
h. Commandments whose obligation differs as between men and women, and as between Israelites and priests and levites.
i. Commandments that are obligatory constantly, such as the commandments to love God, to fear God, and the like.
j. Commandments that must be observed at a specified time, such as the commandments of the Sabbath, *lulab, shofar,* rest on the festivals, the recitation of *shema'*, and the like.
k. Commandments whose observance is contingent upon a given circumstance, and which are therefore not obligatory unless that circumstance should arise; as for example the commandment to give the hired man his wages in the appointed time which is obligatory only upon one who has hired workers.

In the course of his discussion of the commandments, the following additional categories of commandments, which he does not include in this list, become apparent.[21]

a. Commandments that apply only in the time of the Temple, or when the Jubilee law is in force.
b. Commandments that are binding upon all mankind.
c. Commandments punishable by death or by stripes.
d. Commandments not legally punishable, but nevertheless morally binding.

Of the *taryag* commandments, three hundred and sixty-nine are applicable in our day. Of the latter, there are seventy-eight mandatory and twenty-one prohibitive commandments which are contingent upon certain conditions. Of those commandments which are binding upon every Israelite unconditionally and independent of any cause or circumstance, there are two hundred and seventy in all; forty-eight mandatory and two hundred and twenty-two prohibitive commandments. The above commandments, with the exception of six, are not obligatory at all times, but only at specified times during the day or the year.

Commandments Obligatory At All Times

The six commandments which are binding always and of which a man must constantly be mindful during his lifetime are the following:

1. To believe in God.
2. Not to believe in any other besides Him.
3. To affirm His unity.
4. To love Him.
5. To fear Him.
6. Not to stray after wayward thoughts, or after the waywardness of one's eyes.

EXPOSITION OF THE MIZVOT

The very name given to his work by the author of the *Sefer ha-Hinnuk* is an indication of the motive that prompted him to write it. He states:[22] "My intention is to educate the youth, and to impress upon them that there are reasons for the commandments which are apparent to all men and which they can readily understand in their youth. I therefore named the book *Hinnuk*[23] (*Book of Education*)."

The author's objective, therefore, in writing the *Sefer ha-Hinnuk* is to offer the young people of his day a means of satisfying their natural inclination to investigate the nature and the purpose of the divine commandments.[24] It is his desire to present to them satisfactory and cogent reasons for their observance, "that the commandments might not appear at the outset as words of a sealed book, lest they thereby spurn them in their youth and abandon them forever." [25] In pursuing this motive he employs most effectively the literary style of addressing himself to his own son.[26]

The Scriptural Order

Consistently following, as we have indicated, Maimonides' reckoning of the commandments, he deviates only in that he arranges them according to their scriptural order. This is the simplest and most practicable grouping of the commandments. The Hinnuk follows this arrangement in view of his avowed purpose: to present the mizvot in such a way that they may be studied along with the weekly scriptural readings in the synagogue,[27] according to the prevailing annual cycle.[28] Indeed, it is for this very reason that the Sages instituted the reading of Scripture in the synagogue, so as to stimulate the people to study the Torah and to observe its commandments.[29]

Nature of the Exposition

The Hinnuk's exposition of each of the mizvot is based upon a division into four distinct parts. The first part consists of a discussion of the nature of the mizvah, its source in the Torah, and its explanation according to the Sages. The second part deals with the "root" of the mizvah,[30] or the reason that may be advanced for it. In part three, the specific laws of the mizvah are cited, as derived from the Talmud and other sources. Part four, the final part, indicates the conditions of each of the mizvot. It explains where and when a given mizvah applies, to whom it applies and what, if any, punishment is due for having transgressed it.[31]

It should be pointed out that the Hinnuk does not attempt a comprehensive elucidation of the laws. In most instances he offers only a topical outline of the laws on a given commandment, probably intended as an aid to further study.[32] His evident purpose was to present the commandments in a manner that would render them understandable and easily accessible for study and review, not over-encumbered with intricate halakic discussions.[33] At times he goes beyond the bounds within which the commandment legally applies, drawing attention to the wider application of the principle under which the commandment is operative.

The discussion of the reasons for the commandments is clearly the author's major contribution and indeed constitutes the prime objective of his work. The reasons which the Hinnuk offers for the commandments are by no means meant to be taken as final; indeed, he is fully aware that other reasons and meanings may be ascribed to them.[34] His contribution in this respect lies not only in the fact that reasons are offered for the commandments but more particularly in the character of the reasons which he proposes. By and large, he does not dwell upon mystical interpretations, though he appears to have held the Kabbalah in high regard.[35] He likewise avoids abstruse philosophical explanations.

Ethical and Religious Root-Ideas

The Hinnuk is primarily concerned with revealing the ethical and religious root-ideas underlying the commandments, the moral and ethical purposes which the laws are meant to serve, their spiritual quality, and their conduciveness to further the welfare of the individual and the community. In seeking to determine the reasons and meanings of the commandments, while at the same time ascertaining their halakic character, the Hinnuk has evolved a philosophy of mizvot, reflecting his conception of the moral and religious philosophy of Judaism, which we will endeavor to trace and assess in the following chapters.

CHAPTER THREE

THE DIVINE PURPOSE

The Hinnuk's religious philosophy is based ultimately upon certain historically affirmed premises which, as formulated by him, serve as necessary predicates to his investigation of the purpose of the mizvot.

REVELATION OF THE TORAH

At the core of Judaism is the belief in the divine origin of the Torah. Divine revelation is, moreover, an established historical fact, attested to by the entire people of Israel. "When God wished to give the Torah to His people Israel," the Hinnuk states in his Introduction, "He gave it to them in the presence of six hundred thousand men, and a multitude of children and women, so that they would all be trustworthy witnesses to this event." [1] In the course of time, it became an authenticated tradition, handed down by the elders of each generation to the next, establishing thereby an unbroken, living chain which enshrined this great tradition in the collective memory of the people of Israel.

Direct Revelation to the People

The Hinnuk is careful to note that, at the fateful moment of revelation, the whole people attained to the degree of prophecy. This was necessary in order to render their testimony the more reliable, "because that which is known through prophecy is never subject to doubt." [2] A direct revelation to the people, the Hinnuk explains, was designed to allay any doubts that God actually spoke to Moses.

32

Thus, belief in the prophecy of Moses is based on Israel's experience at Sinai.

This view, already advanced by Ibn Ezra and by Maimonides,[3] is sharply disputed by Nahmanides, who points to a long-standing tradition of belief in prophecy received from their forefathers.[4] In the opinion of Nahmanides the entire people were lifted to the level of prophecy in order to instill in them an unwavering faith in the prophecy of Moses forever, so that future generations would not heed anyone who would presume to contradict it. The Hinnuk, significantly, also takes account of Nahmanides' view and, consequently, develops the thesis that the power of prophecy bestowed upon the Israelites at Sinai served the double purpose of removing present doubt, as well as any challenge in the future, regarding the authenticity of God's revelations to Moses. "Once they had attained to prophecy, there no longer remained for them any doubt whatever in the matter . . . Those who witnessed the event and thus had a true knowledge of it, there being no firmer truth for man than this, bore witness to their children who were born afterwards that the whole Torah which they had received at the hand of Moses, from the very first statement 'In the beginning' (Genesis 1:1) to the concluding words 'before the eyes of all Israel' (Deuteronomy 34:12) was true and certain, subject to no doubt whatsoever. The children in turn bore witness to their children, and so on from one generation to the other until our own day. It is evident, then, that our Torah is a Torah of truth."[5]

The truth of revelation is thus predicated on prophecy, on the testimony of the people who witnessed the historic event at Mount Sinai, and on the unbroken, authenticated tradition regarding the revelation transmitted through the generations.

Torah, the Source of Ultimate Truth

The Torah, divinely revealed, is the source of ultimate truth and of the knowledge of God's will, which would have been unattainable by means of reason and speculation. "Since man lacks perfection, his reason does not comprehend the ultimate purpose of things. The preferred path for man is, therefore, to do whatever is commanded in the Torah which was received from trustworthy witnesses, and which the lord of wisdom gave to mankind, for it contains all precious knowledge." [6]

As the repository of great and boundless wisdom, the Torah is often brief and cryptic, leaving the full import of its meaning and intent to the explanation given orally to Moses. Its very words and phrases are cast in a definite and necessary mold, both as to their number and construction, because they possess a meaning and value of their own, quite apart from that which is evident on the surface.[7] For this reason, also, chapters and verses occur in a specifically ordained order.[8] Several laws may be derived from a single scriptural verse, "because of the wisdom contained in the Torah, it being possible to derive many things from one statement.[9] The Sages have therefore said, 'There are seventy ways of expounding the Torah.' "[10]

In his belief that the Torah contains all wisdom, the Hinnuk is reflecting, as he himself notes, the traditional view that the Torah is in truth the revelation of that wisdom which was created by God and which existed before the creation of the world.[11] "So highly have our Rabbis, of blessed memory, exalted the wisdom which God, blessed be He, placed therein that they were moved to say, 'The Holy One, blessed be He, consulted the Torah and created the world.' "[12]

THE PURPOSE OF REVELATION

Having established the first of his premises, namely revelation of the Torah, the Hinnuk proceeds to a consideration of the question of divine purpose, specifically the very purpose of revelation. What, he asks, was God's objective in giving the Torah to man? The simple answer, the Hinnuk avers at first,[13] is that the mind of man is incapable of comprehending the ways of its Creator and hence, while the reason eludes us, we believe that God's revelation of the Torah was for a necessary purpose.[14]

God's Design

Nevertheless, the Hinnuk continues to probe for a more satisfying answer. "Man's knowledge of God's ways," he explains, "is a necessary consequence of God's own perfection." [15] Since God is perfect, the world which He created must carry out to perfection His ultimate design in its creation. Of all creatures on earth, man alone was endowed with intelligence, having been formed of both body and intellect. Man was created in this manner so as to have cognition of God, which he attains through his wisdom and intelligence.[16] "It follows of necessity therefore that man should know and acknowledge his Creator in order to complete the design in his creation. Were it not for the Torah which God gave us, man's intellect would be completely drawn after his material nature, with all its lust, and he would be like the beasts that perish. Consequently, the work of creation would not be complete, since man and beast would be the same in essence though different in form, resulting in a deficiency in creation." [17]

In speaking of man's dual nature, the Hinnuk employs here the term *sekel,* which though usually taken to refer to the rational faculty of the soul, is used here in a wider sense. Speaking elsewhere of the interdependence of body and soul in man,[18] the Hinnuk uses the terms *sekel* and *nefesh* interchangeably. The reference in this context, then, is clearly to man's spiritual nature in contrast to his material nature.[19]

The import of the Hinnuk's argument is that, were it not for the Torah, man's spiritual nature would deteriorate and be drawn after his material nature, thereby thwarting God's design. As to God's purpose, therefore, in giving the Torah to man, we are persuaded by reason to assume that man's knowledge of the ways and the will of God, revealed therein, is thus part of the divine plan. Having willed the creation of the world, it must be perfect, reflecting God's own perfection. The Torah is indispensable in the perfection of man, in that it affords him the means of retaining the distinctiveness of his nature which distinguishes him from other created beings.[20] Hence, the object of the Torah is to enable man to attain his full intellectual and spiritual stature,[21] so that he may know his Creator and serve Him.[22]

The question of divine purpose in revelation is similarly propounded by Saadiah relative to God's motive in creation. Proceeding from the premise that man is the end and "intended purpose of creation,"[23] and consistent with his view that the final aim of God's creation is the good of His creatures,[24] Saadiah maintains that God's intention in revelation was to endow man with the means of attaining happiness and well-being. "Now His first act of kindness toward His creatures consisted in His giving them being—I mean His calling them into existence after a state of non-being ; . . . He also endowed them with the means whereby they might attain complete happiness and perfect bliss . . . the commandments and the prohibitions prescribed for them by God."[25]

Maimonides, on the other hand, in an initial discussion in his *Guide of the Perplexed*,[26] summarily rejects the anthropocentric notion of the world held by Saadiah, and takes the view that the question of purpose in creation invariably invokes a series of successive purposes which resolve themselves only in the final answer, "It is the will of God." He concludes, "This must be our belief when we have a correct knowledge of our own self, and comprehend the true nature of everything: we must be content, and not trouble our mind with seeking a certain final cause for things that have none, or have no other final cause but their own existence, which depends on the Will of God, or, if you prefer, on the Divine Wisdom."[27]

In a later discussion,[28] however, he apparently articulates the more traditional view held by Saadiah and the Hinnuk. Abrabanel, in an attempt at resolving the problem, suggests that the question of purpose may be addressed either in respect of the Creator or of the created. It is only with regard to the former that Maimonides deems it inappropriate to seek any purpose other than the will and wisdom of God.[29] It may be noted that Maimonides is, moreover, in accord with the Aristotelian view which, while it cannot countenance the notion of an ultimate purpose to creation, because it holds it to be the necessary effect of God and not the result of divine intention, yet maintains a teleological view of the world. There is manifest a sense of immanent purposiveness within the created world itself. While paralleling the Aristotelian view in the development of his thesis, Maimonides proceeds from a different premise, to be sure, inasmuch as he accepts the traditional view of creation.

The Hinnuk's methodology here is of interest, in that he follows a line parallel to that of both Maimonides and Saadiah, adopting at first the position of Maimonides and then suggesting substantially the argument advanced by Saadiah in a somewhat modified form.

Why Was the Torah Given to Israel?

The aforegoing discourse leads logically to another fundamental question which the Hinnuk finds it necessary to confront at this point. "Since the Torah is intended for the perfection of all humanity," he notes, "why was it given only to one of the nations in the world, namely Israel, and not to all of them?" [30]

Evidently this question, too, engaged the interest of the medieval Jewish philosophers. Maimonides, characteristically, dismisses it by stating, "We might be asked, why has He revealed the law to one particular nation . . . We answer to all these questions: He willed it so, or His wisdom decided so . . . We do not know why His will or wisdom decided so." [31] Ibn Ezra, addressing himself to the implied obligation that revelation of the Torah imposes in particular upon Israel, seeks to justify the yoke of the Law on the ground that the Jewish people are bound to serve God in gratitude for His having delivered them from the Egyptian bondage. [32] The Law, he points out, is moreover for Israel's own benefit, since it will make of them a righteous people, who may thereby merit the world to come.

The Hinnuk, however, sees the question in a different light. He perceives in the revelation of the Torah to Israel an act of divine favor, and he feels constrained to justify this beneficence for which the Jewish people has been singled out. [33] The Hinnuk prefaces his answer with a tacit acceptance of the view of Maimonides that the intention of the Creator is beyond our understanding, but he contends that the matter is nevertheless to be viewed from a different perspective. To begin with, it is not correct that no Law was given to the other peoples of the earth. In fact, the rest of mankind was also granted the means by which to retain its distinctive human character in the form of the Seven Commandments of the Children of Noah. [34] By means of these universal laws, designed to guide humanity in the fundamentals of human conduct and spiritual attitudes, all mankind is able to attain higher moral and spiritual levels.

THE ELECTION OF ISRAEL

The true answer to the question, the Hinnuk believes, lies in the classic view of Judaism on the election of Israel. "One portion was chosen from among mankind. This is Israel . . . God chose them to be called His people and He gave them all essential wisdom." [35] The divine choice carries with it a special charge. "The people of Israel are the chosen of mankind, created to acknowledge their Creator and to serve him." [36] It is this people, therefore, to whom God revealed His Law.

God's Covenanted People

Intrinsic to the concept of the chosenness of Israel is the correlative concept of an eternal covenant entered into by God with His people. Israel thus enjoys a unique status with respect to the Torah because God selected it to be His covenanted people.

The election of Israel, a form of selectivity that is amply evident in nature, also manifests itself in the selection of the tribe of Levi, "chosen always to serve God." [37] A select status was also accorded by God to the Land of Israel, "to settle therein the chosen of mankind," and to Jerusalem, "chosen to be the sanctuary of the Torah and the place for divine service, whence blessing will go forth for all the earth." [38]

The Hinnuk's approach to this problem and his development, relative to it, of the concepts of the chosenness of Israel and the preeminence of the Land of Israel parallel, to a considerable degree, the approach of Judah Halevi. The question is raised and answered by Halevi, albeit somewhat obliquely, in his *Sefer ha-Kuzari*. [39] In response to the Rabbi's statement as to Judaism's roots in Israel's early history, the King of the Kazars remarks: "Then your belief is confined to yourselves?" [40] To which the Rabbi replies: "The Law was given to us because He led us out of Egypt, and attached His glory to us because we are the chosen of mankind."

Halevi's position in this matter is quite evidently determined by his general thesis regarding the transmission of the spiritual essence from Adam, through the chosen of each generation, to the patriarchs and thence to the children of Israel. [41]

Whether or not the Hinnuk was directly influenced by Halevi is not clear,[42] particularly in view of the prevalence of these concepts in midrashic literature.[43] Halevi, to be sure, adds another significant element, namely, that the Torah was confined to Israel because its laws are rooted in the history of Israel and in its national past.[44] Indeed, he concludes, "if there were no Israel, there would be no Torah." [45]

The belief in the election of Israel constitutes for the Hinnuk one of the pillars of his religious philosophy. Having been chosen by God, Israel is consequently under a special divine providence. "Israel is the people whom God chose from among all other peoples to serve Him and to acknowledge His name. They are, therefore, not under the dominion of the constellation which God assigned to all the rest of the peoples, but they are directly under the dominion of the Holy One, blessed be He." [46] Indeed, it is encumbent upon a Jew to foster a sense of pride in the people of Israel, and to feel "that our nation is the most honored of all, so that he will come to love his nation and his Torah." [47]

In His desire to render Israel worthy of His blessings, God developed within them "a good and noble character," [48] by enjoining upon them such commandments as would train them in these qualities. "A noble soul is prepared to receive goodness, and upon it will blessing always be bestowed. And since God seeks the good of His people, He crowned them with every desirable and noble quality." [49] In the mizvah requiring compassion for the slave, the Hinnuk writes, "God wished His chosen people Israel to be a holy people, replete with and crowned with all good and superior qualities, because in that way blessing will be bestowed upon them." [50]

The Covenant of Torah and Faith

The selection of Israel by God is thus a spiritual one. The choice is moreover inextricably bound up with the Torah. "God, blessed be He, chose the people of Israel and desires, for his righteousness sake, that they shall all occupy themselves in study of the Torah and in the knowledge of His Name." [51] Israel's status of nobility is that of "a kingdom of priests and a holy nation." [52] Thus the Hinnuk asserts with marked emphasis: "The essential honor of Israel is the

Torah, through which they were separated from the rest of the nations and became God's portion." [53] The Hinnuk underscores the learning of Torah as a fundamental principle upon which all the rest of the mizvot are dependent. [54] It is for this reason that the Sages instituted the public reading of the Scriptures in the Synagogue, as well as the reading and study of Torah at home. [55] The concept that the Torah constitutes the reason for the existence of the Jewish people and imparts to them their distinctive spiritual character, is developed by the Hinnuk numerous times, but particularly in his discussion of the mizvah regarding the counting of the Omer during the seven weeks between Passover and Shabuot.

"The reason for this commandment," he writes, "may be explained as follows: The Torah is of the very essence of Israel. Indeed, it is for the sake of the Torah that heaven and earth were created; as it is written, 'If my covenant be not with day and night, if I have not appointed the ordinances of heaven and earth' (Jeremiah 33:25). The main object and purpose of their deliverance from Egypt was in order for them to receive the Torah at Sinai and to keep it, even as God said to Moses, 'And this shall be the token unto thee that I have sent thee; when thou hast brought forth the people out of Egypt, ye shall serve God on this mountain' (Exodus 3:12): that is to say, Israel will receive the Torah which is the essential thing and for which they were delivered. This constitutes their ultimate good, and it is of greater import for them than their liberation from bondage. Therefore, God set their liberation from bondage as a token for receiving the Torah, since that which is of relatively secondary importance is set as a token for that which is of primary importance. Hence, since the receiving of the Torah is the essential reason for Israel's existence, and for its sake they were redeemed and were elevated to the high position which they reached, we were therefore commanded to count the days from the morrow of the festival of Passover until the day the Torah was given. We are bidden to do so in order to demonstrate our great and heartfelt yearning for that notable and longed-for day." [56]

Israel's national character is unique. It is essentially, and primarily, a religious community which "entered into the covenant of the Torah and the Faith." [57] All Israelites are thus united in a spiritual fellowship, bound together by their covenant with God and a common bond of loyalty to His Torah. Judaism draws no distinction, therefore, between religious and national observances. Quite the contrary, the apostate who denies his religious faith and "whose deeds are estranged from his Father in heaven," [58] cannot share in Israel's national festivals.

The Hinnuk develops this concept in his explanation of the prohibition against giving an apostate Israelite to eat of the Passover sacrifice. "The Passover sacrifice is a sign and a remembrance of the time that we came under the shelter of the wings of the Divine Presence, and entered into the covenant of the Torah and our Faith. It is, therefore, not fitting that we give one who has left the community of Israel and denied our Faith to eat of the Passover sacrifice." [59] The same reason holds as well for the alien and the uncircumcised. "It is fitting that none should partake of it except those who have fully entered the Faith; namely, full-fledged Israelites, but not those who have not as yet fully joined us in the covenant." [60]

THE MESSIANIC HOPE

The belief in the election of Israel, however, poses a serious problem. If Israel is truly the Chosen People, in possession of the Torah which is the source of divine blessings, then why must the people suffer exile and affliction?[61] Does this not belie Israel's claim to divine election? This is the final, gnawing question that the Hinnuk feels compelled to answer, doubtlessly reflecting the suffering that was the lot of the Jews in his own time as well as in the past.

The Jewish Eschatological View

In the resolution of this problem, the Hinnuk presents his formulation of the Jewish eschatological view, as well as certain accepted theories on theodicy and human suffering. "It is generally well known among men that the Lord of all created two worlds: the world of corporeal beings, and the world of the souls, and that the world of corporeal beings is considered as nothing and as waste in comparison with the world of the souls, because the former is like a passing shadow while the latter exists forever. Therefore, since the soul is the essence of man, and that part of him which endures and remains forever, whilst the body is only the vessel for the soul, serving it for a brief time and then it is corrupted and destroyed, God therefore caused His people to inherit the world of the souls, which is a world that is eternal and of immeasurable delight." [62]

Thus, God gave to Israel, as its eternal inheritance, the supreme good of the World to Come. But why cannot God's chosen people also have their share of the joys and the blessings of this world as well? The answer is that, in order to be worthy of life eternal, we must first atone for our sins and cleanse and purify our souls in this world in preparation for the world of the spirit to come. [63]

The Hinnuk's view here evidently reflects rabbinic tradition, which regards suffering as effecting a cleansing of man's sins, and as a visitation of divine love. [64] In the divinely ordained scheme of things, suffering and misfortune serve a necessary, even if deplorable, function in life. They must be accepted, therefore, not in a rebellious spirit, but in a spirit of faith. "A man must resign himself to bear whatever suffering or chastisement God ordains for him. Let him not think that he can abolish it or that people can escape it altogether. But let him, rather, beseech God blessed be He, to heal his severe wounds." [65] Hence illness and disease, even harm inflicted by others, are to be considered as possible punishments for our sins and should lead to repentance. [66] The laws of mourning are, in this regard, not only a means of expressing grief, but induce one to reflect upon God's judgments and, consequently, to Teshubah. [67] Suffering, then, purifies the soul. Even if conceived as a punishment, it is yet tempered by its redeeming effect. As such, it is spiritually ennobling, and it can be a purposeful force in the struggle of the human soul to reach perfection.

The ultimate reward for the righteous, consequently, is in the World to Come. [68] This is a doctrine which is in keeping with human expectations and is universally known and acknowledged. Indeed, it is for this reason that the Torah does not make any direct mention of it, apart from the fact that people of little faith would tend to doubt such a promised reward for righteous conduct, not having any evidence of it in life itself. Hence the Torah holds forth the promise of earthly rewards and blessings for observing the commandments, consisting of freedom from cares of sustenance and wars. This, in reality, is in preparation for the ultimate reward. It is to assure man that, if he be worthy, God will protect him and free him from worry about his material needs, so that he will be enabled to continue to serve Him and thereby achieve his share in the World to Come.[69]

Eventually, however, the time will come when all Israel will be freed of suffering and redeemed from exile and, having reached spiritual perfection, will receive their rightful share in this world as well as ultimately in the World to Come. This will be fully realized in the days of the Messiah.[70]

A Biblical Homily

The Messianic hope inspires the Hinnuk to a biblical homily in an eschatological vein. The divine command which forbade Jacob and his descendants from eating the sinew of the thigh vein, following his encounter with the angel, is explained by the Hinnuk as presaging the exile and the ultimate redemption of the Jewish people. "This indeed is the meaning of the sign. For the angel who fought with Jacob our father, and whom tradition identifies as having been the guardian angel of Esau, sought to destroy Jacob as well as his children. But, as he could not prevail against him, he thereupon injured him by striking his thigh. Even thus do the descendants of Esau afflict the descendants of Jacob. But, in the end, they will be delivered from them. As it was with the Patriarch, that the sun rose upon him to heal him and he was relieved from pain, so will the sun of the Messiah rise upon us, and will heal us from our afflictions and redeem us." [71]

The Messianic Era

In the Messianic era, thus envisaged, there will be realized the resettlement of the Jewish people in the Holy Land and the restoration of the Kingdom in Israel. In his discussion of the commandment which requires the king to write a Scroll of the Torah, the

Hinnuk remarks: "It is not necessary to write when this command-ment applies, since we know that there can be no kingdom in Israel except in the time when their Land will be settled. May our eyes speedily behold the coming of the Redeemer who will reign over us in the Land of Israel." [72] The ruler, as prescribed by tradition, will be in the line of Davidic descent. [73] In Messianic times Israel will also expand its territory. [74]

With the advent of the Messiah, mankind will experience a spiri-tual regeneration. The moral and ethical elevation of man will result in the elimination of sin for the most part, since man will virtually free himself of his *yezer hara'*, his evil inclination. [75] In this respect, the Hinnuk appears to have chosen a middle ground between the position of Maimonides, who maintains that life in this world will continue virtually unaltered in the days of the Messiah, and that of Nahmanides who foresees a radical change in man's nature. Maimon-ides' opinion is based upon Samuel's dictum, "There is no difference between This World (the present) and the Days of the Messiah ex-cept for our subjection to the dominion of the kingdoms." [76] Nahman-ides, on the other hand, contends that in the days of the Messiah, man's natural inclination will be to do good only. "From the time of creation, man has been free to act as he pleases, to be righteous or wicked. This has been so all the time since the Torah was given to man so that he may have merit when he chooses the good, and punishment when he wills to do evil. In Messianic days, however, man's natural inclination will be toward the good. He will have no desire whatever for that which is not fitting." [77] The Hinnuk evi-dently does not fully subscribe to this view, but intimates that there will still be some inclination to sin even in Messianic days, except that man's character will have been greatly refined.

Thus, while this is a world of material things and subject to cor-ruption, under ideal conditions of life this world, too, can be re-deemed. The good is attainable and desirable, not only in the world of the Spirit, but also in this world. Abraham, whom God blessed in all things, was blessed with the good of this world as well. [78]

In the final analysis, however, as indicated above, the Messianic days are not to be anticipated by reason of the promise of material blessings which they will bring, but rather because in those days the ideal conditions of life in the world will make it possible to observe the commandments of the Torah and to serve God unhindered, and thereby merit the blessing of eternal life in the World to Come. Maimonides expresses the same view in the *Mishneh Torah* in concluding his discussion of Messianic days: "The Sages and the Prophets longed for the days of the Messiah, not in order to rule over the world, nor to oppress the idolaters, nor that they should be exalted by the nations, nor in order to eat, drink and be merry, but rather that they should be free to study the Torah and its wisdom, and that there should be no one to oppress them or to deter them, so that they would merit the life of the World to Come." [79]

The Hinnuk's conception of the nature of the Messianic era, which substantially follows the traditional view, thus includes the following basic elements: a) Israel's freedom from suffering, and the healing of its afflictions; b) Israel's deliverance from oppression and the conquest of its enemies; c) resettlement of the Land of Israel, and the restoration of the kingdom of Israel; d) the spiritual regeneration of mankind; e) observance of the Torah and the service of God unhindered, thereby meriting eternal life in the World to Come.

In sum, the Messiah will bring redemption to the Jewish people, material prosperity for all people, the realization of spiritual goals, as well as the ethical perfection of humanity. The eschatological doctrine thus presented by the Hinnuk serves to resolve the paradox of Israel's historic martyrdom in the face of its manifest destiny as the Chosen People. Ultimate reward in the form of a life of consummate bliss awaits the people of God in the eternal world of the souls. Yet, even the experience of suffering has a redemptive quality, in that it is a means of purifying the soul, rendering it worthy and fit for its existence in the World to Come. We nevertheless hope for the days of the Messiah when Israel will enjoy the tranquility and the good of this world as well.

The belief in the coming of the Messiah must be nurtured and kept alive in the hearts of the Jewish people. There is grave danger that the afflictions of exile may cause many to lose heart and to despair of attaining the spiritual good that ultimately awaits the righteous. We must assure them of Messiah's coming so that they will remain steadfast in their faith and in their righteous ways.

The Hinnuk speaks of the need for sustaining Israel's faith in the coming of the Messiah as follows: "Although they may, in the course of their exiles, suffer many persecutions at the hand of the nations, and at the hand of the children of Esau, they should remain confident that they will not be destroyed. Their seed and their name will endure forever, and the Redeemer will yet come to them and will deliver them from the oppressor.[80]

It is in this manner that the Hinnuk conceives of the divine purpose as manifest in the unfolding destiny of the Jewish people. Reformulated in axiomatic terms, the divine revelation of the Torah, Israel's election and its covenant with God, the Messianic hope and the promise of the World to Come constitute the major premises upon which the Hinnuk constructs his philosophy of Judaism.

CHAPTER FOUR

THE PREAMBLE OF FAITH

PRINCIPLES OF BELIEF

Though we find a concern with prescribed dogma as early as Mishnaic times,[1] it was not until Judaism came into closer contact with established philosophical systems and creeds that Jewish theologians found themselves impelled to delineate the fundamentals of Jewish belief.[2] While religious philosophers, such as Philo,[3] Saadiah Gaon[4] and Judah Halevi,[5] had already endeavored to define these principles, Maimonides was the first to formulate them in doctrinal form.[6] Maimonides' formulation of the Thirteen Principles of Faith[7] is basically related to an exposition of the Mishnah in *Sanhedrin* which sets forth the doctrinal prerequisites that an Israelite must meet to attain his portion in the World to Come.[8]

In keeping with the philosophic view that the divine commandments can have meaning only within the frame of the whole of Jewish belief, the Hinnuk likewise deemed it necessary to state the principal beliefs upon which the commandments are founded.[9] That the Hinnuk intended his statement of beliefs as a preamble to his exposition of the commandments is intimated by his characterization of them as *'ikarei ha-Torah,*[10] principles of the Torah. We shall define and discuss the Hinnuk's principles of belief, with specific reference to Maimonides' beliefs as set forth in his several works, since they undoubtedly served the Hinnuk as a guide.

THE EXISTENCE OF GOD

The Hinnuk states his belief in the existence of God as follows: "Among the principles of the Torah, which, as we have said, God gave His People through His prophet Moses, are the following: To know that God, blessed be He, who is in heaven above and who gave the Torah to Israel is the Primary Being whose existence is without beginning and without limit; that He brought into being and created by His will and by His power all of creation out of nothing; that whatever He created will endure for as long a time as He wills and not for a moment longer; and that nothing is impossible for Him to do." [11]

Knowing and Believing

The Hinnuk uses the term la-da'at, "to know," only in relation to the principle of God's existence stated above, while the others are prefaced with the term le-ha'amin, "to believe." It is evident that the Hinnuk uses the term "to know" in this connection advisedly, since, in his exposition of the mizvah which requires belief in God's existence,[12] he states that the law requires one to know that He exists and to have a knowledge of all that pertains to this belief as expounded in the books of the theologians. It is again clearly enunciated in his discussion of the duties implied in the commandment to love God, where he states, "And he should toil all day in the pursuit of wisdom, so as to attain a knowledge of Him." [13]

This is patently the position of Maimònides, who presents this principle in his opening statement of the Mishneh Torah in these words: "The basic principle of all basic principles and the pillar of all wisdom is to know that there is a Primary Being." [14] Maimonides adds, "The knowledge of this is a positive commandment, as it is said, 'I am the Lord, Thy God' " (Exodus 20:2).[15] That Maimonides' intent is the attainment of a knowledge of God's existence by means of reason and demonstrable proof is to be seen from his discussion in the Guide of the manner of revelation. Following his statement that Moses alone heard the Ten Commandments, while "the people only heard the mighty sound, not distinct words," he elaborates as follows: "There is, however, an opinion of our Sages frequently expressed in the Midrashim, and found also in the Talmud, to this effect: The Israelites heard the first and the second commandments from God, that is, they learnt the truth of the principles contained in these two commandments in the same manner as Moses, and not through Moses. For these two principles, the existence of God and His Unity, can be arrived at by means of reasoning, and whatever can be established by proof is known by the prophet in the same way as by any other person; he has no advantage in this respect. These two principles were not known through prophecy alone." [16]

It is apparent that the Hinnuk, in his statement of beliefs, followed Maimonides' formulation of this principle in the *Mishneh Torah*. Further evidence of this may be noted in the Hinnuk's reference to God as the "Primary Being" (*Mazuy r'ishon*), a term which Maimonides uses in this connection in the *Mishneh Torah* only.

It is to be noted, however, that whereas Maimonides employs here the term "to know," [17] in his Thirteen Principles of Faith, on the other hand, as well as in the *Sefer ha-Mizvot*, he uses the expression "to believe." [18] In a like manner, the Hinnuk, in his discussion of the mizvah proper, evidently following Maimonides' construction in the *Sefer ha-Mizvot*, states that we are commanded "to believe (*le-ha'amin*) that there is one God in the world who brought into being all that exists." [19]

For the Hinnuk, however, the term "to believe" conveys a somewhat different connotation, reflecting his own conception of the mizvah. Knowing and believing are for the Hinnuk neither contradictory nor mutually exclusive, as is to be seen from his further explanation of the commandment. The divine utterance, "I am the Lord, Thy God" (Exodus 20:2) is to be understood, he states, as though God had said, "Know ye, and believe that there is a God in the world, for the word 'I' signifies His existence." [20]

Reason and Revelation

The view thus maintained by the Hinnuk and by Maimonides is, in fact, the classical position espoused by the medieval Jewish philosophers, already clearly defined by Saadiah, "We inquire into and speculate about the matters of our religion . . . to have verified in fact what we have learned from the prophets of God theoretically." [21] Both the metaphysical, as well as the moral, concepts revealed in

Scripture, Saadiah maintained, are apprehensible by reason. Indeed, the rational pursuit of this truth is itself a religious duty. This approach was generally adopted by the religious philosophers, and it was from this perspective that Jewish medieval philosophy viewed the relationship between revelation and reason.

The use of reason as a source of truth in bolstering religious faith is especially pronounced and even more positively advocated in Bahya's philosophy. Bahya gives voice to this in the Introduction to his *Sefer Hobot ha-Lebabot,* where he declares that, with regard to the root-principles of religion and the pivots of practical conduct, we are obliged to use our faculties and gain clear and definite knowledge, so that "faith and conduct shall rest on the foundation both of tradition and of reason." After indicating that acceptance of the unity of God falls into several categories, according to the differences between human beings in knowledge and intellectual capacity, Bahya states that the acknowledgment of the unity of God with mind and in speech, after one knows how to adduce proofs of His existence and has arrived at a knowledge of the truth of His unity by the method of rational investigation and by arguments that are right and reasonable, is the completest and worthiest category of belief.[22] Nahmanides, apparently aligns himself with this position as he interprets the first of the Ten Commandments, "I am the Lord, Thy God" (Exodus 20:2), as exhorting the people "to know and to believe that God exists and that He is their God."[23] Indeed, both Bahya and Nahmanides base their further construction of this commandment upon the same scriptural admonition, enjoining rational enquiry. Bahya writes,[24] "On the question whether we are under an obligation to investigate the doctrine of God's unity or not, I assert that anyone capable of investigating this and similar philosophical themes by rational methods is bound to do so according to his powers and capacities . . . This duty of investigation has indeed been imposed upon us by the Torah in the text 'Know this day, and lay it to thy heart, that the Lord He is God' " (Deuteronomy 4:39). Nahmanides underscores this point in the opening statement of his treatise, *Taryag Mizvot.* "The first commandment is the positive commandment obligating a man to investigate, to search, to seek and to perceive God and to know Him. For this there is a further positive commandment, 'Know this day, and lay it to thy heart, that the Lord He is God' (Deuteronomy 4:39). This is implied in the command, 'I am the Lord, thy God' (Exodus 20:2), because knowledge is the foundation and the root of everything."

Commitment of Reason and Faith

It is evident, however, that the Hinnuk's position is not an avowal of rationalism. The role of reason and knowledge in matters of belief is distinctly limited. At the basis of religion there must be faith; reduced to its simplest form, an unquestioning faith. This the Hinnuk emphasizes in his further elucidation of the commandment to believe in God. "The essence of this belief is that he establish in his soul that it is the truth and that any contrary view is by no means possible. Should anyone question it, he must answer him that this is what he believes in his heart and that he will not admit anything contrary to it even if they should threaten to kill him . . . And if he should merit further to attain to a higher degree of wisdom, so that he understands in his heart and perceives with his own eyes the convincing proof that this faith which he has is true and proven beyond doubt, and that it cannot be otherwise, then will he have observed this commandment in the very best manner." [25] According to the Hinnuk's conception, this principle thus entails the commitment both of faith and reason. Since God's existence is subject to investigation, it is incumbent not only to believe but also to strive to gain a greater knowledge and a deeper understanding of it. Clearly, however, his objective in investigating religious doctrine and subjecting it to rational analysis is not the rationalization, but rather the refinement and the strengthening of belief.[26]

Specific Principles

The Hinnuk's statement regarding the existence of God includes the following specific principles of belief.

a) God is eternal

The Hinnuk's affirmation that God is the "Primary Being whose existence is without beginning and without limit" conforms to

Maimonides' statement in the *Mishneh Torah*: "He is without existence in time, so that He is without beginning and end." [27] This belief is likewise stated by Maimonides as the fourth in his Thirteen
Principles of Faith, though he refers there to God only as being
primordial.

b) *God is the Creator and the Ruler of all that exists*

This is expressed in the words, "that He brought into being and
created by His will and by His power all of creation out of nothing,
that whatever He created will endure for as long a time as He wills
and not for a moment longer."

This is established by Maimonides as the first in his Thirteen
Principles of Faith as follows: "The first principle posits the existence of the Creator, blessed be He; that is, that there is a Being,
perfect in respect of all ways of existence, who is the cause of all
things that exist, that through Him is their existence possible and
through Him do they continue to exist. We cannot conceive of His
non-existence, for were He non-existent the existence of all other
things becomes an impossibility." It is stated again in the *Mishneh
Torah*.[28]

It will be noted that the Hinnuk also asserts power and will as
predicates of God. Creation denotes God's power and His will. All
existence is subject to God's will, both in respect to its creation and
in its continued existence.[29]

In his *Guide of the Perplexed*, Maimonides found it expedient
first to establish God's existence, unity, and incorporeality without
prior recourse to the belief in creation. Inasmuch as the latter is, in
his opinion, not subject to demonstrable proof, it would offer a weak
foundation upon which to build a belief in the existence of God.[30]
In similar fashion, in the *Mishneh Torah*, God's eternity is affirmed
by Maimonides only subsequent to the affirmations of God's existence, unity, and incorporeality.[31]

c) *God created the world out of nothing*

This principle is an affirmation by the Hinnuk of the belief in
creation *ex nihilo* and a denial of the eternity of the world. Maimonides implies it in Principle Four, "This One Being is primordial in
an absolute sense, and whatever is in existence besides Him, is not

primordial in relation to Him." Significantly, Maimonides does not include this belief in the First Principle concerning God's existence.

In his *Guide*,[32] Maimonides explains his position on this question at great length. He accepts the principle of *creatio ex nihilo* on the authority of prophecy and Jewish tradition, inasmuch as the proofs of Aristotle and his followers in support of the theory of the eternity of the universe are not conclusive and are subject to stronger objections than the theory of creation. Moreover, the belief in God's creation of the universe as an act of His will is more in accord with our conception of God than the view that the universe is but the result of fixed laws of nature.

Maimonides' argument is anticipated by Judah Halevi in its salient points. Halevi contends that the question of eternity and creation is obscure, and the arguments are evenly balanced. The theory of creation derives greater weight from the prophetic tradition "which is more deserving of credence than mere speculation." [33] Halevi asserts that Aristotle inclined to the theory of eternity because he had no reliable tradition to the contrary. "Had he lived among a people with well-authenticated and generally acknowledged traditions, he would have applied his deductions and arguments to the establishment of a theory of creation, however difficult, rather than to one of eternity, which is even more difficult to accept." [34]

For Maimonides, belief in creation is "a fundamental principle of the law of our teacher Moses; it is next in importance to the principle of God's unity." [35] He does not, however, for the reasons indicated, include this belief in the First Principle concerning God's existence. The Hinnuk, on the other hand, unburdened for the moment with philosophical proofs, follows his affirmation of God's existence with the belief in creation *ex nihilo*.

d) *God is omnipotent*

God's omnipotence is, for the Hinnuk, a necessary corollary to creation, which is the supreme demonstration of God's power, leading him to conclude that "nothing is impossible for Him to do." The omnipotence of God is not directly offered as an article of faith by Maimonides in his Thirteen Principles of Faith. It can, however, be inferred from his Third Principle that God is incorporeal. In the

Mishneh Torah, Maimonides explicitly relates God's incorporeality to His omnipotence.[36] It is also implied in the First Principle wherein God is declared to be the cause of all existence, as well as in Principle Five which states that only God may be worshipped. Though this was intended primarily against idolatrous worship, it nevertheless implies that only God is omnipotent and, hence, worthy of worship.

The aforegoing are the specific principles of belief that the Hinnuk postulates relative to the existence of God which, in the words of the Hinnuk, "is the foundation of religious faith. Whoever does not believe in it denies God and has no portion and merit in Israel." [37]

THE UNITY OF GOD

The Hinnuk states this principle as follows: "To believe that He is One and that there is none whatever besides Him." [38] For Maimonides, this constitutes Principle Two of his Thirteen Principles of Faith.[39] "He who is the cause of all things is one . . . This Second Principle is indicated in the words, "Hear O Israel, the Lord our God, the Lord is One" (Deuteronomy 6:4).

In his discussion of the commandment relative to this belief, the Hinnuk states: "We are commanded to believe that God, blessed be He, is the cause of all being, the Lord of all; He is One and there is none besides Him, as it is said, 'Hear O Israel, the Lord our God, the Lord is One'. This is a positive commandment not merely an assertion. The word "hear" (*shema'*) means, 'Accept this from me, know it, and believe in it,[40] that God, who is our God, is One' . . . This is fundamental to all mankind, and it is the firm pillar upon which every intelligent person relies . . . Whoever does not acknowledge the unity of God is as though he denies God Himself." [41]

Both in his *Hakdamah* and in the commandment, the Hinnuk employs the phrase *'ehad beli shum shituf*. The term *shituf,* in the meaning used here by the Hinnuk, occurs in the Talmudic statement, "He who combines (*ha-meshatef*) the name of God with something else will be uprooted from the world." [42] Tosafot notes that the stricture applies only when the intention is to ascribe divinity to something else besides God.[43] We do not find this term in Maimonides' formulation of the principle of the unity of God in his Thirteen Principles of Faith, though he does use it in the *Guide*[44] and in the *Mishneh Torah*,[45] though not as definitively as does the Hinnuk. We may surmise that this possibly points up a specific concern on the part of the Hinnuk with the problem posed by the Christian doctrine of the Trinity and, consequently, his unequivocal rejection of the doctrine.[46]

Commandments of Belief

The general principles of belief defined above regarding the existence and the unity of God constitute specific commandments among the Taryag Mizvot,[47] and are included by the Hinnuk among the six commandments that are obligatory at all times and of which one must be constantly mindful.[48] In this respect the Hinnuk follows Maimonides who lists them as the first two Positive Commandments.[49] Nahmanides, contrariwise, questions the validity of including the belief in God's existence among the commandments,[50] citing the *Halakot Gedolot,* who does not count it as one of the Taryag Mizvot. Nahmanides reasons that this is a fundamental principle which stands in a category all by itself, since all of the commandments are inconceivable without a belief in God who has commanded them. Interpreting the Halakot Gedolot's position, he states: "The belief in His existence, which He made known to us through signs and wonders and through a revelation of the Divine Spirit before our eyes, is the foundation and the root from which the commandments stem, and hence is not to be included in their reckoning."[51] Nahmanides' arguments, to be sure, are only theoretical since, in fact, he accepts the belief in God's existence as one of the Taryag Mizvot.[52]

It is noteworthy that Crescas, reasoning in a similar manner, concludes that this belief cannot be reckoned among the mandatory commandments of the Torah. If we do not assume a belief in God, then by what authority are we commanded to believe in His existence?[53] Belief in the existence of God is the Primary Root which is the source of all the other principles of belief.[54] It will, however, be noted, as we have already indicated, that the Hinnuk and Maimonides conceive of this commandment as a quest for the knowledge of God's existence, and not only as an exhortation to believe.

In defining the specific laws of the commandment to believe in the unity of God, the Hinnuk indicates that it is also implied in the prohibition against idolatry. This would explain the fact that the Hinnuk fails to include among his articles of faith the belief that only God is worthy of being worshipped, which Maimonides lists as the Fifth of his Thirteen Principles. The belief that God is One precludes the belief in the divinity of any other power besides Him, hence none other except God is worthy of being worshipped. This can also be inferred from the belief in God's omnipotence, since the fact of God's omnipotence and the worship of Him alone are inter-related.[55]

The Incorporeality of God

Whereas Maimonides declares the incorporeality of God as the Third of his Thirteen Principles of Faith, the Hinnuk does not make specific reference to it among the principles of belief. It is obvious, however, that he does not mention it because, in his opinion, it is implied in our conception of God as being perfect and not subject to any deficiency whatever, as stated in his first principle. Indeed, in outlining the specific laws relating to the commandment concerning belief in the existence of God, the Hinnuk states that it encompasses the belief that God is incorporeal, because corporeality implies imperfection and deficiency, which would be contrary to our basic beliefs as to the nature of His existence. "The specific laws pertaining to this commandment comprise what we are obligated to believe concerning God; namely, that all power, greatness, might, glory, majesty, and all blessing and existence are with Him . . . and all of the beliefs that follow from this; such as to know that He exists, that He is perfect, that He is not a body nor a force in a body,[56] because corporeal beings are subject to deficiency, while God, blessed be He, is not subject to any kind of deficiency." [57]

It may be noted in this connection, that Bahya, though he follows the method of Saadiah and the Kalam in proving creation, the existence of God, and God's unity, does not endeavor to prove the final proposition of the Kalam, namely incorporeality. We must assume that this is because his conception of the Creator and His absolute unity preclude any notion of corporeality.[58] We find a similar attitude in Scripture. While the unity of God is explicitly stated, the incorporeality of God is not directly mentioned, though it is a fundamental scriptural belief. It is implied, however, in the scriptural doctrine of the incomparableness of God to other beings.[59] In all likelihood, it is on this assumption that Philo, too, makes no mention of the incorporeality of God, though he explicitly mentions the existence and unity of God.[60] Indeed, even Maimonides proceeds on the same assumption in his *Guide of the Perplexed*.[61]

Maimonides parallels, in part, the Hinnuk's line of reasoning in his *Mishneh Torah*.[62] He declares the principle of the unity of God, and reasons as follows: Were there many gods in existence they would necessarily be corporeal beings, because things which are alike in existence are separate beings only in respect to such accidental qualities as are ascribed to corporeal beings. Were God corporeal, He would not be eternal, since there is no corporeal being that is not without end. And whatever is limited in its existence is equally limited in its power. Hence, it follows that God, who is omnipotent, must also be incorporeal.

The first part of Maimonides' sequence of reasoning above is subject to question. The *Kesef Mishneh*[63] doubts that the supposition of many gods necessarily leads to the assumption that they must be corporeal beings. He points to the existence of the Intelligences and the Souls which are stated by Maimonides to be incorporeal. He therefore suggests that perhaps Maimonides meant that if there were many gods they would necessarily be corporeal beings, or one would be the cause of the other and hence the latter, by the very nature of his existence, could not be considered to be God. It is significant, in view of the difficulty cited above, that the Hinnuk, unlike Maimonides, does not draw the conclusion as to God's incorporeality from the fact of God's unity but rather from the fact of God's eternal and omnipotent nature.

On Divine Attributes

With regard to the question of divine attributes, the Hinnuk maintains that we can ascribe no attributes to God, because His wisdom, will, power, and all other attributes are of His very essence. "When I speak of attributes in relation to the Holy One, blessed and praised be He, I follow the opinion of our Masters, of blessed memory, who ascribed attributes to God only in respect to the recipients. But as to God Himself, we are not to ascribe attributes to Him, because He, His wisdom, His will, His power, and His attributes are One." [64] We apprehend God as He manifests Himself in the world. In the course of our recognition of God, we are led to ascribe certain attributes to Him. However, at best, we can only describe God in negative terms, excluding all that detracts from His perfection.

In discussing the specific laws with respect to the commandment to believe in God's existence, the Hinnuk states: "We have not the power or the intelligence to comprehend and to express the greatness and the goodness of God. By the very reason of His transcendence He is knowable only to Himself. With all our might we must negate any deficiency ascribed to Him, or anything that would be contrary to His perfection and His excellence." [65] In the absolute sense, therefore, God is unknowable. We can conceive of His existence, but we cannot comprehend His essence.

It will be seen from the aforesaid that on the subject of divine attributes, a matter of prime concern in medieval philosophy, the Hinnuk follows the classical doctrine, generally accepted in Jewish philosophy, as enunciated by Maimonides,[66] and, in fact, first explicated by Bahya in his classification of the attributes.[67] The concept that God is unknowable in His essence, stated here by the Hinnuk and also emphatically proclaimed by Maimonides,[68] was first introduced into the history of philosophy by Philo,[69] who in turn infers it from Scripture. The verses, "Moses drew near unto the thick darkness where God was" (Exodus 20:18), and "Thou shalt see My back, but My face shall not be seen" (Exodus 33:23) are taken by Philo[70] to indicate that God by His very nature cannot be seen, meaning that He cannot be comprehended by the mind of man.

THE ETERNAL REWARD OF THE SOUL

This principle is stated by the Hinnuk as follows, "To believe that when a man observes that which is written in it [the Torah], his soul will attain to a great delight forever." [71]

The World to Come

There is implied here the belief in the immortality of the soul. Following the traditional philosophic view, the Hinnuk conceives of the soul, "as the essence of man, and that part of him which endures and remains forever." [72] The continued existence of the soul after death, or immortality, is granted by God to the souls of the righteous. It is abundantly clear, from the discussion which precedes these articles of faith in his Introduction, that the Hinnuk refers here to the eternal delight of the soul in the "World of the Souls," also designated by him as the 'Olam Haba', the World to Come. [73]

The concept of a life of consummate happiness with God in the World to Come as a reward for the observance of the mizvot is generally stressed by Jewish religious philosophers. [74] The Hinnuk, however, raises the question: If it is in the 'Olam Haba' that the final reward for the commandments is given, then why is it not specifically mentioned in the Torah? He offers two reasons. The first is because it is universally known and accepted. "The World to Come is something that is known and abundantly clear to every intelligent person. There is no people that does not agree that the soul remains immortal after the body perishes." [75] The Torah, therefore emphasizes the rewards in this life in order to assure man that he will be enabled to serve God and thereby achieve his rightful share in the World to Come. Second, because the Torah promised such rewards for the observance of the commandments as would be readily evident in life and would be convincing even to men of little faith. [76]

The reward of the soul in the World to Come is given to each according to his merit. "In the measure that the soul is good and wise, and its deeds worthy, to that degree is its delight greater." [77] The Hinnuk thus implies that the human soul in its immortal state in the afterlife retains its acquired individuality and distinctive status.

This is clearly apparent in his discussion of the judgment on Rosh Hashanah. "With regard to what the Sages stated, that the one who is found to be perfectly righteous in judgment is sealed immediately for life in the World to Come, do not think that the life in the World to Come will be the same for every righteous person. There are in that life degrees without number, and each righteous person will ascend to the place which is fitting to him in accordance with his individual reward." [78]

DIVINE PROVIDENCE, OMNISCIENCE AND RETRIBUTION

This principle is stated by the Hinnuk as follows: "To believe that God observes the conduct of men and knows all the details of their actions and repays each one according to his works." [79] It includes several points of belief.

a) *Providence*

This is implied in the words, "To believe that God observes the conduct of men." Divine Providence extends to the individual. As regards the rest of creation, it applies only to the species. God concerns himself, in the latter case, with the preservation of the species only. This is indicated by the Hinnuk as follows: "The providence of God, blessed be He, over His creatures extends in the case of the human species to the individual, as it is written, 'For His eyes are upon the ways of man, and all his steps doth He see' (Job 34:21). In the case of all other living creatures, divine providence extends to the species in general; that is to say, that it is His desire that the species be perpetuated. Therefore, none of the created species will ever be destroyed, because its existence will be assured by the providence of the One who lives and exists forever." [80] A number of the mizvot are intended to teach the true nature of divine providence, [81] in view of some of the misconceptions that are commonly held regarding it.

The Hinnuk lists three classes of people who entertain false notions with regard to divine providence. [82] First, are those who think that individual providence is given to man, and to all other creatures as well. Second, are those who believe that divine providence encompasses all creation in the minutest detail; that everything is predetermined, nothing is left to chance, so that "when a leaf falls from a tree, God decreed it should fall." The Hinnuk characterizes this view as absurd. The third class, designated by him as evil and heretical, is comprised of those who deny divine providence altogether and maintain that everything is subject to chance. It is necessary to instill a true belief in God's providence, he maintains, because "it is a great cornerstone in our Torah." [83] The Hinnuk's statements on the nature and the extent of divine providence thus express the generally accepted view, particularly as defined by Maimonides, though he does not stress its contingency upon man's intellectual development as does Maimonides. [84]

The Hinnuk recognizes a distinct form of providence as it applies to the Jewish People. As the people chosen by God, they are directly under the special protection and providence of God Himself. "Israel is the people whom God chose from among all other peoples to serve Him and to acknowledge His name. They are, therefore, not under the dominion of the constellations which God assigned to all the other peoples, but they are directly under the dominion of the Holy One, blessed be He, without the mediation of an angel or planet." [85] The Hinnuk adduces scriptural and historical evidence for the notion of a special providence for Israel. The scriptural proof text that he offers is the verse, "For the portion of the Lord is His people, Jacob is the lot of His inheritance" (Deuteronomy 32:9). He reinforces this by citing the historical experience of Israel's miraculous redemption from Egypt, the result of God's own personal intervention. This concept, he notes, is also conveyed in the Sages' interpretation of another scriptural verse (Exodus 12:12). " 'For I will go through the land of Egypt in that night'; I Myself and not an angel, 'And I will smite all the firstborn in the land of Egypt'; I Myself and no seraph. 'And against all the gods of Egypt I will execute judgment'; I Myself and not a messenger. 'I am the Lord'; I am He and no other." [86] The conditions for meriting this benign providence, with its attendant blessings for the nation and protection

from its enemies, are the upholding of the Torah and the service of
God.

   b) *Omniscience*

This is evident from the second part of the principle stated by the
Hinnuk, "and knows all the details of their actions." The belief in
God's providence and in His omniscience is included by Maimonides
in Principle Ten, "The Lord, blessed be He, has cognizance of the
deeds of men, and is not unmindful of them." [87] This principle is one
of the fundamental beliefs invoked by the Hinnuk in his explanation
of the mizvah to recount the story of the exodus from Egypt,[88] which
demonstrated God's omnipotence and instilled faith in his omniscience and in divine providence.

Miracles and the Natural Order

   The Hinnuk's conception of God as a free and absolute being,
whose will manifests itself in individual providence, includes, of
course, an affirmation of God's supernatural activity in the world.
While the Hinnuk does not entertain any notion of a purely natural-
istic principle in explaining miracles, he nevertheless tends to the
opinion that divine intervention in the order of nature, though strictly
the result of God's own free determination, is yet operative within
the confines of the natural order·itself. The Hinnuk takes occasion
to make known his view on this subject in his discussion of the
scriptural command to light a fire on the altar daily.[89] Miracles, he
states, are performed by God in a hidden way, so that they actually
appear to be in accord with nature or, at least, close to the natural
order. Indeed, he points out, even in the miracle of the dividing of
the sea, which was a manifest miracle evident to all, the Bible states:
"And the Lord caused the sea to go back by a strong east wind all
the night, and made the sea dry land, and the waters were divided"
(Exodus 14:21).[90] In similar fashion, God commanded that a fire
be kindled on the altar, even though fire descended upon it from
Heaven, in His endeavor to hide the miracle.

   While the Hinnuk thus seemingly blurs the boundary between the
natural and the supernatural, he does not fully align himself with
Maimonides' view that miracles were implanted in nature at the time

of creation,[91] or that they are effected according to the fixed laws of nature, as an integral part of the original properties of nature.[92] Miracles are, for the Hinnuk, a suspension of the very laws of nature, but are divinely ordained in a manner that imparts to them an appearance of being part of the natural order.

c) *Retribution*

This is stated in the last part of the principle as follows: "and repays each one according to his works."

God's benign providence for the individual, even as for the nation, is merited by observing the mizvot of the Torah. "A man should know that he who keeps the commandments of his Creator, and is righteous in all his ways, and has clean hands and a pure heart will be under the care of God, and he will have long life in this world and everlasting life for his soul in the World to Come." [93] It follows that when a man strays from the path ordained by God he becomes unworthy of God's watchful care. "When a man divests himself completely of faith in God, blessed be He, and allows himself and his thoughts to be led after vanity, he will be utterly unworthy of any blessing or good. Rather will he deserve the very opposite of blessing; namely, a curse and destruction, disease and all manner of evil, because he has removed himself, in the furthest extreme, from all that is good. Therefore, nothing but evil will overtake him on all sides." [94]

Retribution, whether as reward for the observance of the commandments of the Torah or as punishment for their transgression, is visited upon man in this world to a limited degree only. Punishment is, in this respect, but a means to an end; the end being the betterment of man. Here the Hinnuk reveals a deep moral sense in raising punishment from the level of purposeless, punitive action to that of purposeful moral guidance. Suffering and hardship can have a chastening, purifying effect upon the soul, leading to moral improvement by prompting one to self-searching and a repentance of his sinful ways.[95]

The ultimate penalty for the wicked is that the soul is cut off from life in the World to Come.[96] In a like manner, "the reward for keeping the mizvot is not in this world."[97] The Hinnuk cites the verse,

"Thou shalt therefore keep the commandment, and the statutes, and the ordinances which I command thee this day to do them" (Deuteronomy 7:11), and the exposition of the Rabbis, "This day, to do them; and tomorrow, that is to say in the World to Come, to receive their reward." [98] When God bestows material, worldly, blessings upon one it is to enable him to continue to observe the commandments unhindered so as to earn eternal bliss in the *Olam Haba*, that being the real reward for the good life. [99] Thus, in keeping with the traditional view as expounded by the Sages, [100] the Hinnuk emphasizes that retribution in this world is but of an interim nature. In the final account it involves the life of the soul in the World to Come.

The doctrine of divine retribution forms the Eleventh of Maimonides' Thirteen Principles of Faith. Maimonides, likewise, stresses that the ultmate reward is in the *Olam Haba*. "The Lord, blessed be He, rewards him that fulfills the commandments of the Torah, and punishes him that transgresses its prohibitions, the greatest reward being that of the World to Come, and the severest punishment that of extirpation." [101]

DIVINE REVELATION AND PROPHECY

The Torah which we now possess is divinely revealed. This, in essence, is the primary postulate which the Hinnuk establishes at the very outset of his declaration on the fundamental beliefs of Judaism. "Among the principles of the Torah, which we have said God gave to His people through His prophet Moses are the following: To know that God, blessed be He, who is in heaven above and who gave the Torah to Israel, is the Primary Being . . ." [102]

The Revelation on Mount Sinai

Divine revelation, the Hinnuk likewise asserts, is attested to both by tradition and by prophecy. [103] God gave the Torah in the sight of six hundred thousand adult men, in addition to a large number of children and women, so that they would all be faithful witnesses. Furthermore, in order that the testimony would be more reliable, they were all raised to the degree of prophecy, "because that which is known by means of prophecy is never subject to doubt. Even thus did God, blessed be He, say to Moses: 'That the people may hear when I speak to thee, and may also believe thee forever' (Exodus 19:9). That is to say, they and their children will believe in you and in your prophecy forever, because they will then know of a certainty 'that God doth speak with man, and he liveth' (Deuteronomy 5:21), and that all of your prophecy is true."

The Hinnuk evidently is of the opinion that all Israel heard the first two of the Ten Commandments on Mount Sinai directly and clearly from God. In this he agrees with Nahmanides, who writes: "The motive behind this was that with respect to the belief in God and the prohibition of idolatry all of them should be prophets." [104] This opinion, commonly held, is supported by statements of the Sages. [105] Maimonides, however, maintains that what Moses experienced at the revelation on Mount Sinai was radically different from what the rest of the Israelites experienced. Moses alone was addressed by God, and he heard the words distinctly, while "the people only heard the mighty sound, not distinct words." [106] Maimonides evidently maintains this position in view of his belief that prophecy requires intellectual perfection. He therefore contends that at the time of revelation the people did not have a direct prophetic experience.

The Nature of Prophecy

The Hinnuk's conception of revelation encompasses the belief in prophecy, particularly in the prophecy of Moses. Prophecy is the most reliable source of knowledge. "The highest degree to which a man can rise is that of prophecy. There is no more reliable knowledge in the world for man than the true knowledge of things through prophecy, which is knowledge that is not subject to doubt because it comes from the fountain of Truth." [107]

Prophecy is attainable only by such as are possessed of exceptional moral and spiritual qualities. The necessary attributes are piety, moral character, good works, and the ability to predict future events. The latter constitutes, in fact, the test of the true prophet, but only if the event foretold is of a goodly nature. Should his predictions of some evil fail to materialize, this would not be a clear test since the evil might have been averted through repentance. On the other hand, a divine decree for good proclaimed through the prophet is never rescinded. In view of these requisite conditions that rabbinic tradition attaches to prophecy, the Hinnuk is led to conclude, "Few men are found worthy to attain it, because the ladder is exceedingly high, its base is upon the earth and its top reaches into heaven. Who is the God-fearing man who will merit to ascend the mountain of the Lord and stand in His holy place? One man from among millions of men can attain to this degree, and only in a generation that is worthy of it." [108]

With the exception of Moses, the Hinnuk believes, the prophets were vouchsafed prophetic revelations only intermittently. This, he says, explains the tribulations that the true prophets experienced at the hands of their enemies who constantly denied the authenticity of their prophecies and demanded divine signs as proof that they truly spoke in the name of God. The Torah expressly forbids such harassment of a prophet, [109] once his veracity has been tested and his truthfulness ascertained, lest this lead to contention and rebelliousness.

The revelation at Sinai was unique in one respect, among others, in that the entire people attained to prophecy. "Having been raised to the degree of prophecy there remained with them no doubt whatsoever in the matter, and they knew clearly that everything was done at the command of the Lord of the universe and that all that befell them was from Him." [110] The Hinnuk's statement that the entire people were raised to the degree of prophecy reflects, as we have already noted, accepted Jewish tradition.

The Hinnuk, however, gives additional emphasis to the prophetic nature of the revelation experienced by the people, in view of his desire to establish an unbroken chain of testimony regarding the historical reality of the Sinaitic revelation. The general principle of the veracity of tradition is applied by the Hinnuk, in a manner similar to that of Saadiah, to an authentication of religious tradition, in particular to revelation. Thus, while revelation is distinctly a supernatural phenomenon, it is nonetheless a demonstrable fact, and belief in revelation becomes thereby an aspect of historical knowledge. [111]

The Hinnuk further implies that a state of prophecy was apparently attained by the people while they were still in Egypt, even before the time of the revelation. This was necessary in order to assure their confidence in Moses and to dispel any doubts that they may have had as to the verity of the signs that he performed for them and for Pharaoh. The basic, underlying problem, however, as the Hinnuk indicates parenthetically, centers on the belief that God directly communicated with Moses. As Judah Halevi had noted earlier, "Although the people believed in the message of Moses, they retained even after the performance of the miracle some doubt as to whether God really spoke to mortals, and whether the Law was not of human origin and only later on supported by divine inspiration. They could not associate speech with a divine Being, since speech is a corporeal function." [112] Ibn Ezra more specifically ascribed this lingering doubt on the part of the people to influences emanating from India and prevalent in Egypt at the time, that "it is inconceivable for God to commune with man." [113] Hence, the critical phase of prophecy was reached by the people at Mount Sinai, when the prophecy of Moses and the fact of revelation were thus authenticated.

THE TRUTH OF THE ORAL LAW

The belief in the truth of the traditional exposition of the Torah is stated by the Hinnuk as follows, "Among the principles of the Torah there is also the following: To believe that the true explanation of the Torah is the explanation received by us from the ancient, holy Sages of Israel. Any explanation which is contrary to that which they intended is in error and is null and void, because the Sages received the explanation of the Torah from our master Moses, peace be unto him, who received it from God, blessed be He, when he was in Heaven for forty days." [114]

Unity of Written and Oral Law

The Oral Law like the Written Law is thus equally of divine origin. Together they constitute an organic whole, an inseparable unity. This principle is basic to Judaism. "Whoever denies all of this is not to be included among the Holy People. For we can never arrive at the truth from the literal meaning of the scriptural verses without their authentic explanation and traditional interpretation." [115] The Oral Law is identified by the Hinnuk as being that tradition which was compiled by the Sages as transmitted from generation to generation, from the time it was received by Moses, and finally recorded in the Babylonian Talmud and in the Jerusalem Talmud. The Babylonian Talmud, being clearer and more extensive, is considered more authoritative. The Oral Law, the Hinnuk points out, is further expounded in additional works by some of the early Sages, namely the *Sifra, Sifre, Tosefta,* and the *Mekilta.*

We must be guided in our understanding of the Torah, especially when we are confronted by seeming contradictions, only by the accepted, traditional interpretations as received from Moses and transmitted orally by our Sages and later written down and compiled in the aforementioned halakic works. The Hinnuk cites three examples of apparent contradictions in the Torah which are resolved by the Rabbis on the basis of their traditional exegesis of the Torah. They are: the length of Israel's stay in Egypt; the number of Jacob's family that settled in Egypt; and the number of days during which it is obligatory to eat unleavened bread on Passover. [116]

Implied Principles of Belief

In comparing the Hinnuk's formulation of the principal beliefs with Maimonides' Thirteen Principles, we find that the former does not include certain principles which Maimonides considers cardinal tenets of Judaism. We are certainly not to conclude that the Hinnuk does not affirm these beliefs, as we have already indicated in our discussion above regarding the incorporeality of God and the belief that only God is to be worshipped. Rather, these beliefs are implied, and thus included in other principles that relate to them. Indeed, this is the general conclusion eventually reached by Joseph Albo, the last of the medieval Jewish philosophers, after surveying the discordant, dogmatic theologies of the religious philosophers who preceded him. [117]

Advent of the Messiah

Nevertheless, there remain to be considered, more specifically, three dogmas laid down by Maimonides which the Hinnuk fails to include among his declared principles of belief. The Hinnuk does not include the belief in the advent of the Messiah, which for Maimonides constitutes the Twelfth of his Thirteen Principles of Faith. This is all the more striking since the coming of the Messiah is, as we have seen, of vital importance in the Hinnuk's philosophy. The answer may lie in the nature of the Messianic era which, as characterized by the Hinnuk, is but a prelude to life in the World to Come.[118] The belief in the advent of the Messiah is therefore an integral part of the belief in divine providence and retribution. Thus, after discussing the question of Israel's suffering and the promise of reward for the righteous in the World to Come, the Hinnuk, in keeping with the tradition which viewed the Messianic hope as an answer to the problem of Jewish suffering, concludes significantly, "We must believe, however, that the time will come when we will merit both portions. This will be in the days of the Messiah." [119]

Nonetheless, the Hinnuk's failure to include a belief in the coming of the Messiah explicitly among his articles of faith may perhaps be understood in light of the overriding emphasis given to it in Christian theology. In view of the primacy therein accorded this belief and the christological overtones associated with it, the Hinnuk may have been moved to avoid undue doctrinal emphasis upon it. In this connection, it is interesting that a somewhat similar note is to be discerned in Albo's discussion of the disparity of dogmatic beliefs with regard to the advent of the Messiah. Proceeding from a different perspective, he concludes, "Under providence and reward and punishment comes the belief in the advent of the Messiah, which is a special principle of the law of Moses according to the opinion of Maimonides. But according to our opinion the belief in the Messiah is not a principle. And if it is, it is not special to the law of Moses, for the Christians, too, regard it as a principle, and that, too, in order to abrogate the law of Moses. It is indeed a special principle for them, for their religion cannot be conceived without it." [120]

Resurrection of the Dead

The Hinnuk also does not include the belief in the resurrection of the dead, which is cited in the Mishnah as an essential dogma,[121] and which constitutes for Maimonides the last of his Thirteen Principles. It can be said, of course, with respect to this as well as to the messianic belief, that the Hinnuk is concerned primarily with "principles of the Torah," namely, doctrines that are directly traceable to scriptural sources. Indeed, the Sages raise the question of scriptural evidence for the belief in resurrection.[122] To be sure, they offer several proof-texts, but these must rather be accounted as inferential scriptural support for accepted doctrine. It is probable, however, that the Hinnuk would associate resurrection with immortality of the soul in the World to Come,[123] and hence it would be subsumed under the latter principle.[124]

Supremacy of the Prophecy of Moses

For Maimonides, belief in the divine revelation of the Torah and the Oral Law, in Prophecy, and in the supremacy of the prophecy of Moses are the subject of Principles Six, Seven, and Eight of the Thirteen Principles of Faith.[125] While the Hinnuk does not specify the supremacy of the prophecy of Moses as an article of Faith, it is undoubtedly implied in his general statements regarding revelation and prophecy, and his references therein to Moses leave no doubt as to his superior status.

Immutability of the Torah

Maimonides includes under Principle Nine the belief in the immutability of the Torah. This is also omitted by the Hinnuk. Omission of this principle, again, is obviously not to be construed to mean that the Hinnuk would not affirm the eternal validity of the Torah. It is apparent that for the Hinnuk the belief in the immutability of the Torah is inherent in, and follows as a logical consequence of, his principles regarding the origin and the divine nature of the Torah. "The Lord, blessed be He, Who charged us with the Torah," the Hinnuk states, "is absolutely perfect. All of His works and all of His commandments are perfect and good. Any addition to them, and certainly any deletion from them, is in the nature of a deficiency. This is clear." [126]

Principles Predicated in the Torah

As we have indicated at the outset, the Hinnuk considers the aforestated principles to be essential beliefs predicated in the Torah. Indeed, several of them constitute specific commandments among the Taryag Mizvot. The existence of God and the unity of God are, as already noted, principles of faith that constitute distinct positive commandments which are binding at all times.[127] Among other mizvot that are of a credal nature are the following: the commandment to hearken to a prophet,[128] the commandment prohibiting belief in other gods,[129] and the prohibition against following after the waywardness of one's heart, which is understood as forbidding the harboring of heretical thoughts.[130]

Formulation of Dogmatic Principles

The formulation of dogmatic principles in Judaism was not without opposition, notably among the Kabbalists, who maintained that all of God's commandments are essential principles of faith. In the view of the Kabbalists, all of the Bible, including the narrative portions, is fundamental to our belief, containing as it does great secrets and mystic lore beyond our comprehension.[131]

This view was also set forth by R. Isaac Abrabanel, who points out[132] that the endeavor to establish principles of belief in Judaism was influenced by the other sciences, whose first principles and axioms are deemed essential in order to facilitate scientific inquiry and investigation. This is not the case with respect to the Torah, which is based upon faith and tradition, where there is no necessity to distinguish between elements of faith or to impart greater importance to specific commandments. Inasmuch as the Torah is wholly a divinely revealed code, all of the commandments stem from the same divine authority and have the same certainty. It is a mistake therefore to formulate dogmas, since every precept in the Torah is an essential part of our creed. In Abrabanel's opinion, even Maimonides' stipulation of religious principles, confined to his commentary on the Mishnah which Maimonides composed in his youth, was intended for the general populace, the beginners in the study of Mishnah, and not for the learned. Neither was it intended for those proficient in philosophy, since Maimonides does not devote himself to an explication of the principles of faith in his *Guide of the Perplexed*.[133]

Revelation, the Ground of Faith

It is perhaps significant, in light of the above, that the Hinnuk designates his principles as *'ikarei ha-Torah*, principles of the Torah, and not as *'ikarei ha-dat*, principles of faith, by which term Maimonides characterizes his Thirteen Principles in his Commentary on the Mishnah in Perek Helek. The Hinnuk's apparent reluctance to define them strictly as principles of faith, may reflect a disinclination on his part toward crystallizing religious beliefs in doctrinal form, which would set them apart from other principles of the Torah.[134] In any event, for both the Hinnuk and Maimonides these are not merely principles of faith of a universal character, but fundamental principles of Judaism which define the basic commitment of religious faith of an Israelite.[135] For the Hinnuk, we may regard them as specific elements of belief subsumed under the overall commitment of faith in the Torah as divinely revealed to Israel. This is indicated, as we have already noted, by the fact that for the Hinnuk, revelation of the Torah is a primary postulate of faith, and not merely an individual principle of belief.[136] The ground of faith in Judaism is revelation, not philosophical speculation. Hence, principles of belief, even the root-belief in the existence of God, are derivable from the Torah.

The endeavor to construct a formally defined creed for Judaism, begun by Maimonides and continued by his successors, resulted in a distinctive and varied philosophical literature.[137] However, despite apparent differences as to what would constitute fundamental principles and what are only beliefs that Judaism seeks to inculcate, there is evidently an overall unanimity of belief. It would seem that the doctrinal emphasis given by one or another philosopher to certain beliefs depended, to an appreciable degree, upon the objective in mind, as well as upon the exigencies of the times.[138] It is in respect of this, and the concomitant desire to provide a frame of religious belief for the commandments, that evidently persuaded the Hinnuk to formulate his statement of the principles of belief in Judaism.

CHAPTER FIVE

A RATIONALE OF MIZVOT

Jewish religious philosophy, as we have seen, reveals a sustained effort to probe for the purpose and meaning of the commandments.[1] However, such investigation was generally conducted independently of any definitive study of the mizvot. Even Maimonides, who dealt extensively with this subject, did so not in his halakic works, but rather in his philosophical treatise, *The Guide of the Perplexed.*[2] Thus, in the *Mishneh Torah* he generally assigns no reasons for the observance of the mizvot, except for a few parenthetical observations which are only incidental to his exposition of the laws.[3] It remained for the Hinnuk to pursue the quest for the purpose of the mizvot and their religious and ethical significance through a comprehensive and systematic analysis of every one of the Taryag Mizvot. The Hinnuk, it may therefore be said, pioneered in his endeavor to devise a rationale for the mizvot of the Torah in an halakic work.

The basis of the Hinnuk's approach to an understanding of the mizvot lies in the thesis that there is purpose to the commandments; that in the ultimate sense the commandments are rational and their reasons are capable of being known. It follows, then, that as intelligent human beings we should strive, to the best of our ability, to find a meaning or reason for each of them.

THE PRECEDENT OF THE SAGES

The Hinnuk points out that his thesis has ample support and authority in Jewish tradition.[4] That the Rabbis assumed that the commandments have reasons, and are not merely arbitrary expressions of the will of God, is evident from several statements in the Talmud and in the Midrash. He cites a Midrashic statement concerning the mysterious rite of the red heifer.[5] "Solomon said, All of these laws I have fully comprehended; but as regards the section dealing with the red heifer, I have investigated and inquired and examined, 'I said, I will get wisdom, but it was far from me'" (Ecclesiastes 7:23).[6] To Moses, however, even this was revealed. The Midrash states: "The Holy One, blessed be He, said to Moses: To thee I shall disclose the reason for the heifer, but for anybody else it is a statute."[7] The Hinnuk notes another instance. The Talmud states:[8] "What does ve-li-mekaseh 'atik[9] mean? This refers to him who reveals the things which the Ancient of Days concealed. And what are they? The reasons of the Torah."[10]

The Sages themselves, the Hinnuk maintains, offered reasons for certain commandments, indicating thereby that they were of the opinion that there are reasons for the commandments. While the Hinnuk does not cite examples, some are quite evident. We may cite Rabban Gamliel's dictum regarding the reasons for the Passover sacrifice, the unleavened bread, and the bitter herbs.[11] Another instance is the discussion of the Rabbis as to the reason for blowing the shofar.[12] The Talmud also frequently indicates that Rabbi Simeon expounded the reasons of the scriptural texts.[13] It is to be noted, however, that these instances generally reflect a tendency toward the exposition of scriptural laws rather than a deliberate inquiry into their rational basis. The Rabbis, it is apparent, did not intend to develop a rationale of the mizvot. Their purpose in ascribing reasons for some of the laws was to serve an educational objective and to reveal the Torah as a priceless treasure.[14] Beyond that, they were content in the belief that the mizvot were ordained by God, this being reason enough for their observance.[15]

A Pivotal Mishnah

Pivotal to a consideration of the question of whether or not the attempt to find reasons for the commandments is in keeping with Jewish tradition, is our understanding of the following Mishnah,[16] which is subjected by the Hinnuk to careful analysis.[17]

The Mishnah states: "If a man said, 'To a bird's nest do thy mercies extend' . . . they put him to silence." It is believed that the reference here is to the mizvah of *shiluah ha-ken*, the commandment requiring one to spare the mother bird and to let her go when a nest is taken out (Deuteronomy 22:6, 7). The Mishnah is understood to mean that if a man includes this statement in the course of his prayer[18] he is silenced. The Talmud[19] cites two opinions in this matter. One maintains that he is silenced, "because he causes jealousy among the works of creation." Rashi explains this to mean that he intimates that God's love of his creatures is partial. "He causes jealousy by saying that God has compassion on the birds but not on cattle and animals."[20] The other maintains that he is silenced, "because he makes the *middot* of God to be acts of mercy, whereas they are but injunctions." Rashi interprets the term *middot* in this context to be the equivalent of mizvot, referring to God's commandments. Hence, according to Rashi, the second opinion holds that he is silenced because he is stating that God's commandments are acts of mercy, whereas in reality they are statutes imposed upon Israel for the purpose of demonstrating its willing subservience to God.[21]

Maimonides' view is that the Mishnah reflects the belief that the commandments have no reason but are only the will of God.[22] Maimonides, to be sure, rejects this presumption. In his *Guide of the Perplexed* he writes as follows: "When in the Talmud those are blamed who use in their prayer the phrase, 'Thy mercy extendeth to young birds,' it is the expression of one of the two opinions mentioned by us, namely, that the precepts of the Law have no other reason but the divine will. We follow the other opinion."[23]

Maimonides contends that the mizvah reflects God's mercy, and likewise teaches us compassion. "When the mother is sent away, she does not see the taking of her young ones, and does not feel any pain. The eggs over which the bird sits, and the brood that are in need of the mother, are generally unfit for food. Consequently this commandment will cause man to leave the whole nest untouched. The Torah provides that such grief should not be caused to cattle or birds; how much more careful must we be that we should not cause grief to our fellowmen."[24]

Maimonides' contention finds rabbinic support in a Midrash[25] which mentions several laws in the Torah that are indications of God's compassion for men as well as for cattle and fowl. The Midrash cites the laws with respect to circumcision on the eighth day (Genesis 17:12, Leviticus 12:3), to refrain from parting the young from its mother until the eighth day (Exodus 22:29, Leviticus 22:27), to refrain from slaughtering the mother and its young on the same day (Leviticus 22:28), and to spare the mother bird (Deuteronomy 22:6, 7).

Surprisingly, however, Maimonides' belief, as stated in his philosophic work, would appear to be in contradiction with his own view as expressed in his halakic work. In his *Commentary on the Mishnah* he rejects the belief that this mizvah is because of God's compassion for the bird, but claims it to be a commandment for which there is no reason.[26] It cannot be contended that the above statement is only an exposition of the Mishnah itself and does not necessarily reflect his own view, because in the *Mishneh Torah* he explicitly states that the commandment to spare the mother bird and the commandment forbidding one to slaughter an animal with its young on the same day are not inherently acts of mercy, but are only statutes expressive of the will of God. "If one says in his prayer, 'May He who had mercy on a bird's nest in enjoining one from taking the mother bird with the young, and who prohibited the slaughter of an animal with its offspring on the same day, also have mercy upon us,' and the like, they silence him because these commandments are divine decrees and not acts of mercy. For were they due to compassion for the animal, He would not have permitted us the slaughter of animals altogether." [27]

Nature of Divine Providence

The Hinnuk disagrees with Maimonides in his strict interpretation of the Mishnah, and indicates that it should not be construed as maintaining the view that the commandments are merely expressive of the will of God and have no inherent reasons. In the course of his construction of the Mishnah and the views expressed in the Talmud, wherein he essentially follows the lead of Nahmanides, the

Hinnuk lays down the guidelines for an understanding of certain specific principles of belief and the general purpose of the commandments. The object of this mizvah, the Hinnuk states, is to teach us divine providence, namely that "the providence of God, blessed be He, over His creatures extends in the case of the human species to the individual, as it is written, 'For His eyes are upon the ways of man, and all his steps doth He see' (Job 34:21). In the case of all other living creatures it extends to the species in general; that is, God's desire that the species be perpetuated." [28]

Preservation of the species in the case of all living creatures is, for the Hinnuk, a direct manifestation of divine providence. This is even more clearly stated by him in his discussion of the biblical law prohibiting the slaughtering of an animal and its offspring on the same day. "The purpose of this commandment is that a man should take to heart the fact that God's providence extends generally to all species of living creatures, and that by His providence over them will they continue to exist forever; for divine providence in relation to things constitutes their very existence. Hence none of the species will ever become totally extinct. And though divine providence in the case of the human species extends to the individual, it is not so in regard to other living creatures. In the latter instance God bestows his providence in a general way over the species alone." [29]

Hence we may infer from the above that, since God's providence over all creatures other than man extends only to the species and not to the individual, the form of prayer cited in the Mishnah is inconsistent with the view of Judaism. Though the Hinnuk does not explicitly draw this conclusion, it nevertheless follows from his stated principle regarding the nature of divine providence. This, then, would be the meaning of the first opinion cited in the Talmud. He is silenced "because he causes jealousy among the works of creation." In other words, he errs in his prayer in extending divine providence to the individual among animals.

Nurturing the Quality of Mercy

Moreover, it cannot be said that God commanded us to let the mother bird go when a nest is taken out because He is moved by a special compassion for the mother bird in this instance in the same manner as would a human being. For if this were so, why did God permit the slaughter of animals altogether?[30] The attribute of mercy is of the nature of man. The attempt to apply qualities, such as mercy, to God is erroneous and incompatible with Judaism's conception of the nature of God. "This is not to say," the Hinnuk explains, "that God is not merciful . . . but it means that His mercy is unlike man's. Mercy in man is a necessary consequence of the nature with which God endowed him. God's mercy, on the other hand, is the result of His free will. His wisdom moves Him to be merciful because it is a quality of goodness, and God is the source of all good." [31]

This view is a development of the second opinion cited in the Talmud, namely, that he is silenced "because he makes the *middot* of God to be acts of mercy, whereas they are but injunctions." It is significant, we may note, that the Talmud uses here the term *middot* which, in its stricter sense, means attributes or qualities, a meaning that is eminently pertinent in this context. The statement above is consequently to be understood in this sense, namely, that "these commandments with respect to cattle and fowl are not because of compassion for them, but are rather injunctions intended to train us and to teach us good traits." [32] The object of this mizvah is therefore to teach us to refrain from cruelty, and thereby to nuture within us the human quality of mercy and compassion. For, indeed, the basic purpose of the commandments is to provide man with a means of purifying his soul, thus meriting the good life in this world and in the World to Come.

Hence, in the light of his construction of the Mishnah in question, the Hinnuk believes that it does not mean to indicate that the mizvot are without reason, nor does it reflect a negative attitude on the part of the Sages toward a rational understanding of their purpose. Quite the contrary, it would appear that their attitude in this respect was a positive one.[33] Thus, in summation, the Hinnuk is convinced of the correctness of his thesis, and that it is manifestly in consonance with authoritative Jewish thought.

JUSTIFICATION FOR A RATIONALE OF MIZVOT

The question arises: If there are reasons for the mizvot, why are they not given in the Torah? In answer, the Hinnuk cites[34] the following statement in the Talmud: "Why were the reasons of the Torah laws not revealed? Because in two verses reasons were revealed and they caused the greatest in the world to stumble."[35] The reference is to King Solomon, who did not heed the prohibitions forbidding a king's acquisition of excessive wealth and an inordinate number of wives and horses.[36] He violated these prohibitions, the Rabbis explain, in the mistaken belief that he would not succumb to the resultant evils of which the Torah explicitly warns. His transgression was thus due to the fact that in both instances Scripture revealed the reasons for the prohibitions. Presumably, had no reasons been set forth, he would have simply complied with the biblical injunctions. Hence, had the Torah given the reasons for other mizvot as well, similar miscalculations would have followed. This would be particularly true, for example, in the case of forbidden foods for which the Torah gives no reason, lest those who consider themselves wiser than their fellows be prompted to contend that a harmful effect ascribed to a forbidden food applies only in certain climates, or to certain persons whose nature makes them susceptible to it. By this kind of specious reasoning, they themselves would eventually be misled, and they would mislead others, thus causing incalculable harm.[37]

But if this be so, why does the Hinnuk himself attempt to offer reasons for the commandments? It may be pointed out, as the Hinnuk suggests,[38] that in offering reasons for the mizvot he is but following the precedent already established by the Sages in the Talmud, as previously indicated, and by the great authorities who preceded him. Indeed, as we have seen, both Nahmanides and Maimonides are unequivocally committed to the position maintained by the Hinnuk.

Comprehension of God's Ways

For Maimonides, a comprehension of God's ways and of the purpose of His commandments is man's supreme objective in life. Even as creation and the actions of God are not merely the result of His will, but of His wisdom, so "all commandments and prohibitions are dictated by His wisdom and serve a certain aim. Consequently there is a reason for each one of the precepts; they are enjoined because they are useful." [39] The thesis that the commandments are rational and their reasons are to be probed was not mere speculation which Maimonides allowed himself within the confines of his philosophical work alone. Indeed, he deems it proper and germane to a true conception of Jewish law. In the *Mishneh Torah* Maimonides writes: "Even though all of the statutes of the Torah are divine decrees, as we explained at the end of *Hilkot Me'ilah,* it is nevertheless fitting to reflect upon them and to offer reasons for them wherever possible." [40]

Nahmanides expresses substantial agreement with the general principle established by Maimonides. "The Master's conclusion that there are reasons for the commandments is exceedingly evident . . . The Rabbis have explained that what prevents us from knowing the reasons for the mizvot of the Torah is but our own intellectual blindness. In fact, the reason for the most difficult one among them was already revealed to the Sages of Israel." [41]

Strictly speaking, moreover, the author of the *Sefer ha-Hinnuk* would maintain that he only delineates general objectives which the commandments serve, as in the case of the laws of impurity and of forbidden foods. Indeed, in his opinion, only the essential object of a given commandment should concern us. We may ascribe a reason as regards the general aspects of a commandment, but we need not attempt to explain the purpose of its details.[42] In this way the danger anticipated does not enter into consideration. This view is also expressed by Maimonides. "The repeated assertion of our Sages that there are reasons for all commandments, and the tradition that Solomon knew them, refer to the general purpose of the commandments, and not to the object of every detail." [43]

Commandments Have Purpose

Nevertheless, the above would not be a sufficient answer; for, if ascribing reasons for the mizvot may lead to their misunderstanding and neglect, then why pursue this line of investigation? It would appear that the Hinnuk's justification for advancing reasons for the commandments is his assumption that, in order to assure an observance of the mizvot, we must seek out and offer reasons that are convincing and acceptable. "My intention in writing these reasons," says the Hinnuk, "is to guide the youth, and to impress upon them at the beginning of their studies that the words of the Torah have reason and purpose, so that they may accept them in accordance with their training and to the extent of their limited intelligence. Let not the mizvot appear to them at the outset as words of a sealed book, lest they thereby spurn them in their youth and abandon them forever to follow after vanity." [44]

The fear that a stated reason may be misconstrued is then no longer a valid concern, in view of the total disregard of the commandments which can result from a lack of appreciation of their purpose. In the final balance, the harm that may accrue from misunderstanding must be equated with the infinitely greater harm that comes from the belief that the commandments have no rational basis or intelligent purpose, and hence are of no meaning in our lives. [45]

The Transcendent Wisdom of God

In embarking upon his quest for a rationale of the commandments, the Hinnuk affirms one fundamental condition as a prerequisite. Regardless of whether or not we are successful in fathoming the reason for a given commandment, we must presume the commandments to be of divine origin and their observance in no wise subject to the outcome of our quest. "There is no man in the world," the Hinnuk emphasizes, "who has attained to the ultimate of all wisdom and from whose knowledge nothing is hidden. Of Moses it is said that he had access to but forty-nine of the fifty gates of wisdom. [46] One was closed even to him. King Solomon, the wisest of men, said of himself, 'I said I will be wise, but it was far from me' (Ecclesiastes 7:23) . . . If, then, in our wisdom we attain to an understanding of the purpose which the laws serve, we can be pleased. However, where we do not in our wisdom fathom their purpose, we must nonetheless consider that God in His wisdom, which transcends that of any being, knew the purpose which a given law serves and for that reason did He command us concerning it." [47]

It is from this very premise that Maimonides took his point of departure in his investigation into the reasons of the mizvot. In the *Mishneh Torah* he enunciates this clearly, as follows: "It is proper for a man to reflect upon the laws of our holy Torah in order to understand their final object according to his ability. However, if there is something whose reason he will not have found and whose cause he does not know, let him not consider it as being unimportant . . . Note how strict the Torah is regarding the improper use of sacred property, which is but wood and stone but which has become hallowed by reason of the fact that God's name was bestowed upon it, . . . how much more so must a man refrain from spurning the commandments which God ordained for us, only because he does not know their reasons." [48]

This view is also clearly affirmed by Saadiah and Ibn Ezra. Saadiah concludes his brief analysis of the laws with the statement: "But even though the chief reason for the fulfillment of these principal precepts and their derivatives and whatever is connected with them is the fact that they represent the command of our Lord and enable us to reap a special advantage, yet I find that most of them have as their basis partially useful purposes. I see fit, therefore, to note some of these motivations and discuss them, although the wisdom of God, blessed and exalted be He, is above all that." [49] Ibn Ezra, likewise, states: "God forbid that any of the mizvot should be contrary to reason. However we must keep all that God has commanded us irrespective of whether their reason has been revealed to us or not." [50]

THE OBJECT OF THE MIZVOT

The Hinnuk's approach to an understanding of the mizvot of the Torah is based in the first instance, as we have shown, on the premise that there is reason and purpose to the commandments. To this he adds a second, corollary hypothesis, namely, that the object of the mizvot is to further man's welfare. We shall examine this second hypothesis and endeavor to delineate those principles enunciated by the Hinnuk which reflect his conception of the general object of the commandments.

The Hinnuk indicates this to be a fundamental premise in his rationale of mizvot. "The great benefit that we derive in acquiring virtuous qualities and in avoiding evil is due to the fact that goodness will cleave to the good. And our good God, Who desires our benefit, has therefore commanded His people to choose the good. This is the way that I follow with regard to most of the commandments in explaining their plain meaning."[51]

Mizvot Are for Man's Good

The thesis set forth by the Hinnuk may be stated as follows. The mizvot were given by God solely for man's benefit. Their observance renders man capable and worthy of receiving goodness from God, who is the source of all good, and whose very essence is goodness. In violating or neglecting them, however, he becomes susceptible to evil and grief.

"Know my son," says the Hinnuk, "that God derives nothing from man's observance of all His commandments, other than that it is His desire to do good to us. When man is prepared to receive this goodness by the observance of these commandments, then God bestows it upon him.[52] God, therefore, made known to man the good way that leads him to be good, namely, the way of the Torah, for by it man can be good. We find, therefore, that whoever observes God's commandments fulfills His will since he is then worthy to receive His goodness. On the other hand, whoever does not prepare himself in this way is exceedingly wicked, because he knows what the will of God is, but he acts contrary to His will." [53]

In the final analysis then, the mizvot are for our own good. Some of them are designed to keep our souls pure.[54] Those which designate certain actions or procedures are intended to teach us good traits. We must, therefore, assert that the commandments are given exclusively for our benefit and not for God's benefit. It neither adds to nor detracts from God's honor, for instance, whether we slaughter according to ritual or not, or if we eat unclean and forbidden foods. The same can be said of the other commandments. "The mizvot of the Torah," the Hinnuk concludes, "have the purpose of helping the people to refine their opinions and of training them to improve all of their actions. There is no benefit in their observance to the Creator, blessed be He."[55] This, the Hinnuk emphasizes, is basic to his thesis. "Indeed, this is the view which I maintain in all of my discussions in this book, namely, that the commandments are of benefit to us, but not to Him who commanded them. If you will set your heart to it, you will find this to be the intention of all of them."[56]

The Hinnuk's exposition above is substantially that of Nahmanides,[57] who cites as authority the midrashic statement, "What does it matter to God whether the animal is slaughtered at the throat or at the back of the neck? The Torah has been given only to ennoble mankind."[58] The Midrash bases itself upon the verse, "The word of the Lord is tried [zerufah = refined]. He is a shield unto all them that take refuge in Him" (Psalms 18:31). The verse is understood to mean that the mizvot are intended to purify, refine, and ennoble and, as a consequence, to protect and benefit man.

In this connection he quotes a significant talmudic discussion on the annulment of vows. The Mishnah states: "Rabbi Zadok said: Rather than open the way for a man by reason of the honor due to father and mother, they should open the way for him by reason of the honor due to God."[59] The Jerusalem Talmud[60] proceeds to analyze the Mishnah: "What is honor due to God? If he says I will not make a sukkah, or I will not take the lulab or I will not wear the tefillin, this is a matter of honor to God? Indeed, he benefits himself, as Scripture says: 'If thou be righteous what givest thou Him? (Job 35:7)[61] If thou sin, what dost thou effect against Him?' " (Job 35:6).

This same thought, Nahmanides notes, is expressed in the prayer on Yom Kippur: "Thou hast set man apart from the beginning and acknowledged him that he should stand before Thee. Yet who shall say unto Thee: 'What dost Thou?' And if he be righteous, what boon is that to Thee?"[62] Maimonides, likewise alluding to this prayer,[63] though in a different context, concludes, "The service of God is not intended for God's perfection; it is intended for our own perfection."[64]

THE IMPRESS OF MIZVOT UPON THE SOUL

The mizvot were given by God in order to benefit man materially and to purify and ennoble him spiritually.[65] Certain of the mizvot are quite evidently designed to promote man's physical health and well-being, a condition desirable in itself as well as for its felicitous effect upon his spirit. "God, blessed be He, removed his chosen people from all things which harm the body, because it is the vessel for the soul which has cognition of its Creator." [66] Should the body be subject to any defect, it would impair the function of the mind. Therefore, the Torah has forbidden us anything that would be harmful. "In this way we can explain all of the prohibitions of the Torah regarding forbidden foods." [67]

It is equally reasonable to assume that other mizvot may have as their purpose the preservation of man's spiritual health and well-being. In some way, of which we are not fully cognizant, man's soul and intellect may suffer ill-effects as a result of adverse physical factors. "Do not be dismayed, my son," the Hinnuk contends, "by the laws of impurity, even though their reason is generally unknown to people. For it is possible that impurity is harmful and has some ill-effects upon the soul." [68]

In support of this thesis, he draws upon a statement by the Rabbis wherein they call attention to the injurious effect of transgressions upon the soul, particularly in the case of prohibited foods. Citing the biblical verse, "Ye shall not make yourselves abominable with any creeping thing that creepeth; and ye shall not make yourselves unclean with them, that ye should be defiled thereby" (Leviticus 11:43), the Rabbis conclude that forbidden food "dulls the heart of man," defiling the soul and deadening its finer qualities and its purer nature.[69]

Interrelatedness of Body and Soul

Food is an important factor in man's health. Some foods are demonstrably detrimental to the proper functioning of the body. That *terefah* meat is harmful should be obvious from the fact that the defect resulted in the animal's having become diseased, thus endangering the health of one who would eat such meat.[70] Since body and soul are inseparable, one affecting the other, this will likewise result in a harmful effect upon the soul. For this reason, the Torah forbade certain fats and prohibited the ingestion of blood.[71] In the case of the restriction against blood, he cites an additional consideration: the eating of the life force of another living creature is bound to develop in man a cruel and brutal nature.

As the craftsman depends upon the strength and the quality of his tools, so does the soul depend upon the body in order to function properly. Even those prohibited foods whose harmful effect upon man's physical being is not readily apparent may still be injurious to man's physical and spiritual nature in a way as yet not known to us or to medical science. In the final analysis, the Hinnuk emphasizes, "God knows that all of the foods which He prohibited His chosen people are harmful to the body, which is the vessel of the soul, in which the soul functions and by means of whose good deeds the soul is uplifted. God, therefore, forbade them to us so that the soul might perform its appointed functions without being restricted by the ill disposition of the body or the dullness of the heart."[72]

Hence, until we have acquired conclusive knowledge of the nature of man's soul, we would do well not to question the proscriptions of forbidden foods and impurities. "The human soul may be ill-affected by material things though they are not of its kind. In all probability, this happens because of the interrelatedness of the body and the soul. If we humans, in our limited understanding, do not know the nature of the soul, how can we presume to know, of a certainty, what is beneficial to it or harmful to it merely through investigation? Indeed, the doctors have no means of curing an illness until they first recognize the essential nature of the illness. Therefore, as regards all of the restrictions found in the Torah regarding impurity, we cannot expect to lay bare all of their reasons until we will have first reached an ultimate knowledge of the nature of the soul, its origin and its function. Understand this, and bear it in mind, because in it you will find a partial answer as to the purpose of the laws of impurity and purity."[73]

The Hinnuk here points up the innate interdependence of body and soul, maintaining that the body is "the vessel of the soul, through which the soul functions."[74] The belief in the interrelatedness of man's body and soul, as set forth by the Hinnuk, was anticipated by Maimonides.[75] It is more precisely developed by Nahmanides in his discourse on the prohibition of the blood of animals;[76] the reason for the prohibition being that the coarse animal spirit in the blood would be absorbed and become a part of the spirit of man. "It is well known," Nahmanides writes concerning animals that are forbidden by the Torah, "that they are not beneficial to health, and besides this, they are harmful to the soul."[77] Noting that this is of especial consequence to Israel, he elaborates, "The reason for the statement, 'Thou shalt not eat any abominable thing' (Deuteronomy 14:3), is to indicate that all things which are forbidden are an abomination to the pure soul . . . because forbidden foods, being coarse, give rise to a denseness and a dullness in the soul."[78] Ibn Ezra, in like manner, understands this to mean that Israel, as a holy people, must abjure anything which defiles the purity of the soul.[79]

This approach to mizvot, which views them in terms of the interdependence of body and soul, is particularly evident in the writings of the Kabbalists. Thus, Menahem Recanati, a Jewish mystic who was a disciple of Nahmanides, writes: "In connection with all of these prohibited foods it states, 'Ye shall be holy unto me' (Leviticus 20:26). This is in order that the soul, which draws its substance from food, be kept pure in accordance with its essential refinement and purity."[80] This conception was also anticipated by Saadiah,[81] who explains that forbidden foods and prohibited forms of cohabitation have a debilitating and defiling effect upon the soul. While the effect may, at times, not be evident to men, it is perfectly clear to God.

MAN IS AFFECTED BY DEEDS

There remains to be considered one further hypothesis that is essential in the Hinnuk's rationale of the mizvot—his belief that the deepest impressions upon a man's soul are made not by thoughts alone but by overt acts. "You must know that man is affected by his actions. His heart and all of his thoughts invariably follow the deeds with which he is occupied, whether they be good or bad." [82] The Hinnuk advances this as the reason why God commanded the performance of so many acts in remembrance of the exodus from Egypt, when it might seem that one act of remembrance would suffice to bring the miraculous event to mind.

The notion that man's character is molded by habitual acts and conduct, also propounded by Aristotle,[83] is affirmed by Maimonides in his discourse on the acquisition of moral dispositions. "How shall a man train himself in these dispositions, so that they become ingrained? Let him practice again and again the actions prompted by those dispositions and repeat them continually till they become easy and are no longer irksome to him, and so the corresponding dispositions will become a fixed part of his character." [84]

Moral and Spiritual Effects of Mizvot

The Hinnuk takes this to be a guiding principle to be followed in explaining the commandments, which are designed to promote man's well-being and to cultivate the moral and spiritual phases of his personality. The object of the Torah, he asserts, is to envelop us with mizvot and righteous deeds, thereby directing our thoughts to holiness and guiding us to the good life. "Our Sages, of blessed memory, have therefore said, 'The Holy One, blessed be He, was minded to make Israel worthy; wherefore He gave them a copious Torah and many commandments,' [85] in order to occupy therewith all of our thoughts and activities for our own ultimate good, because through good deeds we will be inclined to become good and to merit life everlasting." [86]

Even a man's garb and dress can have an effect upon his attitude and conduct. Thus, the priests were commanded to wear prescribed garments while performing the service in the Temple, the Hinnuk observes, because apart from the fact that the garments were a means of according honor and respect for the divine service, they were also intended as a constant reminder of their sacred duties and their dedication to God. [87]

The Hinnuk evinces a keen insight into the psychology of the human personality and the effect of habit upon human actions and feelings. Echoing rabbinic dicta, he maintains that even the inveterate sinner, who makes a sincere effort to follow the commandments of the Torah, can in the course of time incline toward a good life even if his motives initially are not pure. "Were he to rouse his spirit and endeavor to occupy himself diligently with the Torah and the commandments, even if not for the sake of Heaven, he would immediately incline toward the good and by the power of his deeds he would destroy his evil nature, because men's hearts are drawn after their actions." [88]

A man's character has a quality of pliability and is not completely impervious to sustained pressure resulting from certain factors and conditions in life, be they for good or for evil. No man may consider himself impenetrable to the corroding influence of evil habits and morally degrading situations. Hence, says the Hinnuk, "Even if a man be wholly righteous, upright and wholehearted, delighting in the Torah and the commandments, were he perchance to occupy himself continually with shameful things—let us say, for example, that the king imposed upon him an appointment to an evil occupation, and if he were indeed engaged all day continually in that occupation—he would in due time turn away from the righteousness of his heart and become a completely wicked man, for it is a known and true fact that every man is affected by his actions." [89]

For this reason the observance of the commandments, even if in a perfunctory and mechanical manner, is beneficial both in the inherent goodness achieved and in the strengthening and cementing of good habits. Thus, the Hinnuk writes, "In accustoming themselves to that which is good and upright, even if at first out of fear, they will train themselves eventually to do justice and righteousness out of love, once they perceive the way of truth. This is in accord with what the Sages say, that habit becomes second nature; that is, just as a person's nature compels him to gratify his wants, so will a strong habit become a part of his very nature, impelling him to follow in the way in which he has become accustomed. Hence, when people walk in the ways of uprightness and faith and choose the good, then goodness will cleave unto them and God will rejoice in His works." [90]

The Hinnuk thus bases his conception of the mizvot on what he believes to be the consensus of opinion held by the Sages and the religious philosophers, namely, that the commandments, divinely ordained, are purposeful and capable of being rationally comprehended, and that they were designed by God to promote man's welfare. That some of the mizvot are beyond our understanding is due, as we have noted, to the limited knowledge which man presently possesses. Since our knowledge is still too meager to allow us fully to apprehend the manner in which they influence and determine our well-being, we must observe unquestioningly all of the commandments, even the *hukim* for which no reason is given and which baffle and elude our comprehension. "No intelligent person," the Hinnuk contends, "will doubt that God, Who is the source and embodiment of all wisdom, and the source of all goodness, will command His creatures anything except it be for their good and for their benefit." [91] The Torah laws thus demand unqualified obedience and implicit faith in God's superior wisdom. The knowledge of God in these matters far transcends the limits of human intelligence.

Having thus established that the mizvot are rationally comprehensible, the Hinnuk accordingly proceeds to probe the reasons for all of the Taryag Mizvot.

CHAPTER SIX

MAN'S ETHICAL DUTIES

In the history of moral philosophy two conceptions of ethical theory may be distinguished; the one philosophical, reflecting Greek thought, and the other religious, reflecting the biblical ideal. Philosophical ethics, which is speculative and antinomian in nature, holds itself to be independent of religion and removed from theological considerations, relying solely upon reason or some other human faculty for its moral judgments. Religious ethics, on the other hand, encompasses the totality of man's human and religious experience. More significantly, it is based upon a belief in a Divine Being who manifests His concern for man's conduct in life. While certain acts or motives may commend themselves to the intelligence or to conscience, moral conduct, in the ultimate sense, is not determined by human reason or the natural intuitive judgment of man, but by divine will.

In Judaism, the ground of moral duty, as of religious obligation, is the mizvah which bespeaks the will and wisdom of God. Ethical ideals and moral principles are of divine origin, and are thus invested by the Torah with the authority and sanction of divine commands.[1] As the mizvot are all-pervasive and, by their very nature, exhortative and pragmatic, they become the pattern for moral conduct and the working rules of moral action. Even as each individual mizvah has its own inner ethical core, so every ethical concept of the Torah has its concrete expression in Halakah. Jewish ethics is thus integrated into Jewish Law.

THE WAY OF GOD

The Hinnuk's methodical exposition of the mizvot reveals a moral philosophy firmly based upon the broad foundations of Halakah, and deeply rooted in traditional ethical and religious doctrine.

God's ultimate aim, whether in creation of the world or in revelation of His Law, is the good and well-being of His creatures, especially of man. Of prime concern to the Torah, therefore, in addition to man's own welfare, is the cultivation of his proper relationship with his fellowman. A man ought to set as a prime object in life to do good on earth. He will thereby not only bring God's blessing upon himself, but he will be instrumental in the fulfillment of God's design in the world, which is to vouchsafe good to all beings.

Man is thus cast in the role of God's agent, serving God's purpose. "And this is the great principle underlying all of man's good deeds in this world, and such is his reward from God because he fulfills God's will, inasmuch as God desires the welfare of His creatures." [2] This is why we are bidden to help the poor, says the Hinnuk, "for were it not for this reason, God would amply provide for the poor man's wants without us. But it is of God's kindness that we are become His agents so that we may merit thereby." [3] It is of the very essence of God's nature "that He is abounding in kindness, and that He desires the welfare of His creatures and wishes them to be worthy and meritorious in order to receive the good from Him." [4]

The Emulation of God

In order to be the instrument of divine goodness, man must strive to emulate those attributes which we understand to be of the essence of God's ethical nature. This, in substance, is the principle of *Imitatio Dei,* which as developed in talmudic and midrashic literature is the virtual fountainhead of Jewish ethics. [5] For the Hinnuk, this emulation is not only an ethical maxim, but one of the Taryag Mizvot.

"We are commanded to act in a righteous and goodly manner to the best of our ability, and to conduct all matters between ourselves and others in a kindly and merciful way, even as we know from our Torah that this is the way of God and this is His desire for His creatures so that they merit His goodness, for He desires kindness. Concerning this it is said, 'And walk in His ways' (Deuteronomy 28:9). This commandment is repeated again elsewhere, as it is said, 'To walk in all His ways' (Deuteronomy 10:12). The Rabbis, of blessed memory, explained this commandment as follows:[6] As the Holy One, blessed be He, is called merciful, be thou also merciful; as the Holy One, blessed be He, is called righteous, be thou also righteous; as the Holy One, blessed be He, is called holy, be thou also holy. Their intention is to indicate that we should learn to emulate such good deeds and honored qualities which are ascribed to God, blessed be He, in dealing with His creatures."[7] The *Mekilta* draws this lesson from the scriptural verse: "This is my God and I will adorn Him" (Exodus 15:2). The Sages comment, "Is it then possible to adorn God? Yes, by resembling Him. As He is compassionate and gracious, be thou likewise compassionate and gracious."[8]

Maimonides, likewise, lists the imitation of God as one of the commandments.[9] The principle of *Imitatio Dei* is explained by Maimonides in the course of his discussion of the scriptural passage regarding Moses' request to know the true nature of God (Exodus 33:18-23). While it is not given to man to know the true essence of God's metaphysical nature, God does reveal His ethical nature. After making it clear that all attributes, as ascribed to God, are attributes of His acts and do not imply that God has any qualities, Maimonides states: "For the utmost virtue of man is to imitate God as far as possible; which means that we liken our actions to His actions."[10] In the concluding passage of his *Guide of the Perplexed*, Maimonides states: "The perfection in which man can truly glory is attained by him when he has acquired, as far as possible, a knowledge of God and of His providence over His creatures in their creation and continued existence. Having acquired this knowledge, he will then be determined to seek lovingkindness, justice and righteousness, and thus imitate the ways of God."[11]

The Doctrine of the "Mean"

Following the Aristotelian view as explicated by Maimonides,[12] the Hinnuk believes that one should adopt the "mean" as the norm in human conduct. "A man should choose the good road and the middle course in all matters and in all activities, whether it be eating, drinking, business, study of Torah, prayer or speech, and he should never tend to extremes in all these things." [13] The doctrine of the "golden mean," signifying harmony and balance in life, reflects the indigenous Jewish teachings of the Sages[14] and the medieval Jewish philosophers, such as Saadiah,[15] Bahya ibn Pakuda,[16] Halevi,[17] and Maimonides.[18] For Maimonides it is "the way of God," the legacy of Abraham.[19]

Important in this regard is the strengthening of man's spiritual nature and the exercise of control over his grosser nature. "Most of man's sins," writes the Hinnuk, "are the result of excessive eating and drinking," [20] and similar gratification of bodily desires. Man ought nourish his soul by fostering a reverence for God and by observing the mizvot.[21]

Refinement of Moral Character

The "good way," leading to the good life, is the "way of Torah." [22] The Torah predisposes the people of Israel to a wise disposition of their innate resources, for "by conducting themselves in accordance with its commands, they will be prepared for wisdom and understanding, and will perceive what is necessary for their proper conduct in life." [23] Thus, echoing the view of the Sages that "the commandments were given to refine the people," [24] the Hinnuk envisages a refinement of character and the attainment of moral qualities through the mizvot.

Some commandments, primarily intended to make us cognizant of our religious beliefs and duties, are also designed to guard us from lustful and impure thoughts. "In His desire to render His holy people worthy, God enjoined us to surround ourselves with mighty guardians. We were therefore commanded to study the Torah unceasingly day and night, to affix four fringes upon the four corners of our garments, and a *mezuzah* upon our door, and to place *tefillin* upon our arms and heads—all in order to remind us to desist from robbery, and to keep us from straying after the waywardness of our eyes and the evil inclinations of our hearts." [25]

Concerning our need for these guardians, the Hinnuk states: "Since man is a material being he would perforce be drawn after his passions . . . were it not that the soul which God, in His grace, gave us restrains us from sin, as far as it is able to do so. And since the soul dwells in man's domain, on earth, and very far from its own natural domain, in heaven, it has need, therefore, of many guardians to protect it in its evil environment." [26]

Notwithstanding, man is capable of exercising control over his desires and emotions. Indeed the Torah proceeds on this assumption when it states in the last of the Ten Commandments: "Neither shalt thou desire thy neighbor's house, his field, or his manservant, or his maidservant, his ox, or his ass, or anything that is thy neighbors" (Deuteronomy 5:18). The Hinnuk notes the distinction between the term "desire" (tit'aveh) in the commandment as given in Deuteronomy and the term "covet" (tahamod) in the commandment as stated in Exodus (20:14). The latter prohibition applies only to the actual acquisition, even upon payment, of that which is coveted. [27] The former, however, prohibits the entertaining of covetous desires altogether, inasmuch as they will lead one to scheme and to resort to all means to acquire that which is in the possession of another. [28] The Tenth Commandment thus comprises two prohibitions; the one moral, directed against the harboring of sinful desires; and the other legal, where the transgression is committed upon acquisition of what is desired. [29]

The contention that the Torah cannot legislate against evil thoughts and desires over which a man presumably has no control must be rejected. If man makes a sincere effort he can succeed in refraining from such thoughts. "Do not question," says the Hinnuk, "how can a man restrain himself from harboring desires for a veritable treasure of delightful vessels which he sees in his neighbor's possession while he is utterly bereft of all these things, and how can the Torah presume to forbid a man something over which he has no control? Such a contention is specious, and only fools and men of wicked intent will argue so. It is within man's power to control himself and

to restrain his thoughts and desires from whatever he pleases." [30] In
the final accounting, God, who alone knows the innermost recesses
of a man's heart, will determine whether or not he has made a
genuine effort to do so.

The Nazirite and Asceticism

The Hinnuk's call for self-restraint and control over man's natural
passion is not to be construed as an espousal of asceticism. While
he does affirm the duality of man's nature, noting that "our intellect
is forced to dwell within the body that is the source of man's lusts
and sinfulness," he nonetheless recognizes the responsibility "to provide for the material needs of its physical abode." [31]

His view of the Nazirite who takes a vow of abstinence is of interest in this regard. The Nazirite is considered to be holy in that
he endeavors to subdue the cravings of his physical nature so as to
allow for the full development of his intellectual and spiritual nature,
without however resorting to extreme measures of self-denial. The
laws requiring him to abstain from wine and to refrain from cutting
his hair are but moderate restraints that he takes upon himself in
order to divert his thoughts from indulging in vainglory and in physical pleasures. Indeed, the sin-offering which Scripture orders him to
bring upon completion of the period of his vow (Numbers 6:14),
which the Rabbis consider to be in atonement for his abstinence,[32]
is understood by the Hinnuk to be necessary since the Nazirite may
have misjudged his own nature and needlessly subjected himself to
these restrictions. The Hinnuk pointedly differs from Nahmanides,
whom he also cites, who believes that the Nazirite must bring a sin-
offering because he has resumed a normal way of life, and subjected
himself to the contamination of worldly desires, after having been
consecrated to God, a condition that he should have sought to maintain all his life.[33] The Hinnuk argues forcefully for a rational evaluation of life, its multi-faceted demands and legitimate needs. In opposition to ascetic practices, he quotes from the Talmud.[34] "R. Jose
says: An individual may not afflict himself by fasting. Rab Judah
said in the name of Rab: R. Jose's reason is because it is written,
'And man became a living soul' (Genesis 2:7). Scripture thereby

implies, Keep alive the soul which I gave you." To this the Hinnuk appends a verse from Kohelet, "Be not righteous over much; neither make thyself overwise; why shouldest thou destroy thyself?" (Ecclesiastes 7:16).

MORAL VIRTUE

The goodness exemplified by God that is to be emulated by man is not passive but active, "because only the one who does good to others besides himself can be considered perfect in his goodness." [35] The truly good men are, therefore, to be distinguished by certain moral virtues that the commandments are intended to develop. Though no attempt to classify these moral virtues is discernible in rabbinic tradition, nevertheless certain of them are given preeminence. Righteousness or charity and justice stand out in Scripture as the two essential *middot,* or moral attributes of God in his dealing with man. [36] They are, consequently, the primary ethical norms of human conduct.

Cultivation of a Charitable Nature

The mizvot requiring that a portion of a man's field or vineyard and their gleanings be left for the poor, apart from aiding the needy, tend to nurture within man a good heart and a charitable nature. The reason for these commandments is that "God wished His chosen people to be adorned with all good and noble qualities, and that they should have a benevolent soul and a generous spirit." [37]

In his development of the concept of charity, the Hinnuk follows the classic view as enunciated by the Rabbis[38] and later formulated by Maimonides.[39] The highest form of charity is to lend money to the poor. "One whose impoverished condition is evident and known and who has been reduced to begging from people does not suffer as much as the one who has not yet reached such a state of humiliation but fears lest he may yet come to it. Had he but some support through a loan by which he might profit somewhat, perhaps he would never have to resort to begging."[40] The Hinnuk does not, however, take as broad a view in ascribing ethical meanings to such precepts,

as giving the second tithe, and donating to the Sanctuary the valu-
ation of a life, as does Maimonides who cites them as being "based
on the principle of charity," [41] since man must develop a liberal disposition. Maimonides also considers the heave-offering, the dough
offering, the first fruit, the first of the shearing, the fruit of a tree in
its fourth year, as also all gifts to the priests and levites and things
devoted to the Temple, as means by which "man accustoms himself
to be liberal." [42] The Hinnuk views these precepts essentially as serving spiritual purposes.

The Hinnuk stresses that the prime object, of greater importance
even than the actual help accorded the poor, since God is capable
of providing for them in other ways, is man's cultivation of a charitable and compassionate nature so as to be worthy of God's beneficence. [43]

The Sabbatical year, aside from the concepts of faith that it incul-
cates, is thought by the Hinnuk to provide training in benevolence
and liberality. "Whoever finds it in his heart to renounce possession forever, and give away all of the produce of his fields and of
the inheritance of his fathers that grow in the course of a full year,
a practice to which he and his whole family become accustomed all
their lives, will never be prone to an avaricious nature, nor to a lack
of trust." [44] Cultivation of a spirit of generosity and the prevention
of covetousness and robbery will result from the laws of *Shemitah*
and the Jubilee year[45] which call for release of the land,[46] and the
remission of debts,[47] the latter necessitating a specific prohibition
against withholding loans from the poor for fear that the money
would not be repaid in the seventh year. [48]

Compassion for All Creatures

As God's "mercies are over all His works" (Psalms 145:9), embracing the whole of existence, so man in emulation of God must
be equally universal in his ethical concern. In forbidding the practice of cruelty to or the infliction of unnecessary pain upon animals,
the Torah seeks to cultivate humane and compassionate feelings for
them as well as for human beings. [49] This is the object of several
commandments of this nature. Such is the manifest intent of the

law prohibiting the slaughter of an animal and its offspring on the same day.[50] Similarly, it is forbidden to muzzle the ox when it treads corn,[51] a prohibition that applies to all animals employed in labor. "When a man becomes accustomed to have pity even upon animals who were created only to serve us, and he gives them a portion of their own labors, his soul will likewise grow accustomed to be kind to human beings and he will refrain from depriving them of anything that is due them. He will pay them their rightful wages, and he will satisfy them from the fruit of their labors. This is the proper way for a holy and chosen people to follow."[52]

The Hinnuk insists upon his own construction of these mizvot, despite the different view of Maimonides, as is markedly evident in the prohibition against yoking an ox and an ass together.[53] Maimonides is of the opinion that it is intended to prevent cross-breeding, an act he believes is forbidden by the Torah because it is degrading, since it involves vulgar and indecent practices.[54] After citing Maimonides and giving due deference to his opinion, the Hinnuk expresses his view, also held by Ibn Ezra,[55] that the pairing of two animals of diverse species is forbidden because it must result in anguish and pain to one of them. Significantly, the Hinnuk draws the lesson applicable to relations among men. "Every wise person will learn from this never to appoint, in regard to any matter, two people who differ greatly in their nature and conduct, such as a righteous man and a wicked man, or a base person together with an honored person. For if the Torah is concerned lest pain be caused to creatures that have no intelligence, certainly this would be so in the case of human beings who possess an intelligent soul capable of comprehending their Creator."[56]

The desire to refrain from causing pain to a living creature likewise figures as a factor in the law of shehitah,[57] prescribing the method of slaughter. The Hinnuk cites it as his second reason, the first being the need to assure the full flow of blood from the slaughtered animal. Maimonides makes the same point. He notes that while shehitah is primarily a test of man's obedience to the will of God, it is intended specifically "to ensure an easy death and to effect it by suitable means."[58] Slaughtering an animal is, moreover, viewed by the Hinnuk as a divine dispensation, it being permitted only when it serves a human need, such as food or health, or if it is for the purpose of atonement, as in sacrifices. Killing an animal needlessly is "wanton destruction and is to be considered as spilling blood." [59]

As already indicated, the mizvah of sparing the mother bird when a nest is taken serves to teach us the quality of mercy.[60] It is note-worthy that the tractate *Hullin,* which deals in the main with the slaughter of animals and the laws pertaining to their use for human consumption, ends with an entire chapter devoted to this mizvah of *shiluah haken* and its concomitant reward, thereby underscoring the basic ethical character of the commandments. This mizvah is, fur-thermore, singled out by the Rabbis as indicative of the inherent reward that obtains in the case of all of the commandments. The concluding Mishnah in *Hullin* states: "If then of so light a precept concerning what is worth but an *issar* the law has said 'that it may be well with thee and that thou mayest prolong thy days' (Deuteron-omy 22:7),[61] how much more shall the like reward be given for the fulfillment of the weightier precepts of the Law." [62]

The Hinnuk's explanation of these laws reveals a tendency that is indicative of his approach generally. While he is cognizant of the element of humaneness implicit in these mizvot, a factor that is par-ticularly stressed by Maimonides,[63] he consistently points up and emphasizes that their essential purpose is the refinement of man's ethical nature.

The Acquisition of Torah Knowledge

Along with the development of man's moral character and the inculcation of certain moral virtues Judaism, as we have seen, seeks the cultivation of intellectual virtue, as well, through the acquisition of wisdom, the highest of the virtues. Wisdom, or *hokmah,* in Jew-ish tradition, however, is not the exercise of reason in mere con-templation,[64] but the intellectual pursuit of the knowledge of God. "The main cause of man's having been created in the world is wis-dom, in order that he would know and acknowledge his Creator." [65] It is the "wisdom of the Torah" that one is duty-bound to learn and to teach, says the Hinnuk, because a knowledge of Torah will afford a knowledge of "the ways of God." [66] He should honor the Sages,[67] and associate with men learned in Torah so that he will learn from them its commandments and true opinions about God.[68] The support of the tribe of Levi is required under scriptural law, thus enabling the Levites to devote themselves to learning and "to acquiring wisdom and an understanding of the righteous ways of God," so that they might serve the people as teachers and as spiritual guides.[69] In His desire to make Israel "a wise and understanding people" (Deuteronomy 4:6), God sought to have them constantly occupied with the study of Torah, "that they would learn to know the Lord, from the least of them even unto their greatest." [70]

It is evident that the Hinnuk associates wisdom with a knowledge of the divine truths imparted by the Torah, whose object is to provide instruction in the moral laws and to foster faith in God. Maimonides, similarly, in discoursing on the meaning of wisdom, says that it denotes the apprehension of those truths which lead to the knowledge of God, and that it is also applied to acquiring moral principles. Thus, "one who has a true knowledge of the whole of the Torah is called wise in two respects; in respect of the intellectual virtues comprised in the Torah, and in respect of the moral virtues included in it." [71] Hence, in the moral philosophy of Judaism, as taught by the Hinnuk, the ultimate good and the highest objective in life is the acquisition of moral and intellectual virtue, leading to the cognition and the service of God.[72]

Insofar as moral law must accord with God's will and is based upon divine authority, the Hinnuk thus predicates a theonomous ethic. This does not obviate a concern with man's happiness and well-being. Indeed the Hinnuk views the moral objective in terms of an ethical idealism that conceives moral goodness to be related to man's striving for virtue and perfection, and holds moral action to be directed toward the improvement of man's condition in life and the betterment of society.

LAW AND JUSTICE

The welfare of the individual and of the community requires maintaining peaceful relations among all men. This is attainable by means of the establishment of a judicial system under which equal justice would be administered to all in accordance with the Law,[73] and by the appointment of officers and leaders to govern the people.[74]

Administration of Justice

Jewish law and tradition set high moral and spiritual standards both for judicial and temporal office. While exemplary qualities are to be acquired by all people, they are particularly requisite for one who is in a position of leadership and responsibility. It is moreover, essential that "he have compassion for the people, so as not to oppress them in any way, and that he love truth, justice and righteousness." [75] Inasmuch as these characteristics are deemed to be native to the children of Abraham,[76] the Hinnuk believes this to be the reason for the commandment requiring that the ruler, or any other designated leader among Jews, whether temporal or spiritual, be of the seed of Israel.[77] The Hinnuk emphasizes the responsibility for the appointment of worthy leaders at all times and in all positions of communal trust. "It is forbidden to appoint wicked and cruel men as leaders of the community. If one appoints them because they are relatives or because he fears them, or in order to flatter them, there will not depart evil from his house and the violence of that wicked man will come down upon his head. However, he who fears no man but seeks with all his might to benefit the people, will always receive his reward from God in this world, and his soul will in goodness rest in the World to Come, and his children will inherit the earth." [78]

The administration of public justice entailed a judiciary comprised of local tribunals of three judges for civil cases, a *Bet Din* of twenty-three judges in each city with jurisdiction in capital crimes, and a high court, or Sanhedrin, of seventy-one with appellate jurisdiction, as well as original jurisdiction in certain cases.[79] The constitution of these courts was subject to two preconditions, namely, residence in the Land of Israel and *Semikah,* the latter being a distinctive ordination which preserved an unbroken chain of religious and judicial authority.[80] While *Semikah* itself could be bestowed only in Israel, those who were duly ordained in Israel had the power to judge even outside of Israel. Jurisdiction in the case of capital crimes was further restricted to the time of the Temple and the Sanhedrin in Jerusalem. The Hinnuk points out that although we do not have *Semikah* in our day,[81] there is a duty nonetheless to appoint qualified judges to administer justice in every community.

God is the Source of Justice

Justice is, in Judaism, regarded as morally binding upon both God[82] and man, and is considered to be the foundation upon which human society is based.[83] "Were it not for justice," says the Hinnuk, "men could never live together. Without justice the world could not exist." [84] The Hinnuk is, nevertheless, not unmindful of the moral problem inherent in man's arrogation of authority in assuming the power of judgment over a fellow human being. He resolves this question by acknowledging that, assuredly, it is God alone who is the true judge and the source of all justice, as it is written, "for the judgment is God's" (Deuteronomy 1:17).[85] Such authority as we have is, therefore, delegated to us by God. The exercise of this authority must be in accordance with divinely ordained principles and prescribed limitations. With certain exceptions, the law requires the testimony of at least two competent eyewitnesses in all cases, whether criminal or civil.[86] Circumstantial evidence is, as a rule, not admissible. Witnesses are to be subjected to severe interrogation and searching cross-examination and, in capital cases, solemnly charged with their grave responsibility.[87] The court is to proceed with its deliberations on the basis of a presumption of innocence, requiring unimpeachable proof of the crime and of criminal intent. The accused is accorded the full protection and benefit of the law in order to facilitate his acquittal.[88]

Justice and Mercy

In dispensing justice we must seek, moreover, to pattern ourselves after God. As in God's judgment of man justice is tempered with mercy, so must we be guided as we administer justice to our fellowman. This concept is developed by the Hinnuk in discussing the law which stipulated that, while a simple majority of one is sufficient for acquittal in capital cases, a clear majority of at least two judges is required for conviction. "The reason for this mizvah is that we are commanded to model our actions after the attributes of God, blessed be He. And it is of the nature of God that He is abounding in kindness; that is to say, He deals with men beyond the line of strict justice. We are, therefore, commanded to do likewise, so that in capital cases the chances of acquittal shall be more favorable than for conviction, for a misjudgment in this instance is irreparable." [89]

There is, it appears, a broader moral and legal implication in this law. The decision involving taking the life of a human being belongs only to God. Where that authority is delegated to man, it must be in accord with a fixed principle of law. The Torah, by necessity, concedes such authority arbitrarily on the strength of two witnesses.[90] "At the mouth of two witnesses or three witnesses shall he that is to die be put to death" (Deuteronomy 17:6). The *Mekilta*,[91] which is referred to by the Hinnuk in discussing this commandment, intimates that in our case the judgment must follow the principle fixed in the case of witnesses which requires a minimum of two on whose testimony a man may be put to death. Hence, a minimum majority of two judges is, likewise, required in a court of law for conviction in capital cases. Jewish law, furthermore, imposes a distinct moral responsibility upon every court of law involving a case of capital punishment. While the court is under obligation to protect society as directed by the Torah, "And thou shalt put away the evil from the midst of thee" (Deuteronomy 17:7), it is nevertheless bound by a higher moral obligation to preserve life, equally enjoined by the Torah, as it is written, "Then the congregation shall judge . . . and the congregation shall deliver . . ." (Numbers 35:24, 25).[92]

The Hinnuk makes it clear, however, that justice must be served and society protected against criminal elements. The Bible enjoins that one who commits murder or inflicts physical harm upon his fellowman must receive punishment commensurate with his crime. The Hinnuk warns that the judge must not thwart or pervert justice because he is swayed by misguided feelings of pity engendered by the criminal's impoverished condition. The courts have a solemn duty, even under their present limited jurisdiction in capital cases, to punish the guilty to the utmost extent of their power and authority, and as demanded by the times and circumstances. The certainty of punishment for criminal acts, in full and just measure, he believes, serves as a deterrent to crime and is essential to the existence of society. Failure on its part to punish the criminal and to excise such evil from its midst can only lead to a state of lawlessness, where "men would swallow one another alive," and to society's ultimate destruction.[92a]

Judicial Procedure

The principle that a decision involving human life is not to be left to one man is invoked by the Hinnuk to account for the procedure designed to prevent domination of the court by the opinion of one of its members. In discussing the commandment prohibiting a judge from arguing for conviction in capital cases when he had first argued in favor of acquittal, the Hinnuk states: "The object of this commandment is, as we have stated at the outset, that none of the judges should merely follow the opinion of another of his colleagues, but should understand the facts himself. The reason for this is that, otherwise, it is possible that a decision may sometimes be rendered solely upon the opinion of one judge, and God, blessed be He, did not wish to surrender the decision on a human life to one man's judgment." [93] This procedure applies only to the deliberations during the course of the trial. In the final judgment, each judge is no longer bound by his prior opinion but is free to render his decision on the basis of his present construction of the law in the case.[94] The scriptural verse, "Neither shalt thou speak in a cause to incline after many to wrest judgment" (Exodus 23:2), which is cited as authority for this law, is likewise construed, with respect to court procedure in capital cases, as a directive to the judges that they may not open their deliberations with an argument for conviction, and that arguments are to be heard first from the less prominent members of the court in order that they may not be influenced by the expressed opinion of their elders.[95]

It is of interest to note the Hinnuk's consideration of the talmudic law, "If the Sanhedrin is unanimous in its opinion for conviction, he is freed." [96] This provision of the law has been difficult to understand. At first glance it appears to be illogical and unreasonable to assume that, while a man may be convicted when only a majority holds for his conviction, he is to be freed if there is unanimity on the part of the court for his conviction. The Hinnuk includes this provision among the specific laws which pertain to this commandment but, significantly, he states it as follows: "If they all began with arguments for conviction, he is acquitted." [97] It would seem that he here follows Maimonides, who evidently construes this law to apply in a case where the arguments are all for conviction, and no argument is heard in the defense of the accused. Maimonides states: "If a Sanhedrin in a capital trial opened with a unanimous opinion for conviction, and all proclaimed that he is guilty, he is freed until there be some who will study what might be said in his favor and argue for his acquittal. Then, if the majority is for conviction, he is put to death." [98]

The reasoning behind the view of Maimonides and the Hinnuk, we may suggest, is that in the case where no argument for acquittal is heard, a man's legal right to an adequate defense had been denied him. [99] According to Jewish law the responsibility for providing a defense for the defendant lies with the court. The Talmud itself emphasizes this responsibility when, in explanation of this law, it cites the fact that the court procedure in capital cases provides for postponing the verdict until the next morning, expressly for the purpose of reviewing and reexamining the evidence with the object of trying to find some legal basis for acquittal. [100] In view of the above construction of the law given by Maimonides and the Hinnuk, it is probable, in our opinion, that the law in this instance would require that the case be declared a mistrial. [101]

Capital Punishment

Jewish law is, thus, so construed as to tend to favor acquittal of the defendant. The moral justification for the death penalty, where all legal constraints have been exhausted, is to be found in the obligation to ensure the welfare of society as a whole. Evidently concerned with the moral question involved in capital punishment, the Hinnuk offers in explanation the following graphic illustration. [102]

Let us suppose that a man builds a city for his many children and settles them there. In order to promote their welfare he would perforce, have to promulgate strict laws, prohibiting one from killing the other on the pain of death. Let us further suppose that one of them violates this command and kills his brother. If he would forgive him, then the community would eventually be destroyed, because there would be nothing to restrain the rest from committing similar crimes. What is the father to do? He can try to find some legal basis for the acquittal of the accused, but if he cannot find it, then he must order his execution for the preservation of the rest. The principle is clear. While human life is sacred, and all legal safeguards must be resorted to in order to protect it, justice must nevertheless prevail for the very preservation of society. Maimonides gives voice to the same sentiment in a general way in his *Guide of the Perplexed*. While we must always help those who seek it, we may not extend such help to sinners and evildoers when it would interfere with the course of justice. We should not be persuaded by those who, through misplaced pity, fail to distinguish between the oppressor and the oppressed, because under these circumstances "pity for wrongdoers and evil men is tantamount to cruelty" with regard to all others.[103]

The Principle of Majority Rule

Central to the concept of justice and the entire judicial structure is the principle of the rule of the majority which the Hinnuk characterizes as "the pillar upon which the Torah rests."[104] It is a fundamental principle in Jewish law which we are commanded to maintain "in order to strengthen and preserve our faith."[105]

From a pragmatic point of view, this principle is justified because it offers a practicable procedure indispensable for an equitable system of justice, and because the opinion of the majority is more likely to approximate the truth. A requisite condition for the operation of this principle, of course, is that the majority be comprised of people competent and qualified to render judgment. The Hinnuk takes this principle to apply in specific cases and also, in a wider sense, in controversies regarding the law in general.[106]

In considering the principle of majority rule from a broader per-

spective, the Hinnuk recognizes man's moral obligation to abide by
the truth as his reason dictates. He underlines first the functional
aspect of the principle, pointing out that it is essential for the unity
of the people and the preservation of the Torah. Though we must
strive for the truth, we must also realize the danger that would ensue
if each one were permitted to render judgment and to act in accordance with his own opinion as to the truth in a given instance. The
result would be disunity and confusion which would threaten the
very existence of the Torah.[107] He then draws attention to the
deeper theological implications of this principle. Under it no man
can argue that he cannot violate his conscience and act contrary to
what his reason indicates the truth to be, because in submitting to
the will of the majority and in acting accordingly, he is obeying the
dictates of a higher, Divine Law whose object is the welfare of all.[108]

"The purpose of this commandment," the Hinnuk states, "is to
strengthen and preserve our faith. For, were we to have been commanded as follows, 'Keep the Torah as you are able to comprehend
its true meaning,' every Israelite would say, 'My reason tells me that
the truth of this matter is such.' Hence, even if the entire world
expressed a contrary opinion, he would not be free to act contrary
to what his reason tells him to be the truth. The result would be
chaos, because the Torah would be as many Torahs, since each one
would render judgment in accordance with his own limited understanding. But now that we are expressly commanded to accept the
opinion of the majority of the Sages, we all have one Torah which
is a great factor in our preservation. We should therefore not deviate
from it, come what may. Consequently, in carrying out their commands, we fulfill the commandment of God. Hence, even if the
Sages should, God forbid, sometimes not arrive at the truth, the
guilt would be upon them and not upon us."[109]

Significantly, the Hinnuk thus justifies the principle of the rule
of the majority on moral grounds by contending that submission to
divine authority permits the suspension of the dictates of a man's
own reason and enables him to clear with his own conscience an
action which he deems to be contrary to it. It should be noted that
involved in this question are a man's actions, not his thoughts or

private opinions. The Torah does not prohibit or restrict one from maintaining whatever views on the law he considers to be true. Even in the case of "a rebellious elder," who refused to abide by a decision of the majority of the Sanhedrin, the law was not operative and he was not subject to punishment unless he himself acted, or rendered a decision calling upon others to act, contrary to the decision of the court.[110] Beyond that, he is free to continue to teach his private views to his disciples. The Mishnah states: "If he returned to his own city and again taught as he was wont to teach, he was not punishable, for it is written 'And the man that doeth presumptuously' (Deuteronomy 17:12), he is not punishable unless he gives a decision concerning what should be done." [111] The law, it is to be seen, does not aim at uniformity of thought. What it does aim at, in order to preserve the Torah and the unity of Israel, is a unanimity of action, based upon the acceptance of the judgment of competent Torah authority.

CHAPTER SEVEN

THE INDIVIDUAL AND SOCIETY

The ethical norms that govern the conduct of society, as of the individual, are hypostatized within the Halakah in a regimen of specific laws and mizvot. The latter are themselves grounded in certain principles which reflect moral and religious, as well as socio-logical, objectives. A principle that is, for the Hinnuk, fundamental in the evolvement of society in a manner envisioned by the Torah is that of *yishub ha-'olam,* the welfare of society.

MARRIAGE AND THE FAMILY

The very first mizvah in the Torah relates to this principle in its primary and fundamental sense.[1] Man is commanded to propagate the human race, as the Bible states, "Be fruitful and multiply" (Genesis 1:28), since "it is God's will, blessed be He, that the world be inhabited, as it is written, 'He created it not a waste; He formed it to be inhabited'" (Isaiah 45:18).[2] Specifically the mizvah in-volves the obligation of marriage and the procreation of children. The duty of procreation, in a strictly legal sense, devolves upon the man, and not upon the woman. Within the marital relationship as envisaged by the Torah the act of cohabitation is to serve the pur-pose of propagation of the human race, and of fulfilling the mizvah of *'onah,* or intimate companionship in marriage.[3] In his appraisal of the laws of family purity, which prohibit cohabitation during a woman's menstrual period and following childbirth, the Hinnuk takes account of the psychological and emotional factors that affect marital relations. Apart from the purely hygienic concerns that present themselves in consideration of her condition at such times, he notes the effect of the laws in fostering moderation in conjugal relations, and in enhancing a woman's charm and allure in the eyes of her husband, thereby insuring marital felicity and fidelity.

Faithfulness in Marriage

Husband and wife are committed to maintain their marriage in a spirit of faithfulness and mutual trust, so that they may be worthy of God's beneficent care.[4] The Hinnuk explains the significance of the wedding ring prescribed by custom as a token of the solemnity and sanctity of the marriage and as a constant reminder to be faithful.

It is expected that the wife be a "man's help-mate and the object of his delight."[5] The husband must, in turn, cultivate his relationship with his wife. The biblical law requiring that the bridegroom be free to devote the first year of marriage to rejoice with his wife (Deuteronomy 24:5), while originally intended to free him of military and state service, is in its broader intent, the Hinnuk believes, applicable at all times. It obligates the husband to refrain from absenting himself for any extended period of time during the first year, unless it is for a mizvah or a matter of similar urgency. He must devote himself to his wife, "concentrating his thoughts upon her, and cherishing her image and her works in his heart," so that he will come to love her and remain faithful to her.[6] By logical extension, and in its broadened meaning, this principle constitutes the basis for the commandments designed to preserve natural and amicable relations between husband and wife. Thus, it is the root of the prohibition of adultery, a prohibition that applies to all, both Jews and non-Jews.[7]

The ideal is a marriage where peace and harmony prevail. However, where the relationship turns to "bitterness of spirit and loathing," and peace departs from the home, the law provides for divorce, since Judaism does not view the marriage bond as indissoluble, as do some other religions.[8] The dissolution of the marriage is effected by means of a bill of divorcement which the husband causes to be written and delivered to his wife.[9] Nevertheless, divorce should not be lightly undertaken. A man should consider instituting a divorce only for serious and sufficient cause, as Scripture states, "because he hath found some unseemly thing in her" (Deuteronomy 24:1).

Child Training and Education

The family is manifestly the beginning of man's social relationships, since it is primarily in the home that the individual first learns to relate to others. It is evidently in respect of this that a strict moral discipline is imposed upon the child, both within the family as well as within the frame of society. He is admonished against rebelliousness, stealing from his parents, indulgence in excessive food and drink, and consort with wanton and worthless company.[10] The extreme punishment that Scripture stipulates for a stubborn and rebellious son (Deuteronomy 21:18-21)[11] is because of the fear that such conduct, if unchecked, would inevitably lead to his committing worse crimes. Effective control and discipline are particularly necessary in early youth when character and personality are being molded. At this time the child must learn to value intellectual and spiritual pursuits, and develop a reverence for God and a regard for His commandments.[12]

The duty to teach his son the commandments of the Torah falls upon the father, but the mother, though legally exempt, is still morally obligated to educate her child.[13] Moral and religious instruction should commence as soon as the child begins to talk. He is first taught to recite the verses, "Moses commanded us a Law, an inheritance of the congregation of Jacob" (Deuteronomy 33:4), and "Hear, O Israel, the Lord our God, the Lord is One" (Deuteronomy 6:4). Informal instruction is continued at home until the child is six or seven years old, whereupon he should be entrusted to a teacher of young children. The Hinnuk takes care to caution the parent to adopt a sensible attitude toward the education of his child, not to burden him or to endanger his health at an early age, when the child is still in a weak and delicate condition, but to wait until he is older and stronger. At such time, when he is ready and capable of enduring a strict discipline, "he must bring his neck under the yoke of Torah, not slackening it even a hair's breadth, and continually give him to drink of its spiced wine, and to eat of its honey." [14] Girls, too, are to be instructed in their religious and moral duties, though they are not obligated to learn Torah since that commandment does not apply to women. Nevertheless, a woman who studies Torah will be recompensed. [15]

Women's Religious Duties

As a general rule, women are equally obligated as men in the observance of all commandments, whether prohibitive or mandatory. With certain exceptions, women are exempt from those affirmative commandments for whose performance a fixed time is set. In practice, the law recognizes further exceptions in both categories, by reason of the nature of the applicability of the precept or because of certain halakic considerations. Women may, of their own volition, assume the obligation of performing certain religious duties. Indeed, the Hinnuk is of the opinion that a woman may observe the mizvah of *tefillin*, and will receive due reward for her religious devotion. In this connection, he cites the example of Michal, the daughter of King Saul, who wore *tefillin*. Her action was evidently sanctioned by the Sages, as the Talmud notes, as was that of the prophet Jonah's wife, who assumed the obligation of making the pilgrimage on the Festivals. [16] It should be noted however that, notwithstanding the above, it has not been the practice for women to wear *tefillin*.

Moral and Spiritual Guidance

The Hinnuk evinces special concern for the moral conduct of the youth. Ever mindful of the weakness of human nature in the face of temptation, he counsels that social contact between the sexes should be of such a nature as to insure the purest of relations. [17] Time and again he reveals himself as the wise and devoted father gently, but firmly, admonishing his son. "Let not your imagination lull you into false confidence, and lead you to say, 'Since I am whole-hearted and upright in my faith in God, what harm can there be if I indulge occasionally on the streets and in the market places in the customary pleasures of men, such as joking with the frivolous or speaking coarsely, and the like, which most assuredly are not sins that need to be atoned for by guilt-offerings or sin-offerings? Have I not a will of my own, and is not my spirit stronger, then why should I fear that they will draw me after them?' Nay, my son, guard yourself against them lest you be caught in their net. Many have in this way drunk their cup of poison. As for you, save your soul!" [18]

The obligation to guide the child and to control his activities is thus primarily that of the parents, though society itself is not altogether free of responsibility. Maimonides also considers it the clear duty of the parent to restrain and guide his child in religious matters "in order to train him in holiness." [19] However, while he specifically states that the *Bet Din* is not obliged to restrain minors in religious matters,[20] he nevertheless rules that they are to be punished by the court for transgressions of a social nature, such as theft and damages, in order to restrain them from further anti-social behavior, and to train them in proper moral conduct.[21] Maimonides' decision, for which there is incidentally no talmudic precedent, has been construed as indicating a graver view on his part of social sins as compared with religious sins.[22] In our opinion this is rather a recognition of the respective areas of responsibility of the *Bet Din* and the parents with regard to children who are legally not punishable, but whose extra-legal punishment is justifiable on the grounds of character training and protective restraint. Where the minor's misdeed affects the well-being of society, it comes within the prerogative and the duty of the court to impose the necessary restraints. On the other hand, where the sinful action is of a distinctly religious nature, it remains the duty of the parent to give his child the spiritual guidance needed.[23]

Honoring Parents

The paramount duty of children is to honor their parents. The Hinnuk's exposition of this mizvah is most instructive in that it yields certain concepts that are basic to all human relations. "The reason for this commandment is that it is proper for a man to acknowledge and to repay with kindness the one who treated him with goodness. One should not act in an ignoble, or estranged and ungrateful manner, for this is the most evil and contemptible trait before God and man. But he should take to heart the fact that his father and mother are the cause of his being in the world, and therefore it is really fitting for him to give them all the honor and to help them in whatever way he is able. For it is they who brought him into the world and also endured so much trouble for his sake in his childhood." [24] The Hinnuk notes here two factors which motivate this mizvah, one explicit, and the second implicit. A person ought to feel a sense of gratitude to his parents who gave him life and provided for his needs. Implied in this is quite evidently a prior sense of dependence. Feelings of dependence and gratitude which express themselves in active concern for the welfare of another are likewise the elements necessary for good relations in society. Man's very existence depends upon a recognition of his reliance upon his fellowman and, consequently, a mutual concern for each other's well-being. [25]

LOVE OF FELLOWMAN

This concept is further amplified in the Hinnuk's exposition of the biblical command, "Thou shalt love thy neighbor as thyself" (Leviticus 19:18), which, as the foundation sustaining man's entire moral edifice, is likewise the ethical motive underlying many of the commandments. "Rabbi Akiba said, 'This is a fundamental principle of the Torah,' [26] that is to say, many commandments of the Torah are dependent upon it, for whoever loves his fellowman as he loves himself will neither steal his wealth, nor commit adultery with his wife, nor wrong him in money matters or in words, nor will he encroach upon his livelihood, nor harm him in any way." [27]

Parity of Human Concern

In its concrete expression, the mizvah requires a parity of concern for one's fellowman as for oneself, motivated in part by enlightened self-interest, which must result in peaceful relations among men. "For as he does unto his fellowman, so will his fellowman do unto him, and in this manner there will be peace among men." [28]

The specific obligations that this mizvah entails, as explained by the Sages, is spelled out by the Hinnuk. One must respect his fellow-man's property, and refrain from harming him, or wronging him in deed or in words. The mizvah is also the basis for several rabbinical laws which stress additional obligations that we owe to our fellow-men. In enumerating them, Maimonides writes, "It is a positive rab-binical precept to visit the sick, to comfort mourners, to attend the dead, to provide a bride with a dowry, to escort one's guests, to perform all that is necessary for burial, namely, carrying the de-ceased upon the shoulder, going before him, bewailing him, digging his grave, and burying him; and likewise to rejoice before the bride and the bridegroom and to provide for all their needs. These are personal acts of lovingkindness which are without a prescribed limit. Though all of these precepts are rabbinical ordinances, they are nevertheless included in the commandment, 'Thou shalt love thy neighbor as thyself.' " [29]

This is essentially the halakic construction of the mizvah as it bears upon man's social obligations.[30] Love for one's fellowman is to be translated into compassionate feelings and deeds; helping him in respect of his material needs, safeguarding his property and per-son, and protecting his rights as a human being. Nahmanides fur-ther underscores this aspect of the relationship when he suggests that, by nature, man is incapable of actually loving his fellowman as he loves himself. What the Torah commands, therefore, is that he love his fellowman with regard to all that pertains to him.[31] The term "as thyself" is hyperbolic, and means to convey the thought that one should seek his fellowman's well-being in all respects, without reservation or envy, enabling him to achieve his most cherished goals in all areas of human endeavor.

It is significant to note, therefore, that the Hinnuk introduces a singular nuance in the relationship. He contemplates that compliance with the mizvah would bring about a deeper, more personal relation-ship, which he characterizes as 'ahabat nefesh, "a love of the soul." This would express itself in "love, friendship and peace, and rejoic-ing in his fellowman's good fortune." [32]

Whether or not love manifests itself to the degree of 'ahabat nefesh, the law demands due regard for the human dignity of our fellowmen. We must be solicitous of their honor and speak of them only with favor.[33] "Whoever glorifies himself by humiliating another person," say the Rabbis, "will have no portion in the world to come." [34]

The Divine Image in Man

The *Sifra*,[35] cited by the Hinnuk for Rabbi Akiba's declaration that "Thou shalt love thy neighbor as thyself" is a fundamental principle of the Torah, is likewise the source for the correlative moral postulate ascribed to Ben Azzai. An even greater principle, Ben Azzai states, is expressed by the Bible in the verse, "This is the book of the generations of Adam; in the day that God created man, in the likeness of God made He him" (Genesis 5:1).[36] Love of fellowman is thus ultimately predicated upon consideration of the kinship of all men and the common inheritance of humankind created in the image and likeness of God. It is the divine image in man which underlies our common humanity.

EQUITY AND PURSUIT OF PEACE

Of prime concern, in this regard, is the assurance of respect for all men and fair treatment of those who, by virtue of their inferior social and economic status, may otherwise be disadvantaged. This concern is clearly impressed upon the laws pertaining to relations between master and slave and between laborer and employer.

Equity in Human Relations

Scriptural and rabbinical law distinguishes between the Canaanite slave and the Hebrew slave. The latter was, in actuality, to be treated like a hired servant. He was to be dealt with in kindness and mercy. "God admonished us," says the Hinnuk, "to be merciful to one who is under our authority and is beholden to us, and to deal kindly with him." [37] He was not to be subjected to excessive labor or to demeaning or useless work, but was to be shown every consideration in being provided with a respectable, useful job and favorable conditions of labor and maintenance.[38] In stipulating that he was to be considered "as a hired servant, and as a settler" (Leviticus 25:40), the Torah meant to emphasize that the relationship between the master and his Israelite servant was to be on the same basis of a free and voluntary agreement as in the case of other servants.[39]

In the case of a Hebrew maidservant the law stipulated that a father may place his daughter in servitude only when driven by poverty and desperation, with a view toward providing for her maintenance until the age of her maturity. Upon her consent, the master or his son was to marry her, or failing that, to enable her to go free. These laws, the Hinnuk points out, are due to God's compassion for the poor father and his unfortunate daughter in their desperate plight.[40]

Though the essential laws governing employer-employee relations are to be found in the Talmud and the later codes, the spirit underlying them is already evident in the Torah, as noted by the Hinnuk. While the employer is entitled to benefit in due measure from the work of his employee and to receive an honest day's work, special consideration under the law is accorded the worker in order to protect him from exploitation and to safeguard his material and human rights. He is to receive his wages at the stipulated time, the employer being biblically enjoined from·withholding it, "for he is poor and setteth his heart upon it" (Deuteronomy 24:15).[41] The Halakah gives the worker the advantage when claiming his wages. While, ordinarily, the law provides that one can deny a claim and be freed of the obligation by taking an oath, in this case the employee has the right to take the oath and receive his wages.[42]

Significantly, the law guards his rights due him as a free agent. In exercise of this freedom the Rabbis allow the worker to quit his job on the principle, "For unto Me the children of Israel are servants" (Leviticus 25:55), and not servants of servants.[43] This right is limited, however, in consideration of equity, to prevent injustice and undue loss to the employer. The welfare of the common worker merits the Hinnuk's special consideration. Thus, he advocates that we should follow the practice today of granting severance pay to one who has provided service for a period of time, even though the law was, strictly speaking, limited to the Hebrew servant in the time of the Temple.[44]

Certain of the mizvot are intended, the Hinnuk believes, to normalize human relations. The commandment not to hear the case of a litigant in the absence of his opponent[45] serves to teach the virtue of truthfulness and to urge upon us the Torah's abhorrence of falsehood. In this, too, we must seek to emulate God, who is "a God of truth, and His very essence is truth." [46] In business the Law demands fairness and honesty, so that no one be wrongly deprived of what is rightfully his. "It is wrong to take a man's money through falsehood and deceit. Every man should be entitled to the fruits of his labor with which God favored him, and which he obtained in a truthful and rightful manner. This is of benefit to everyone, because as he will not wrong others, so will others not wrong him." [47] This is also the object behind the several commandments prohibiting usury, the prohibition extending to all of the parties to the arrangement; namely, the lender, the borrower, as well as the witnesses, the scribe, and the guarantor. "The reason for this commandment is that no man shall be permitted to swallow up the wealth of his fellowman, without the other even noticing it until he finds his house emptied of all his worldly goods." [48] The scriptural admonition, "In righteousness shalt thou judge thy neighbor" (Leviticus 19:15), though primarily a directive for the judges in matters of law, applies as a guide in human relations as well. In practical terms it means that every man must judge his fellowman benignly, and seek to interpret his actions and his words in a favorable manner. "The essential purpose of this commandment is to further the common welfare by righteous judgment, and to establish peace by removing distrust between one man and another." [49]

Protection of the Orphan, Widow, and Stranger

Three classes in society, the orphan, the widow and the stranger, are marked by the Bible for special solicitude by reason of their weak and pitiable condition.[50] The orphan and the widow are deserving of consideration and gentle treatment because of their depressed spirit, having no one to provide for them or to plead their cause. It is expressly forbidden to oppress them in any manner, or to hurt them physically or wound their feelings with harsh words.[51] They are the charges of the community, with the Bet Din specifically responsible for the protection of their property and their legal rights.

All who have dealings with them are obliged to show them compassion and respect, being answerable, as the Hinnuk notes, "to God who will demand accounting for any anguish caused them." [52] "For if they cry at all unto Me, I will surely hear their cry" (Exodus 22:22).

The stranger, often mentioned in Scripture, is taken by the Hinnuk and by Maimonides to be the *ger zedek*, the true and righteous proselyte, who has embraced the Jewish faith and cast his lot with the Jewish people. [53] Though he is in all respects an Israelite as far as his duties and privileges are concerned, the Bible still singles him out for particular consideration. He is entitled to share in all of the "gifts to the poor," such as the tithe given to the poor, the gleanings, and the corner of the field. [54] It is similarly forbidden to wrong him or to harm him in any way, since his spirit is low and "he has no one to help him or to support him." [55]

We are doubly charged in the Torah regarding love of the *ger*. He is included under the command to love one's fellowman, and he is the subject of an additional commandment, as it is written, "Love ye therefore the stranger" (Deuteronomy 10:19). [56] This is in recognition of his self-sacrifice. It is our obligation "to bestow lovingkindness upon one who has left his people and family and comes to take refuge beneath the wings of another nation because of his love for it, spurning falsehood and choosing the truth." [57] Characteristically, the Hinnuk views the commandment within a broader ethical frame. "We must learn from this precious mizvah to have compassion upon every stranger who finds himself alone in an alien city, away from his country and from his family." [58] Scripture itself intimates this when it bids us remember that we were strangers in Egypt" (Deuteronomy 10:19). It reminds us, says the Hinnuk, "that we already experienced the great pain felt by every person who sees himself among strange people, in a foreign land, his heart heavy with worry." [59]

Peaceful Relations in Society

Since the ways of the Torah are "ways of pleasantness and all her paths are peace" (Proverbs 3:17), [60] it is the special object of some of the mizvot to maintain peace between individuals and in society in general. Thus the law prohibiting marriage with two sisters, either together or in the lifetime of the other, is to avoid a situation that would most likely lead to continuous strife. "The Lord of Peace desires the peace of all his creatures. Most certainly does he desire that there be peace between those of his creatures that nature and reason demand that they live in peace." [61]

For this reason the Torah prohibits one from wronging his neighbor in any way, irrespective of whether the wrong be done through an act, as in defrauding one in business, or whether the injury be inflicted by word. "We are commanded," writes the Hinnuk, "not to wrong a fellow-Israelite in speech, that is, one should not say to a fellow-Israelite such things that will cause him pain and distress whilst he is helpless to defend himself." [62] One should take care not to cause distress and pain in this way even to his own children and the members of his household. However, if one is provoked and grieved by another, he may resort to a suitable rejoinder in order to defend himself against abuse, just as he is permitted to defend himself against physical attack. It is not expected of one to be silent and "immovable as a stone," although those who practice extreme restraint and are silent in the face of their revilers and detractors are to be praised for upholding the high standard of *hasidut*. [63]

The commandment to admonish and reprove one who is guilty of wrongdoing[64] is likewise intended to preserve peaceful and amicable relations among people. This is indicated by the very sequence in the scriptural verses, "Thou shalt not hate thy brother in thy heart; thou shalt surely rebuke thy neighbor, and not bear sin because of him. Thou shalt not take vengeance, nor bear any grudge against the children of thy people, but thou shalt love thy neighbor as thyself" (Leviticus 19:17, 18).[65] The commandment requires due regard for the feelings of the other person; one must reproach one's neighbor with kindness and consideration. While one is to persist in admonishment until repulsed or until its futility is clear, one may not put the other to shame.

Talebearing and slander are twin evils that are expressly forbidden because they lead to "quarrel and strife." [66] Not only is the individual protected by law against this insidious evil which destroys all those who are caught in its web,[67] but the community also has a right to protection from calumny. The Hinnuk enters into a discussion of one who turns informer against his fellow Israelites. He is deemed a pariah and is subject to the death penalty.[68] His extensive treatment of the subject betrays a concern with this problem, which evidently plagued the Jewish community in his day.[69] The manifest object of these commandments is to establish peace upon which "all blessings in the world are dependent."[70]

War and the Call for Peace

In its relations with other nations, Israel is likewise commanded to call for peace before resorting to war, and to offer terms for a peaceful settlement.[71] Adopting the broader view of Maimonides and Nahmanides, rather than the limited view of Rashi, the Hinnuk takes this to apply to all nations, and under all conditions of war. The offer of peace was to be made not only in the case of *milhemet reshut*, the permitted war, such as that waged by Israel against its implacable enemies,[72] but also in the case of *milhemet mizvah*, an obligatory war, such as that waged against Amalek, the first to attack Israel without provocation, or against the seven nations who polluted the Land with "all forms of idolatry and other abominations hateful to God," or in defense of an enemy attack.[73] In defining the specific laws that pertain to this commandment, the Hinnuk pointedly states, "According to our Sages, of blessed memory, the law requiring that an offer of peace be made applies under all circumstances."[74] The Hinnuk further emphasizes the need for cultivating a feeling of mercy and an awareness that even the enemy, however unworthy, should be dealt with mercifully.

Nonetheless, when Israel finds it necessary to wage war, it should do so resolutely, and every man must set aside all personal interests, and go forth to battle with the thought that the safety of all the people depends upon him. The Hinnuk views the biblical command, "Fear not nor be alarmed, neither be ye affrighted at them, for the Lord, your God, is He that goeth with you to fight for you against your enemies, to save you" (Deuteronomy 20:3,4), as an exhortation

to courage and trust in God in defending the nation and in upholding the honor of God.[74a] Thus, while Judaism accepts war as justified
and necessary under certain conditions, its prime objective is still
peace and the preservation of man's qualities of humaneness and
compassion.

A UNIVERSAL MORALITY

A question that is highly significant in its implications and in our
understanding of the moral philosophy of Judaism bears consideration at this time. Is the Jewish ethic parochial, in that it is operative
distinctively within the Jewish community, or is it universal? It is
likely that this question does not admit of an unequivocal answer,
insofar as it reflects the inherent antinomy in the dual character of
Judaism as a national and as a universal religion. The universalistic
nature of its religious conceptions and aspirations, in conjunction
with its firm resolve to preserve the unity and the particular national
character of the Jewish people, would naturally manifest itself in
a certain tension in the ethical sphere as well. It is of interest to
explore the subject in the light of the Hinnuk's formulation of the
Halakah relative to the mizvot that pertain to this area of Jewish
ethics.

Relations Between Jew and Non-Jew

The relationship between Jew and gentile, as envisaged by the
Torah and delineated in Jewish law, is necessarily limited and restricted. The object, quite evidently, was to preserve the distinctive
character of Israel and to protect the moral and spiritual life of the
Jewish community from inimical influences. The scriptural command, "And ye shall not walk in the customs of the nation which I
am casting out before you; for they did all these things, and therefore I abhorred them" (Leviticus 20:23), is understood to apply
with respect to all heathen and gentiles. "The reason," the Hinnuk
notes, "is because they turn aside from God and worship idolatry."[75]
The law, in application, prohibits not only alien religious practices,
but also their moral habits and social customs and institutions which

are associated with deranged and repulsive conduct, immorality, or idolatry.[76] This commandment, together with the laws prohibiting intermarriage[77] and drinking the wine of gentiles,[78] was designed to keep the Jew apart, in the avowed hope that "he would direct all his heart and his thoughts toward God and His precious commandments."[79]

Notwithstanding the relative curtailment of contact between Jew and non-Jew thus effected, Jewish law did not contemplate, by any means, a state of total isolation or estrangement. On the contrary, it makes ample provision for normal relations and an active interchange in all areas of life and endeavor. These are to be governed by the principles of law and equity. The protection of the law and basic human rights are accorded by the Torah to all men, Jew and non-Jew alike, "Ye shall have one manner of law, as well for the stranger, as for the home-born, for I am the Lord your God" (Leviticus 24:22).[80] The latter part of the verse is revealing, in that it asserts the universality of God as the basis for the equality of both the native-born Israelite and the stranger before the Law. The stranger referred to is the *ger toshab,* the resident alien,[81] who undertook not to engage in idolatrous worship and who conducted himself in a civilized manner.[82] While he was not bound to observe Jewish religious law,[83] he had to abide by the Noahian laws, or as they are more specifically termed, the Seven Commandments of the Children of Noah.[84]

The Noahian Laws

The Hinnuk's conception of the Noahian laws as universal concepts meant to guide mankind in its relationship with God and with man is evident from his exposition of the commandments involved. The Noahian laws, which are obligatory upon all humanity as descendants of Noah and which the Jewish people are duty-bound to promulgate among all men, are the following:[85] (1) To establish courts of justice; (2) not to blaspheme the name of God; (3) not to worship idols; (4) not to commit incest or adultery; (5) not to murder; (6) not to rob; (7) not to eat the flesh cut from a living animal.

These laws are, in reality, categories of laws which are the counterparts of similar laws in the Torah which apply to Israelites. Thus, with respect to the commandment to believe in the unity of God the Hinnuk states: "This is the essential belief of all mankind. It is the firm pillar upon which every intelligent person relies." [86] In delineating the specific laws relating to this commandment, he notes that it is "included in the prohibition against idolatry." His position on this point is stated clearly in his discussion of the law prohibiting covetous desires. Although the law is not included among the seven Noahian laws, yet the Hinnuk states: "All of mankind abide by it because it is a branch of the prohibition against robbery, which is one of the seven commandments obligatory upon all of mankind." [87]

The Hinnuk continues to explain that the reference in the Talmud to "seven Noahian commandments" is not to be understood as limiting the number of these laws. "These seven are, in truth, in the nature of general principles, which include many specific laws." [88] He cites as an example the Noahian law prohibiting adultery which includes incestuous as well as unnatural relationships. The intent of the law, therefore, is to preserve the inviolability of family relationships and to prevent sexual perversion.[89] Similarly, the commandments concerning robbery and idolatry include many specific laws, whose object is, in the former case, to protect a person's rights and property, and in the latter to remove all forms of idolatrous worship. Thus the laws which govern man in the basic areas of human conduct and spiritual attitudes apply, with certain legal distinctions,[90] to Jews and non-Jews alike.

Acknowledgment of Divine Origin

Although the Noahian Laws are rational in nature and can be arrived at independently through reason, the talmudic Sages nevertheless deem them to be divinely ordained, and they indicate the scriptural source wherein God is said to have commanded them to Adam (Genesis 2:16; 9:4).[91] Acknowledgment of their divine origin is, as Maimonides points out, a prime condition in the attainment of the ultimate reward of eternal life for their observance. "Whoever accepts the seven commandments and is careful to observe them is deemed to be among the saints of the nations of the world and he has a portion in the World to Come, providing he accepts them and observes them because the Holy One, blessed is He, commanded them in the Torah, and made it known to us through Moses our master that the children of Noah were previously commanded them. But if he observes them merely by reason of his own judgment, he is not considered a *ger toshab,* and he is not of the saints among the nations of the world, but of their wise men." [92]

Maimonides apparently distinguishes here between one's voluntary assumption of these laws as autonomous, ethical laws demanded by reason, and their acceptance as laws commanded by God. While the former would surely be considered an ethical person, only the latter, who views the laws as heteronomous in nature and responds to them in compliance with the divine will, would qualify as a pious, saintly person.[93] The Seven Commandments of the children of Noah thus represent a universal code of morality based upon recognition of a Divine Being.

Even as the Taryag Mizvot were enjoined upon Israel at Sinai, so were the Seven Commandments enjoined upon the rest of mankind.[94] Gentiles who abide by these commandments are classed among the righteous of the world who are assured of their portion in the World to Come.[95] They constitute the touchstone of Israel's relations with other peoples. Thus the Torah forbids Israel from entering into an alliance or effecting a covenant with those who do not abide by the Seven Noahian Laws. An idolater who persists in the practice of idolatry in violation of one of these laws is to be refused permission to settle in the Land of Israel. He is not allowed to acquire property or to lease a house for residence, although he may lease it for storage of his merchandise. In the latter instance, he is further restricted so as to prevent the establishment of a neighborhood of idolaters.[96] The Hinnuk believes the object of the prohibition was to prevent the spread of idolatry in the Land, as indicated in the scriptural verse which he cites for the mizvah, "They shall not dwell in thy land, lest they make thee sin against Me, for thou wilt serve their gods, for they will be a snare unto thee" (Exodus 23:33). Maimonides, on the other hand, derives the prohibition from the scriptural admonition *ve-lo' tehanem* (Deuteronomy 7:2), which the Rabbis interpret to mean "thou shalt not grant them a settlement in the Land." [97] He construes the verse cited by the Hinnuk to indicate that they are to be denied even transient privileges so long as they do not forswear idolatry and accept the Noahian Laws. [98]

The Rights of a Resident Alien

However, Judaism assumes an obligation under the law for the welfare of the non-Jew, and in particular the alien resident in the Land, who by his abstinence from idolatry and his acceptance of the Noahian Laws qualifies as a *ger toshab*. [99] He is to be granted equal rights and benefits along with his fellow Jew. [100] He is entitled to his wages on time, [101] and to the administration of justice in the courts. [102] Moreover, Judaism imposes a moral obligation upon every Jewish community to provide for the needs of the non-Jews who are domiciled among them. They are to share equally in all gifts and portions allocated to the needy. [103] The Mishnah specifies that the poor among the gentiles are to be allowed to gather the gleanings, the forgotten sheaves, and the corner of the field. [104] The Talmud adds that the gentile poor must be supported, and that in sickness and death they are to be afforded equal treatment with the Jews. [105] The impelling moral principle behind the law is stated by the Sages to be *mipnei darkei shalom* "in the interests of peace." Taking note of this principle, Maimonides indicates the moral and legal obligations that Judaism places upon the Jew in his relations with the non-Jew. [106] "It also appears to me that we are to conduct ourselves toward resident aliens with good manners and deeds of lovingkindness, as we would toward an Israelite, because we are commanded to sustain them in life . . ." [107] Even as regards the heathen, the Sages have decreed that we are to visit their sick and to bury their dead as we do the Jewish dead, and to provide for their poor together with the poor of Israel, in the interests of peace. Behold it is said, 'The Lord is good to all, and His tender mercies are over all His works' (Psalms 145:9), and it is also said, 'Its ways are ways of pleasantness, and all its paths are peace' " (Proverbs 3:17).

Status of the Alien Slave

Jewish law is concerned with safeguarding the integrity and personal rights of the individual, whether Jew or non-Jew. This is most clearly manifested in its outlook upon slavery, which is particularly striking when contrasted with the attitude fostered by other cultures, from the Greco-Roman era until nearly contemporary times. While the latter considered the slave the personal property of his master, on a level with his cattle, Jewish law invested him with personality and will in his own right.[108] For the Hebrew slave, as already indicated, the laws pertaining to the terms of his servitude[109] and his ultimate release from slavery[110] are set forth in Scripture and explicated by the Rabbis. An alien or Canaanite slave, whose status was basically similar to that of slaves among other peoples, was yet accorded certain rights of person under Jewish law which he did not have elsewhere. These afforded him protection of life and limb, and prescribed humane conditions of servitude.[111] Thus the law provides that a master is forbidden to treat him in a cruel or brutal manner. If he should maim him, he must grant him his freedom; if the master kills him, he is punishable by death. The law also provides that the alien slave may redeem himself or be freed by his master.[112]

Lack of provision in the law for a prescribed period of servitude, as provided for the Hebrew slave, is in part attributable to the desire to accord him material security. In the main, however, it enabled the slave to attain a higher spiritual level by giving him the opportunity to join his master's household in a quasi-Jewish capacity. Once freed, he was considered an Israelite in all respects. The status of alien slaves, as the Hinnuk notes, is an ambivalent one, inasmuch as "they have already emerged from the status of heathens, but have not yet come into the status of Israelites." [113] The alien slave was allowed the first year to make the transition. During this year, he could voluntarily qualify himself, by renouncing idolatry and by submitting to circumcision and ritual immersion, after which he was bound by religious duties in the same manner as an Israelite woman. Should he fail to avail himself of this, the master could not retain him in his household.[114] If the master sells his slave to a non-Jew or even to a Jew who takes him out of the Land of Israel, the slave goes free, because in either event he will be deprived of the opportunity to observe the mizvot.[115] Indeed, the master is encouraged to free him altogether so as to make it possible for him to reach to the full status of an Israelite.[116] In general, Judaism was inimical to the institution of slavery,[117] and as a result of this, and the cumulative effect of the restrictions imposed by both scriptural and rabbinical law, the institution eventually lapsed into desuetude in Jewish life.

Exemplary Ethical Conduct

A moral commitment to maintain the image of Israel as the holy people of God, tempered and indeed often bolstered by the struggle for survival amidst hostility and intolerance, motivated the Jew to a high level of ethical conduct towards the non-Jew. Jewish law calls for exemplary ethical conduct by Jews particularly in their business transactions with non-Jews, forbidding any dishonest dealing, robbery, cheating, or manipulation with the intention to defraud.[118]

In his dealings with gentiles, the Jew is bidden not only to be concerned with the legal and ethical considerations, but he must also be constantly mindful of the element of *kiddush ha-shem* that is involved. To defraud the gentile is to desecrate the name of God; to deal honestly with him, thus demonstrating that Jews are honorable and trustworthy, is to sanctify the name of God and bring glory to Israel.[119]

The Principle of Reciprocity

Reciprocity is an important factor in the relationship. This is evident in the law which allows a Jew to take interest on a loan incurred by a gentile.[120] The Hinnuk's explanation of this law,[121] which is sometimes mistakenly viewed as discriminatory, is instructive. While he takes the injunction "unto an alien thou mayest lend upon interest" (Deuteronomy 23:21) to be a positive commandment, following the strict view of Maimonides,[122] he nevertheless believes the law is not applicable where it is to his benefit to lend without interest or when it would serve peaceful relations.[123] It is very likely that

Maimonides would agree to the Hinnuk's modification of the law in these instances.[124] In any event, the exacting of interest from an alien was reciprocal, conforming to the non-Jewish practice of usury, and was thus calculated to maintain an equitable basis for trade between Jews and non-Jews.

A policy of realism based upon a form of limited reciprocity seems to have prevailed, so that in litigation one who was not a *ger toshab* was judged either in accordance with Jewish law or with his own law, with the option given to the Jew.[125] The assumption, it would seem, is that equity in law is possible only where there is a common ground of ethics. Maimonides makes this clear as he formulates the law in a case cited by the Mishnah.[126] "If an ox of an Israelite gored the ox of a heathen, whether it was accounted harmless or an attested danger, the owner is not culpable, because the heathen does not hold a man responsible for damage caused by his cattle, hence we judge this case according to their own laws. If an ox of a heathen gored the ox of an Israelite, whether it was accounted harmless or an attested danger, the owner pays for the damages in full. This is a penalty imposed on the heathen because they are not observant of the commandments and they do not take any measures to prevent damage. If they were not held responsible for the damage caused by their cattle, they would not guard it and would thereby inflict a loss upon other people." [127] Adherence to a minimal moral code, represented by the seven Noahian laws, was presumed, in the final analysis, to be the realistic basis for any dealings with other peoples.[128]

It may be pointed out that Halakah in the post-talmudic era has tended toward a reevaluation of the legal status of the non-Jew, in view of the fact that the preponderant majority of the people in the world are no longer idolaters.[129] The non-Jew, especially in contemporary times, is held to be in the category of a *ger toshab*, who observes the Noahian laws and "conforms to the ways established by his religion and morality." [130]

The Aspect of Kedushah

The position of non-Jews in the Jewish community, with particular regard to the imposition of legal sanctions to enforce moral standards, bears further clarification. The seven commandments by which all men are bound include, as we have already noted, the prohibition of adultery, as well as incestuous and unnatural sexual relations.[131] However, while the *Bet Din* is required to take measures not to allow prostitution or homosexual practices among Israelites, they are not constrained to assume such responsibility with respect to non-Jews.[132] The Hinnuk refers to the common practice of sodomy among the Ishmaelites of his day, but he nevertheless states, "If any one among the other nations should be a sodomite, even if he should dwell among us, we are not responsible for him, inasmuch as we are not bound to enforce these laws upon others, except in the case of idolatry."[133] This would indicate a remarkable tolerance of the moral aberrations of others, which appears to be rather inconsistent with the imperative and universal nature of these moral laws. It would seem, upon reflection, that Judaism is inclined to view the Noahian laws, ultimately, as moral and religious standards for which it seeks a free and voluntary commitment, resulting from eventual recognition of their intrinsic value to society, rather than mere compliance due to compulsory measures. While the non-Jew has such a tacit, if not moral choice, the Jew has none. He is bound by the yoke of the commandments.

The key to a proper understanding of the problematical status of the gentile from the perspective of Halakah is the principle of *kedushah,* the ideal of holiness imposed upon the people of Israel. The divine exhortation to *kedushah* (Leviticus 19:2),[134] entails religious duties and moral restraints of a distinctive nature, as set forth in the Torah, that are mandatory for Israelites, but not for other peoples.[135] This distinction between Jew and non-Jew, with respect to the moral and religious obligations of the Torah, is delicately drawn by Rabbi Akiba in a statement attributed to him in the Mishnah.[136] "Beloved is man for he was created in the (divine) image.[137] . . . Beloved are Israel for they were called children of God . . . for to them was given the precious instrument . . . as it is written, 'For I give you good doctrine; forsake ye not My law' " (Proverbs 4:2). Thus, while it is incumbent upon every non-Jew, insofar as he bears the divine image, to submit to the universal moral law that was divinely ordained for all men, he is not subject to the unique duties and constraints that devolve upon the Jew by virtue of the *kedushah* with which Israel alone, as the covenanted people, is invested.[138] A gentile, therefore, does not keep the Sabbath holy in the manner prescribed by the Law,[139] nor does he study Torah, other than the laws pertaining to the mizvot with which he has been charged.[140] He may voluntarily undertake to observe other mizvot, in addition to the seven Noahian commandments, but not those mizvot which are characteristic of the *kedushah* of Israel, such as *tefillin, mezuzah,* and the like.[141]

Jewish ethics, therefore, with the exception of that area which is indigenous to Israel and expressive of its particularistic character of *kedushah,* is largely non-parochial in nature. Certainly, in its wider ethical imperatives, the Torah directs itself to the non-Jew as well as to the Jew. Significantly, the Hinnuk considers the ethical principle embodied in the commandment not to covet part of the Seven Commandments of the Children of Noah.[142] It is surely revealing that this commandment, which within the frame of the ethical idealism of the Torah is designed to effect the moral improvement of man, is deemed to be of general import, applying to Jews and non-Jews alike. It is apparent, then, that both in its broad, human concerns, as well as in its moral philosophy, Judaism is manifestly universal in its scope, embracing all of mankind.

CHAPTER EIGHT

MAN'S SPIRITUAL DIMENSION

The classical division of scriptural commandments is between *mizvot bein 'adam la-makom,* commandments which govern man's relation to God, and *mizvot bein 'adam le-habero,* commandments that direct man in his relationship with his fellowman.[1] This division is largely theoretical; in actuality the lines are not rigidly or arbitrarily drawn. Ethical and religious duties are closely inter-related, the one often serving to reenforce the other.

It is precisely in the Ten Commandments, the preeminent example of this division,[2] that we already have an indication of the connection between the two classes of mizvot. In his discussion of the miz-vah of honoring parents, the Hinnuk affirms the basic interrelated-ness of mizvot. One should honor his father and his mother, even as he must honor God, because parents are God's copartners in the creation of man.[3] By acknowledging parental kindness in bringing him into the world and providing for his needs "he will come to acknowledge the goodness of God, blessed be He, who is the cause of his being . . . and he will realize how proper it is for him to be zealous in serving God."[4] Hence, the Hinnuk concludes, if one does not honor his parents "it is as though he has estranged himself from his Father in heaven." More essentially, however, the interrelated-ness of mizvot, which we have noted initially on the functional level, lies ultimately on the teleological level. Both categories of com-mandments, religious and ethical, are motivated and directed by an identical purpose, namely, to serve God.

133

THE HIGHER MOTIVE IN SERVING GOD

The religious disposition that a man is expected to cultivate in his relationship with God, as the ground for serving Him and fufilling His divine will through mizvot, is characterized in the Bible as the fear of God and the love of God. "And now, Israel, what doth the Lord thy God require of thee, but to fear the Lord thy God, to walk in all His ways, and to love Him, and to serve the Lord thy God with all thy heart and with all thy soul; to keep for thy good the commandments of the Lord and His statutes which I command thee this day" (Deuteronomy 10:12, 13). The two, as the Hinnuk indicates, are in effect complementary; the fear of God[5] acting as a deterrent from sin, and the love of God serving to bestir one to take heed of God's commandments.

The fear of God, which follows on an awareness of God's providence and His retribution, constitutes a tolerable basis for compliance with the divine will. But, "a man will not observe the commandments of God, blessed be He, in the best manner unless it be for the love of Him." [6] Contemplation of the Lord's works and of His commandments, and reflection on the Torah will lead a person to love Him, and thus to serve Him out of a feeling of love, which is the supreme degree attainable, as exemplified by the patriarch Abraham.[7] Indeed, Abraham's binding of Isaac, of which we are reminded by the blowing of the *shofar* on Rosh Hashanah, is to serve as an example for us to be willing to make the supreme sacrifice "for the love of God."

As the expressed will of God, it is the mizvah which is in essence the medium for the service of God. In the observance of mizvot two motives are possible. The first is to be worthy of receiving the divine beneficence which is their reward. This is an acceptable motive, and those who keep the commandments for this reason will have "their portion in life and will merit Eden, the garden of God." [8] There is, however, the more commendable and impelling motive of those "who, in their great love of God, dedicate themselves to the fulfillment of His will unmindful of any personal reward." [9] This is the greater virtue and constitutes the purest motive in serving God.

ACKNOWLEDGING GOD AS MASTER

The service of God entails a true conception of God as Creator and Master of the universe. The thesis, frequently propounded by the Rabbis, that man must acknowledge God's proprietorship is at the basis of several of the mizvot.[10] The reason we are commanded to dedicate our first-born and our first-fruits to God is "that we may know that all is His, and that man has nothing whatever in this world but what God in His grace gives him." [11]

Similarly, we are to take cognizance of God's mastery of the world by counting the Sabbatical years up to the Jubilee year when all property must revert to the original owners. "The reason for this mizvah is simply that God wished to make known to His people that everything belonged to Him, and that in the end it must return to the one to whom it pleased God to give it in the first place, for the land is His." [12]

The Meaning of Blessings

This concept is more fully developed in the course of a discussion of blessings and benedictions. By means of the blessings that we recite we acclaim God's proprietorship of all that is in the world. Quoting the rabbinic dictum, "It is forbidden for man to derive any benefit from this world without first offering a blessing," [13] the Hinnuk takes the blessing to be of the nature of "a request for permission from the master of the house to eat of that which is in his house." [14]

He expatiates on this, as well as on the condition requisite for God's benign providence, in his introductory statement relative to the commandment to bless God in the Grace after meals.[15] When we say, "Blessed art thou, O Lord," our intention is certainly not to bestow blessings on God who most assuredly needs no blessing from us. The expression is rather to be understood in a descriptive, adjectival sense; an avowal that God is the source of all blessings, thus rendering us worthy of His beneficence.

This is the meaning of the benediction of Grace and of the traditional formula, "Blessed art thou, O Lord," used for the opening and closing of the blessings. The Hinnuk puts it as follows: "The blessing which we recite before God is in the nature of a reminder, the words designed to make us aware that He, who is to be blessed, embodies all goodness. By thus affirming that God is master of all, and by acknowledging that He has the power to bestow the good upon whom He pleases, we will thereby be worthy of His blessings. After this reminder and thanksgiving, we proceed to petition Him for our needs . . . When the Sages say that 'The Holy One, blessed be He, desires the prayers of the righteous,'[16] they mean that it is His desire that they perform this deed whereby they would be found worthy of His goodness."[17]

MIZVOT TO INCULCATE DOCTRINES OF FAITH

The commandments that are generally classified as "between man and God" are designed to foster faith and to impart religious truths. Of these there are the mizvot which directly enjoin belief in the existence of God, "the foundation of faith,"[18] and the unity of God, which represents "the essential belief of all mankind,"[19] as well as the prohibition of idolatry. The latter is characterized by the Hinnuk as "the great principle of the Torah upon which everything hangs,"[20] inasmuch as one who practices idolatry controverts the whole of the Torah.[21]

Scripture likewise forbids all manner of superstitious practices. This, the Hinnuk points out, is not only because of the prohibition of idolatry, but also because such practices inevitably lead to false beliefs and distorted notions regarding man's fate and God's governance of the world. Resorting to superstitions in the belief that one can thereby invoke good fortune or escape divine punishment for sins committed constitutes a denial of divine providence and divine justice.[22] Thus the practice of divination is forbidden because it represents a denial of divine providence and misleads people into thinking that "God has forsaken the earth" and human events are determined by the heavenly constellations.[23]

Passover and the Exodus

Many other mizvot, especially those of a commemorative or ritualistic nature, serve similarly to inculcate religious beliefs and to strengthen the faith. The Hinnuk notes that the laws of Passover [24] are intended to commemorate the miracles wrought by God at the time of the Exodus; Israel's freedom from bondage; its going forth to become "a kingdom of priests and a holy nation"; and its covenant of Torah and faith with God.

The multiplicity of commandments relating to the Exodus from Egypt, the Hinnuk explains, is intended to reinforce our belief in creation and in the providence, omniscience, and omnipotence of God. "One should not wonder that so many mandatory and prohibitive commandments bear upon this event, because it constitutes a great foundation and a strong pillar in our Torah and in our Faith. This is the reason we always say in our blessings and in our prayers 'in remembrance of the departure from Egypt,' because the Exodus is for us the conclusive sign and proof of creation, that there is an eternal God who is free and omnipotent and the cause of all that exists, and that God has the power at any given time to change as He pleases whatever exists, even as He did in Egypt where He altered the nature of the world for our sake and wrought miracles that were unprecedented, great and powerful. This, indeed, silences all who deny Creation, and substantiates our belief that God is omniscient, and that His providence and His omnipotence encompass all things collectively and individually." [25] Maimonides stresses other aspects of belief that are kept in focus by perpetuating the memory of the departure from Egypt, namely, a verification of prophecy and the doctrine of reward and punishment. He nevertheless concurs in a recognition of the evident utility of those commandments which, as he states, serve "to keep certain miracles in remembrance, or to perpetuate true faith." [26]

The Sabbath and Festivals

The laws of the Sabbath are similarly intended to inculcate religious beliefs. We are bidden to sanctify the Sabbath with the benediction over the wine so that "we should be stirred by means of this act to remember the greatness of the day and to affirm our belief in God's creation of the world." [27] Such is also the intent of the commandment that prescribes certain limits beyond which it is forbidden to go on the Sabbath.[28]

Relative to the prohibition of work on the Sabbath day, the Hinnuk states, "We should be free of our affairs in honor of the Sabbath so that we may be imbued with a belief in Creation, which is a principle of faith that encompasses all of the fundamentals of our religion. Thus we recall on one day of each week that the world was created in six separate days and that on the seventh nothing was created, and that each day things were created individually, thereby demonstrating God's free will . . . Apart from serving as a reminder of Creation, it is also in remembrance of the miracle in Egypt, namely, that we were slaves there and could not rest when we pleased, but God delivered us from the Egyptians and bid us rest on the seventh day." [29]

The Sabbath and the Festivals are to be devoted to educating the people in the tenets and traditions of the Jewish faith. Of the commandment prohibiting work on the first day of Passover, he states: "Another of the many benefits to be derived from a cessation of work on this day is that all the people will gather in the Synagogues and in the Houses of Study to hearken to words of Torah, and their spiritual leaders will guide them and instruct them." [30]

The Sabbatical Year

The laws of *Shemitah,* which call for resting the land and abandoning its produce on the Sabbatical year, while serving to promote certain social and humanitarian ends, such as to help the poor [31] and to develop traits of benevolence and generosity,[32] are in like manner primarily designed to inculcate fundamental concepts of faith. "Apart from the duty to allow the land to rest," says the Hinnuk, "God commanded renouncing possession of all that it produces during that year, so that man would remember that not of its own power and nature does the land bring forth its fruit each year, but that there is One who is Lord of the land and its Master." [33] This mizvah also strengthens belief in God's creation of the world, banishing "any notion of the eternity of the universe which is held by those who deny the Torah and seek thereby to demolish its pillars and to breach its walls." [34]

In its very essence *Shemitah* is to be a demonstration of "implicit trust in God." [35] In terming it "a Sabbath unto the Lord," (Leviticus 25:4) [36] the Torah itself intimates the bond between the Sabbath and *Shemitah;* both testify to basic tenets of the Jewish faith. [37]

The Assembly of Hakhel

The Sabbatical year was climaxed by a great assembly, known as *Hakhel,* which took place in the Temple in Jerusalem. [38] In expounding upon the mizvah of *Hakhel,* the Hinnuk states: [39] "We have been commanded that all the people of Israel, men, women, and children, shall assemble on the second day of the festival of Sukkot at the close of the Sabbatical year, and that portions of the Book of Deuteronomy shall be read to them. Of this assembly the Torah states: 'At the end of every seven years, in the set time of the year of *Shemitah,* in the festival of Tabernacles, when all Israel is come to appear before the Lord thy God in the place which He shall choose, thou shalt read this law before all Israel in their hearing. Assemble the people, the men and the women and the little ones, and thy stranger that is within thy gates, that they may hear, and that they may learn, and fear the Lord your God, and observe to do all the words of this law' " (Deuteronomy 31:10-12).

The ancient assembly, by its dramatic quality and the presence of such a large multitude, was calculated to create a lasting impression upon the people, inspiring them to a stronger and deeper loyalty to the Torah. Having been sustained by the mercy of God through the year of *Shemitah,* Israel would feel moved to gather and to renew its faith in God and its allegiance to His law. *Shemitah* was an expression of the firm belief that the Land belonged to God and that Israel lived upon it by His grace alone. *Hakhel* was a massive demonstration of that faith. As the Hinnuk explains, *Hakhel* was to manifest that "the whole essence of the people of Israel is the Torah, whereby they are distinguished from all other peoples." [40] The eternal covenant between God and his Chosen People is founded upon the Torah, [41] and Israel's sojourn in the Holy

Land is predicated upon its acceptance of the Torah as the constitution of the Land.[42]

Renewal of the Covenant

The Bible records a reenactment of the covenant between God and Israel at various times in its early history.[43] The covenant made at Sinai was sealed again before the Israelites crossed into the Promised Land (Deuteronomy 28:69). It was later renewed by Joshua (Joshua 24:25), and later still by King Solomon at the dedication of the Temple, which probably took place at a *Hakhel* assembly (I Kings, chapter 8). The assembly convened by King Josiah, subsequent to finding the Book of the Covenant in the Temple, when as the Bible states, "all the people stood to the covenant," (II Kings 23:3) is taken in halakic literature to have been an assembly of *Hakhel*. When Ezra and Nehemiah led the people back to the Holy Land from exile in Babylonia, they assembled and renewed the covenant (Ezra, chapter 10; Nehemiah, chapters 8-10).[44] The assembly of *Hakhel* derives its greatest importance from this concept of a periodic renewal of the covenant.

Maimonides defines the basic objective of *Hakhel* in a similar manner. He points out that all were to hearken to the readings from the Torah with the same feeling of awe and reverence "as on the day it was given on Sinai," because "the Torah established *Hakhel* in order to strengthen the true Faith, and every one present must imagine that he were now receiving the Torah and hearing it from the Lord himself." [45]

Whether or not the mizvah of *Hakhel* is binding today is from the halakic point of view uncertain.[45a] The question would turn, in large part, on the extent to which *Hakhel* is dependent upon *Shemitah*, which is not biblically in force at this time. Maimonides writes in his *Sefer ha-Mizvot*, at the end of his exposition of the Positive Commandments, "Of these commandments there are some that are not in force except in the time of the Temple, such as the Festival offering, the Pilgrimage, and the mizvah of *Hakhel*." The Hinnuk, however, makes no reference to *Hakhel* as being confined to the time of the Temple, but only stipulates that it is to be observed "at the time that Israel is upon its Land."

SYMBOLIC ACTS AND OBSERVANCES

Tefillin, Mezuzah, Zizit

Following traditional, midrashic exegesis, the Hinnuk indicates the function that ceremonial and symbolic acts fulfill in maintaining faith and in developing religious and moral attitudes and opinions. Thus, the *tefillin* serve to guard us from impure thoughts, to convey basic beliefs, and to remind us of our dedication to the service of God. "Among the mizvot which God commanded us in order to direct our thoughts to serve Him in purity is the mizvah of *tefillin*. The phylacteries are placed opposite those organs of man which are known to be the seat of the intellect, namely, the heart and the brain. By this act one will concentrate all of his thoughts for good and be careful to remember always to act uprightly and righteously." [46] The *tefillin* contain four sections of the Torah specifically chosen "because they embrace the acceptance of the kingdom of heaven, the unity of God, and the exodus from Egypt, the latter compelling a belief in Creation and in divine providence on earth." [47] The Hinnuk adds: "These are all fundamental doctrines of Judaism which we are commanded to keep before us always . . . to strengthen our faith and to remind us of the ways of God, so that we may merit eternal life." [48]

Such is also the object of the mizvot concerning *mezuzah* and *zizit*. The commandment to affix a *mezuzah* upon the doorpost of the house is "to remind a man of faith in God every time that he enters or leaves his house." [49] The *zizit*, or fringes, which we are commanded to attach to the hem of our garments are "to remind us always of all the commandments of God, there being no better reminder for one than to carry the seal of his master on the garment which he wears constantly." [50] This commandment also serves to remind us that "a man's body and soul belong to God." [51] The Hinnuk bases this upon a symbolical interpretation of the colors blue and white which are in the Bible associated with the *zizit* (Numbers 15:38). The white signifies the body, while the blue thread is symbolic of the soul. This, he believes, is also intimated by the Rabbis when, in explaining the thread of blue, they say, "The blue resembles the sea, the sea resembles the heavens, and the heavens resemble the Throne of Glory." [52] The souls of the righteous are sheltered beneath the Throne of Glory. [53]

Observances on Sukkot and Passover

Characteristic of these mizvot is that they give tangible expression to fundamental ideals in Judaism and serve as constant reminders of our religious duties. Of this category, too, are the commandments in observance of the Festivals. On Sukkot the *sukkah*, or booth in which every Israelite is required to dwell, is in remembrance of "the great miracles which God, blessed be He, wrought for our forefathers in the desert, when He brought them out of Egypt and covered them with clouds of glory so as to protect them from the sun by day and the frost by night." [54]

Since Sukkot is the festival of rejoicing in the harvest, we are bidden to take the *'etrog* and the *lulab,* together with the myrtle and the willow, so as to "remind us that all of the joy in our hearts should be in His name and in His honor." [55] These four species are waved in all directions betokening that all things belong to God and that His dominion is everywhere. [56] The Hinnuk states that he believes that the Kabbalists are aware of profounder and more esoteric meanings to this mizvah. [57]

Passover has its commandments of a similar nature, [58] such as the *mazah,* the bitter herbs, and the like, which are in remembrance of the Exodus and the miracles wrought by God. Shabuot needs no additional remembrances "because the festival is essentially in commemoration of the revelation of the Torah, and the Torah itself is our greatest reminder to be upright in our ways." [59]

CHAPTER NINE

THE SERVICE OF GOD

THE SANCTUARY

The belief that man's nature, both spiritual and moral, is perfected through deeds that are ethically and spiritually charged receives its foremost expression in the Hinnuk's explanation of the biblical injunction, "And let them make Me a sanctuary that I may dwell among them" (Exodus 25:8). This command is not to be construed as indicating God's need for an earthly abode, for as Solomon said in his prayer of dedication of the Temple, "Behold heaven and the heaven of heavens cannot contain Thee, how much less this house that I have builded" (I Kings 8:27). It is rather to provide man with a means to uplift himself spiritually and to enable him to draw near to the Divine Presence. "The object in building the House of God, where we would offer up our prayers and sacrifices," says the Hinnuk, "was wholly in order to prepare our hearts to serve Him . . . He, therefore, commanded us to establish a place which would be consummately pure and clean, where the thoughts of men would be purified and where they would direct their hearts to him." [1]

Presence of the Shekinah

It is in the Sanctuary that man, mindful of the presence of the *Shekinah,* would reach out to cleave to God, his soul "rising to *debekut* with the Supreme Intellect." [2] The sanctity of its already sacred precincts is to be enhanced by the people's service therein. By their devotion they will themselves render the House of God a potent force

143

in their lives and a source of divine blessing. "It is their goodly actions which will open for them the well-springs of goodness." [3]

With the erection of the *Bet ha-Mikdash,* the Temple in Jerusalem, in place of the Tabernacle which had accompanied the Israelites in their earlier wanderings, no other temple could ever again be built or sacrifices offered in any other place.[4] The Hinnuk views the Temple in Jerusalem both as a spiritual center and as a national center, as the focus of the Festival pilgrimages and as the center for the periodic gathering of the people.[5]

Jerusalem and the Land of Israel

Special holiness is ascribed as well to Jerusalem and to the whole of the Land of Israel.[6] The Hinnuk points out that it is by reason of its holiness that the Land of Israel constitutes an asylum to a fugitive slave. Having fled for refuge into this "chosen valley of purity, there to serve God," he may not be returned to his master. The Hinnuk envisions Jerusalem, the seat of the Sanhedrin, as the center of Torah learning, whence the knowledge and wisdom of Torah would spread throughout the land. He explains that one of the reasons for the stipulation that the second tithe, the tithe of cattle, and the fruits of the fourth-year plantings be consumed in Jerusalem[7] was to assure the presence of at least one member of every family who, while residing there, would avail himself of the opportunity to study Torah. Thus there would always be individuals capable of teaching Torah and providing spiritual guidance in each household and in every community.[8]

Holiness of the Temple

The Temple itself represents the greatest *kedushah,* or holiness. An aura of reverence, conducive to supplication and penitence was to surround the Temple, in keeping with the biblical injunction, "And ye shall reverence My sanctuary" (Leviticus 19:30). The Halakah therefore sets forth specific directives regarding respectful demeanor in the Sanctuary and on the Temple Mount.[9] A feeling of reverence was, moreover, instilled by ceremonial acts, such as kindling the lamps,[10] and burning the incense,[11] as well as by the distinctive garb that the High Priest and the common priests were required to wear during the Temple service.[12] This also was the reason for stationing guards around the Temple, consisting of priests within the Temple grounds and levites on the outside. They were essentially a mark of honor and reverence.[13]

The *kedushah* represented by the Temple is not confined to the structure alone. Indeed, as the Rabbis point out, the reverence enjoined by Scripture is not really for the Sanctuary, but "for Him who commanded the building of the Sanctuary."[14] Hence, the very grounds of the Temple site remain holy forever, retaining their holiness even when desolate.[15] The Rabbis derive this from the verse, "And I will bring your *sanctuaries* unto desolation" (Leviticus 26:31), which they expound to mean that "their sanctity endures although they lie desolate."[16] The eternal sanctity of the Temple grounds is furthermore inferred from the scriptural verse, "Ye shall keep My Sabbaths and reverence My sanctuary" (Leviticus 19:30). The Sages note, "Just as the observance of the Sabbath is binding forever, even so is reverence for the Sanctuary binding forever."[17] The Hinnuk, in accord with the view of Maimonides, maintains that the law prohibiting an unclean person from entering the camp of the Levites, later designated as the Temple Mount, continues in force.[18] It is, consequently, forbidden to enter the Temple Mount, that is, the grounds on which the Temple once stood, even to this day.[19] Maimonides explains this, "The holiness of the Sanctuary and of Jerusalem is due to the presence of the *Shekinah*, and the *Shekinah* has not departed."[20]

PRIVATE AND COMMUNAL SACRIFICES

The Meaning of the Sacrifices

The principal feature of the Temple service is the offering of various kinds of expiatory and propitiatory sacrifices, both public and private. Their object is necessarily in accord with the general object of the Temple. "The purpose of the sacrifice," the Hinnuk states, "is to refine the soul of the man who offers it," thereby rendering him worthy of God's beneficence.[21]

Where the sacrifice is brought for the remission of sins it is a means of atonement effected through a cleansing of the soul. "We have said before that the inclinations of the heart are dependent upon actions. Therefore, when a man sins he cannot thoroughly cleanse his heart merely with words alone, by saying to himself: 'I have sinned and will sin no longer.' However, by performing a great deed to atone for his sin, by taking rams from his fold and troubling himself to bring them to the Temple, and giving them to the priest and performing the entire rite as prescribed for sin-offerings, he will thereby impress upon his soul the extent of the evil of his sin and will avoid it in the future."[22]

The Hinnuk's thesis is fundamentally at variance with the one propounded by Maimonides. The institution of sacrifices, Maimonides believed, was in the nature of a divine concession intended to wean the Israelites away from idolatrous worship, and gradually to draw them to the true service of God. Maimonides explains that the sacrifice of animals was the general mode of worship among all people, hence it was not deemed practicable to demand of the Israelites to discontinue such a universal practice to which they were accustomed. This kind of worship was therefore allowed to continue, but it was transferred to the service of God and confined to the Sanctuary. "By this divine plan," Maimonides states, "it was effected that the traces of idolatry were blotted out, and the truly great principle of our faith, namely, the existence and unity of God, was firmly established. This result was thus obtained without deterring or confusing the minds of the people by the abolition of the service to which they were accustomed and which alone was familiar to them."[23]

Apparently not satisfied with this view of sacrifices which fails to ascribe to them any intrinsic value, a criticism which Maimonides anticipates,[24] the Hinnuk adopts rather the view of Nahmanides as the basis of his own thesis. In his criticism of Maimonides, Nahmanides points out[25] that in the Bible sacrifices are characterized as being "of a sweet savor unto the Lord" (Numbers 28:2), which indicates that they represent of themselves, certain positive spiritual values. Hence they are divinely ordained acts which constitute an integral part of the divine service.[26]

Nahmanides explains the sacrifice in terms of a vicarious offering.

Having sinned before God, a man would stand to forfeit his own life were it not for God's grace in accepting the animal as a substitute. The parts of the offering are symbolic of the organs involved in committing the sin. "Inasmuch as the deeds of men are carried out by means of thought, speech and action, God commanded that when one sins and brings a sacrifice he should lay his hands upon it and confess by word of mouth, in recognition of the act and the utterance that accompanied the sinful deed, and burn in the fire its innards and kidneys which represent a man's thought and desire, as well as its legs which recall his own hands and feet that do his work. He also sprinkles the blood upon the altar as a symbol of his own life's blood. In doing all this the sinner will bethink himself that he sinned before God with body and soul, and that he would deserve to have his blood spilled and his body destroyed by fire, were it not for the mercy of God who accepts his sacrifice as a substitute in atonement for his sin."[27]

To this conception of the meaning of sacrifices, the Hinnuk adds the following thought. People are greatly stirred by the sacrifice of animals. This is due to the similarity between man and animal who resemble each other in all respects and differ only in that man possesses intelligence. Consequently, when a man sins he has forsaken reason. He must therefore be made to realize that with the sinful act he lowered himself to the status of the animal, because it is intelligence alone which distinguishes him from the animal. "For this reason," the Hinnuk writes, "man is commanded to bring a body resembling his own to the place chosen for the elevation of the intellect, and there to burn it and destroy it completely, leaving no trace of it, in order to impress indelibly upon his heart that his body bereft of reason is subject to utter destruction. Then, he will rejoice in the portion which God granted him, namely, his intellect which is eternal." [28]

The psychological impact of the ritual and its symbolism, it is anticipated, will move the transgressor to repentance and therewith effect his moral and spiritual rehabilitation. Both the Hinnuk and Nahmanides imply that, apart from the aforestated, the sacrifices are bound up with mystical meanings and reasons which are known to the Kabbalists.

It is of interest to note the Hinnuk's view regarding the fire that was to burn continually upon the altar. It was symbolic of the fire that is deemed to be the chief component of the four elements comprising man's nature. The fire on the altar thus invoked the special blessing of God, enabling man to possess it in proper measure for his well-being and the perfection of his nature.[29] As to the fire which was kindled for the sacrifices, the Hinnuk believed it to have been for the purpose of concealing the miraculous fire that descended upon the altar from heaven, "since great miracles which God, in His abundant goodness, performs for men are always wrought by Him in secrecy." The Hinnuk views this in light of the principle that miracles are generally brought about in a manner as to appear to be part of the course of nature.[30]

The *Tamid*, the daily burnt-offering brought upon the altar in the morning and at dusk, was the sacrifice offered for the entire nation. Noting that the scriptural injunction concerning the *Tamid* is prefaced with the statement, "Command the children of Israel" (Numbers 28:2), the Hinnuk stresses that "this is of the mizvot that are incumbent upon the community."[31] It is the whole of Israel that is hereby commanded; with the priests, "the ministers of God," performing the service on behalf of the people. The *Bet Din*, as the delegated authority of the people, is charged with seeing to it that the continual offering is instituted, "since upon them devolves the responsibility for communal acts." Hence, with regard to the daily sacrifice the nation acts as a corporate entity, with halakically defined duties and prerogatives. In the worship of God in the Temple, the People of Israel is thus invested with a distinct halakic and spiritual personality.

The Temple Service

The divine service in the Temple was conducted by priests and levites who were divided into twenty-four divisions, with a different group in attendance in rotation each week.[32] The priests were to minister in strict purity, and serve God with profound reverence and great devotion so that the people whom they represented would meet with divine favor and forgiveness. In view of their holy calling, it was fitting that the priests be of good appearance and upright conduct.[33] As "the deputies of Israel before their Father in Heaven," they received the priestly gifts, were accorded particular solicitude and honor and, by virtue of the constancy of their devotion, were deemed worthy of bestowing the divine blessings upon the people of Israel.[34]

The High Priest, "whose soul dwelt constantly among the celestial Beings," was to live secluded from worldly affairs, consecrated in the holiest ministry and dedicated to the exclusive service of God.[35]

While the Temple service was conducted chiefly by the priests, the levites were also engaged in the service of God as attendants at the gates and guardians of the Temple, and particularly as singers on the occasion of the daily, Sabbath, and Festival offerings.[36] In addition to the divine service, the levites were to devote themselves to acquiring divine wisdom, to teaching the Torah and to guiding the people in the Law throughout the land.[37] Inasmuch as they were thus likewise occupied with their sacred duties, and moreover received no portion in the Land, the levites were provided for by the tithes which they received from their fellow Israelites and the levitical cities apportioned to them for their residence.[38]

In consideration of their higher spiritual calling, the entire tribe of Levi, both priests and levites, were not to share in the spoils of war "so that only what was gotten in a peaceful, righteous and trusting manner would be brought to the House of the Lord."[39]

In addition to the priests and levites, a deputation of Israelites, referred to in the Talmud as 'anshei ma'amad, consisting of "honorable, God-fearing men," was designated to represent the entire people as the daily communal sacrifices were brought in the Temple. The Israelites who were present in Jerusalem, and others who were assembled in synagogues throughout the land, offered prayers and engaged in fasting and in reading the Torah.[40] The ma'amadot attendant upon the twenty-four courses instituted by the First Prophets were, in all likelihood, the origin of the synagogue service that eventually replaced the sacrificial service in the Temple.[41] In its time, however, the Temple was "the place that God chose to bless mankind" and to bestow the light of His countenance upon His people, and the sacrifices the means by which their souls rose to ever greater heights, and they were thus rendered worthy of God's beneficence.[42]

PRAYER: SERVICE OF THE HEART

Man has been afforded a means other than sacrifices by which to draw near to God and to serve Him. That means is prayer. Indeed, as the Hinnuk points out, the object of the Temple itself was to provide a place "where we would offer up our prayers and sacrifices." [43] In considering prayer an essential part of the Temple service, the Hinnuk, as noted, reflects recorded tradition concerning the various prayers offered at the time of the public sacrifices by the priests[44] and by the *ma'amad* of Israelites which stood by for the daily offerings,[45] as well as the formal and private prayers offered by individuals.[46]

The Essence of Prayer

That the essence of prayer is service of God is readily evident from the manner in which it is derived as a scriptural command. The Hinnuk derives the mizvah to pray[47] from the verses, "Him shalt thou serve" (Deuteronomy 6:13; 10:20); "And ye shall serve the Lord your God" (Exodus 23:25); "And to serve Him with all your heart" (Deuteronomy 11:13). The commandment, as stated, is broad and indeterminate and can be taken to include all of the mizvot of the Torah whose general purpose it is to serve God.[48] The fact that it is understood to refer specifically to prayer is due to the latter verse cited above, "And to serve Him with all your heart." The Rabbis explain: "What is service of the heart? It is prayer." [49]

The Hinnuk views the commandment regarding prayer in terms of the basic principle which applies to all of the *Taryag Mizvot*. "The reason for this commandment," the Hinnuk writes, "as I have many times stated at the outset of my discussion of the commandments, is that good and blessings are bestowed upon men according to their deeds, the goodness of their hearts, and the worthiness of their thoughts. The Lord of all, who created them, desires their welfare and therefore He guided them and enriched them by His precious commandments so that they would be rendered worthy. He also informed them[50] of a door which He had opened to them whereby they could attain all of their wishes for good, namely, by petitioning for their needs from God, blessed be He, who has the means and the power to grant them, for He answers from heaven all those who call upon Him in truth." [51]

Aside from being a means of petitioning God for personal wants, prayer serves also to uplift man spiritually. Through prayer, man acknowledges God as the author of all good, and as his ever-vigilant guardian. "Apart from attaining our heart's desire, prayer is of great benefit to us in that it stirs our spirit and we impress on our minds that He is the Lord of all that is good and beneficial to us, that He is watchful of all of our ways, and that at all times and at any moment He will hearken to our cries to Him." [52]

The Nature of Prayer

Two primary conditions apply to prayer. First, it is to be, as we have noted, a service of God. Second, it must be an expression of the heart. Both of these are implied in the term "service of the heart" which the Rabbis use to describe prayer. If prayer is indeed to be a service of the heart, it must be attended by true, inner devotion. The Talmud states: "He who prays must direct his heart towards heaven." [53] The Hinnuk clarifies the nature of this inner devotion which the Rabbis call *kavanah*. "A man should bear in mind that he is praying before God and that he is calling upon Him. He must banish from his mind all other worldly thoughts and concentrate upon this alone." [54]

The Talmud further states [55] that "when ten men pray together the *Shekinah* rests among them, for it is written, 'God standeth in the congregation of God'" (Psalms 82:1), hence prayer with a congregation is the most desired form of prayer. "Every man," says the Hinnuk, "is obligated to endeavor as far as possible to worship with the congregation, because the prayers of the congregation are more readily answered than the prayer of the individual." [56] Thus, not only is there greater assurance of genuine devotion, but the prayer of the individual does not remain in the realm of private petition and concern; it reaches out to be joined with the prayers of others in a communal expression of divine worship and supplication.

The Torah commandment on prayer specifies neither the number of prayers to be recited nor its form, nor does it designate a set time of day for prayer. It does, however, obligate us "to implore God's favor each day, and to acknowledge that He is ruler of all and that He has the power to fulfill all of our requests."[57] In interpreting the scriptural command as ordaining daily prayer, the Hinnuk accepts the halakic ruling of Maimonides,[58] rather than that of Nahmanides who believes that the Torah does not obligate one to pray every day.[59] In the opinion of Nahmanides, the Torah obligates one to pray only in time of distress.[60]

Since prayer is an act of divine service prescribed in the Torah, the Sages thereupon ordained its bounds and requisite conditions by law, as they did with all other commandments. Thus prayers are to be recited at times and in the manner as fixed by the Sages.[61] The *Shemoneh Esreh*, which serves as the basis for every worship service, as well as other occasional prayers and benedictions, were formulated by Ezra and his *Bet Din* at the time of the restoration of the second Jewish commonwealth.[62] The divine service in the Temple in Jerusalem constitutes the pattern for our prayers. The three daily prayers, in the morning, afternoon and night, and the additional prayers on Sabbaths, Festivals, and Holy Days are intended to correspond to the sacrifices offered daily and on these special occasions in the Temple.[63] In this way, the Halakah lifts prayer from the plane of mere personal whim, and imparts to it the character of religious duty which one is called upon to perform as a member of the community of Israel.

THE WAY OF THE PIOUS

Serving God entails more than worship and the periodic performance of mizvot. A man must devote all his heart and thoughts to God.[64] The verse, "In all thy ways acknowledge Him" (Proverbs 3:6) is considered by the Sages to be the quintessence of the Torah.[65] This is expressed more concisely in the statement of the Mishnah, "Let all your deeds be done for the sake of heaven."[66]

Constant Awareness of God

The Hinnuk enumerates six commandments that involve principles to which a man must commit himself, and of which he must always be mindful throughout his lifetime.[67] These mizvot which, in a mnemonic, scriptural allusion, he terms the "six cities of refuge" (Numbers 35:13), are the following:

To believe there is One God, who created and wills all being, and who brought us out of Egypt and gave us the Torah.

Not to believe in any gods besides Him, but that He alone exercises His providential care over the world.

To affirm His unity, as it is said, "Hear, O Israel, the Lord our God, the Lord is One" (Deuteronomy 6:4).

To love Him, which entails reflection upon God's actions and His commands, seeking as far as one is able to attain a knowledge of Him.

To fear Him, and thereby to be deterred from sinning for fear of divine punishment.

Not to stray after the waywardness of the heart and the eyes, which means not to entertain thoughts contrary to fundamental views of the Torah, and not to pursue worldly desires for the sole purpose of sensual gratification.[68]

Religious and Moral Commitment

In his discussion of the latter commandment,[69] the Hinnuk discourses upon the integrity of religious and moral commitments demanded in Judaism. In the first instance, the mizvah bids one to refrain from thoughts that may lead to evil deeds and the undermining of faith, but to concentrate rather upon wholesome thoughts and the cultivation of true values based on the guidelines of the Torah. The mizvah also enjoins one not to incline toward a materialistic outlook on life, seeking mere physical and sensual indulgence, but rather to develop a sense of balance and restraint, and pursue moral and spiritual uprightness.

The Jew must, furthermore, insulate himself against alien cultures lest he be ensnared by the blandishments of their idolatrous cults and the allure of their immoral practices. The Hinnuk understands this to be the intent of the biblical admonition, "And ye shall not walk in the customs of the nation which I am casting out before you; for they did all these things and therefore I abhorred them" (Leviticus 20:23).[70] The mizvah, he believes,[71] entails guarding against the adoption of their heathen customs and their aberrant habits and life styles.

Life's true objective is to serve God and observe His commandments. In order to achieve this goal there must be a constant awareness of Israel's elect status and its distinctive character of *kedushah*. Every Jew, says the Hinnuk, should be conscious of the fact that he belongs to "God's holy and chosen people, the guardians of His testimony, the most treasured of all peoples under the heavens, charged with observing His laws and keeping the Faith." [72]

The Study of Torah

The ideal is a life devoted to piety, charitable works, and study of the Torah. The latter is, in Judaism, itself deemed an act of religious devotion, since it leads to love of God and a knowledge of God's ways. The Hinnuk quotes[73] the *Sifre*. "It is said, 'And thou shalt love the Lord thy God' (Deuteronomy 6:5). Since I do not know how a man can love God, Scripture continues, 'And these words which I command thee this day shall be upon thy heart' (Deuteronomy 6:6), intimating that in this way you will come to acknowledge the Creator. That is to say, through meditation upon the Torah the heart will of necessity be filled with love of God." [74]

Study of the Torah is therefore a mizvah which is in reality "the foundation of all of the mizvot." [75] In defining the mizvah, the Hinnuk states, "It is a positive commandment to learn and to teach the wisdom of the Torah; that is to say, how we are to observe the commandments and refrain from doing what God has forbidden us. We must also acquire a correct knowledge of the laws of the Torah." [76] Every Israelite must engage in the study of Torah throughout his lifetime, regardless of his material or physical condition, [77] not only for the knowledge to be gained, but because learning Torah is a way of serving God.[78]

The Pursuit of Life

Piety does not involve an ascetic denial of human needs and seclusion from society. Indeed, the Hinnuk points out, "There is no difference between the priest and the rest of the people, except that at appointed times he serves in the House of the Lord." [79] At other times he conducts himself in a manner similar to all others, joining with his family and friends at joyous and festive occasions.

Although the Hinnuk evinces a fairly tolerant attitude toward the Nazirite,[80] in apparent recognition of a positive element of *kedushah,* viewing his self-imposed abstinence as a means of "breaking his passions" and "subduing his evil inclinations" in order to improve his soul, he agrees substantially with Maimonides that Judaism does not extol asceticism as an expression of piety, but seeks rather to foster a life of moderation.[81] The Nazirite, Maimonides notes, is reproached by the Sages for having "sinned against his own soul" by denying himself the drinking of wine.[82] He cites another statement of the Sages, in disapproval of those who take upon themselves restrictive oaths and vows. "Is it not enough for you what the Torah has forbidden that you must prohibit yourself other things?" [83]

God is to be served in joy. It is a mizvah to rejoice on the festivals, which literally means eating meat and other delicacies, drinking wine and wearing new clothes.[84] The Hinnuk explains this simply by indicating that "a man by nature requires occasional enjoyment, just as he must have food, rest and sleep." What this mizvah does is to keep the rejoicing within moderate and proper limits and direct it toward the service of God.[85]

While shunning excess and striving for holiness, the pious man will yet engage in the normal pursuit of life and share the concerns of the world together with his fellow human beings. "This is the way of the pious and the saintly," says the Hinnuk. "They love peace, and rejoice in the good of their fellowmen, and draw them near to the Torah." [86] In this way "they inspire other people to serve God from love." [87] This, the Hinnuk emphasizes, is inherent in their duty to serve God. In further interpreting the biblical exhortation, "And thou shalt love the Lord thy God" (Deuteronomy 6:5), the Sages say, "Make Him beloved to all people, even as your father Abraham did." [88]

All Are Equal Before God

In the service of God, all men, whatever their calling or station in life, are equal. The equality of all in the spiritual fellowship of Israel, was especially marked during the three pilgrimages to the Temple for Passover, Shabuot, and Sukkot. In defining the laws pertaining to the commandment to celebrate these festivals in Jerusalem, the Hinnuk states: "All men should make the pilgrimage even if, in pursuit of their calling, they must be engaged in such repulsive tasks as collecting the excrement of dogs, smelting, or tanning. Let them cleanse their bodies and their clothing, and let them go up before the Lord, blessed be He. They will be received by God in common with the rest of Israel, because it is defilement of the soul that renders men repulsive in His Presence, and not one's calling, so long as it is pursued faithfully." [89] Purity of soul and nobility of character are the qualities that count in God's estimation of each man. Every man stands with his fellowmen on a common footing before God.

CHAPTER TEN

THE DIVINE IMPERATIVE

RETRIBUTION AND DIVINE GRACE

Divine Retribution

The commandments are intended to enable man to achieve the perfection of his moral and spiritual nature. Viewed positively, they are the means by which a man attains to divine blessing. Conversely, neglect of the commandments renders him unworthy of God's beneficent providence and subject to the dire consequences of his errant ways.[1] Divine retribution is, therefore, a cardinal doctrine in Judaism, underpinning, as it were, the Torah's framework of mizvot.

The Rabbis see a form of retributive parity operating inexorably in the divinely ordained scheme of reward and punishment. The Mishnah enunciates this as a principle: "In the measure with which a man measures, it will be meted out to him."[2] The Hinnuk cites the man stricken with the dread disease of leprosy as representative of this.[3] Since, by his calumny and evil talk "he estranged husband from wife and created enmity between friends," the Torah commands that he be treated as an outcast. This accords with the rabbinic view which presumes that the leper has been punished for the sin of slander. The Rabbis deduce this from the fact that in Scripture the exhortation to heed the prescribed directions with regard to leprosy is followed by the statement, "Remember what the Lord thy God did unto Miriam" (Deuteronomy 24:8, 9). Scripture means to teach us that leprous afflictions come as punishment for slander,[4] since Miriam was smitten with leprosy because she slandered Moses (Numbers 12:1-16).

The Torah's conception of divine retribution differs from the commonly conceived notion. Among men, to be sure, a form of reciprocity generally obtains; favor is repaid with favor, and harm elicits retaliation. Such reciprocation cannot, however, be ascribed to God, "because God brings only goodness, kindness and mercy to the world, and His goodness is always available to the one who is prepared to receive it." [5] Whatever befalls man, is, therefore, the consequence of his own actions. "According to man's deeds," the Hinnuk points out, "whether they be good or the opposite, in that measure will he receive his recompense, and invariably according to the nature of his thoughts or his actions will he bring upon himself a like measure of blessing or the opposite." [6]

God does not of His own will condemn any of His creatures. This thought, the Hinnuk notes, is expressed in the scriptural verse, "For He doth not afflict willingly, nor grieve the children of men" (Lamentations 3:33), and in the verse, "For Thou art not a God that hath pleasure in wickedness: evil shall not sojourn with Thee" (Psalms 5:5). It is also enunciated by the Rabbis in the statement, "No bad thing comes from on high." [7] Hence, when we speak of divine punishment for man's transgressions we are but resorting to language understood by men. In reality punishment is a direct result of a man's own wicked nature and his deviate actions. "It is man who condemns himself when he departs from righteousness and thereby strips himself of all that has rendered him fit and worthy to receive goodness." [8] The Hinnuk explains this in a parable which depicts a man walking along a straight path, cleared of all stones and obstacles, with a fence of thorns on either side. [9] If he brushes against the fence and wounds himself, it should not be imputed to God. He can only attribute it to the fact that he was not careful to walk in the straight path.

Hiding of God's Countenance

Divine punishment is essentially a withholding of God's grace. Whatever evil fortune befalls the sinful man is the effect of God's having removed His divine care and protection from him. Scripture underscores this moral principle as it applies to the Jewish people. Should Israel sin and stray after false gods, God will abandon them and leave them to their evil fate. "And I will forsake them, and I will hide my face from them, and they shall be devoured, and many evils and troubles shall come upon them; so that they will say in their day: Are not these evils come upon us because our God is not among us?" (Deuteronomy 31:17). [10]

The concept of *haster panim,* concealment of the Divine countenance, or the denial of divine favor, which in the Bible is held forth as a dire punishment for the people of Israel as a whole, is developed by the Hinnuk to apply to the individual, as well, as a punishment for his sins until such time as they are expiated and forgiven. "The sum total of our contention is that every misfortune that befalls a man is the effect that results from the hiding of God's countenance from that individual. That is to say, that God deprives him of divine protection because of his sinfulness until he receives the punishment due him according to his sin." [11]

A similar approach is indicated by Maimonides.[12] "Divine Providence is constantly watching over those who have obtained that blessing which is prepared for those who endeavor to obtain it. If man frees his thoughts from worldly matters, obtains a knowledge of God in the right way and rejoices in that knowledge, it is impossible that any kind of evil should befall him while he is with God and God with him. When he does not meditate on God, when he is separated from God, then God is also separated from him; then he is exposed to any evil that might befall him. It is clear that we ourselves are the cause of this hiding of the face, and that the screen that separates us from God is of our own creation. This is the meaning of the words: 'And I will surely hide My face in that day, for all the evils which they shall have wrought' (Deuteronomy 31:18). There is undoubtedly no difference in this regard between one single person and a whole community. It is now clearly established that the cause of our being exposed to chance and abandoned to destruction like cattle is to be found in our separation from God." While Maimonides thus conceives of providence as a form of divine guidance through intellectual communion, the Hinnuk stresses the moral character of the relationship and the ethical factors that would bring about a hiatus between man and God.

Providence and the Course of Nature

It should be noted, in any event, that divine providence does not ordinarily mean a suspension of the laws of nature or an interruption of its normal processes. "For God created His world and erected it upon the foundations and pillars of nature, and decreed that fire should burn and water should quench the flame." [13] The Hinnuk takes cognizance of the principle of causality which, he believes, operates in a kind of conditional determinism as it affects human fate. Man is at all times subject to the normal course of nature and its established laws. Indeed this is the expressed will of God and, hence, is not to be deemed contrary to divine providence. It follows, therefore, that a man must take all measures to protect himself from the ravages of nature, or the threat posed by natural conditions or events, in order to insure his welfare and survival. The Hinnuk points out[14] that Scripture clearly indicates that even in the instances where the people of Israel went forth to battle at divine behest, in a *milhemet mizvah,* they still had recourse to weapons, and they had to wage war in reliance only upon their own might and the human resources that they could muster.

As indicated above, the Hinnuk views determinism as conditional and not absolute, insofar as God reserves the right to override the very laws that He has implanted within nature. Thus, in exceptional circumstances God performs a miracle or, as in the case of saintly men, grants an individual supernatural powers. The Sages, however, caution that one may not rely upon a miracle,[15] but he must exercise his God-given intelligence to protect himself and secure his own well-being.

REPENTANCE

In pondering the implications of the withdrawal of divine providence from man, the Hinnuk is also concerned with man's finding his way back into God's grace. Punishment, he believes, is intended to bring the sinner to reconsider his evil ways and to repent of them. It is essential, therefore, that a man view all events and experiences in life in the light of a divine governance of the world. Hence, should he suffer any misfortune, he must look upon it as retribution and be moved to repentance and a betterment of his ways.

Turning again to the leper, whose disease as indicated above is taken to be a providential affliction in punishment for slander, the Hinnuk draws the moral lesson further by maintaining that the leper's condition of impurity and the isolation imposed upon him is designed to prompt him to repentance. "The Torah warns us that if a man is afflicted with this terrible disease of leprosy he should not ascribe it to chance but he should bethink himself at once that it could be due to his sinfulness. He must therefore withdraw from the company of people, just as one who is banished because of his evil deeds, and he should come and show the plague of leprosy to the priest, who is designated to make atonement and to heal the wounds that result from sin. By means of the priest's guidance and advice, and by a searching of his deeds, he will be able to remove the plague from himself, because God, blessed be He, whose surveillance is always upon him, will take notice of this act of repentance and will heal him." [16]

Repentance, the Object of Punishment

Teshubah, repentance, is thus the real objective of divine punishment. It is God's desire that the sinner repent and endeavor once more to be worthy of divine protection. Citing the classic example of God's pardon of Israel, following their idolatrous worship of the molten calf (Exodus 32:11-14), the Hinnuk concludes that so great is the power of *teshubah* that the most wicked of men may seek and obtain divine pardon. "God's mercy is infinitely greater than we think. He forgives everyone who returns to Him with a sincere heart, however, unforgivable his sin may appear to us." [17]

Teshubah is equally the main object of temporal punishment administered by the judicial authorities to those who transgress the laws of the Torah. "Since the people of Israel are called the children of God," the Hinnuk writes,[18] "it is His wish that they be chastised for their sins, in order that they may return to Him and in the end merit the world that is all good, even as it is written, 'Chasten thy son, for there is hope' " (Proverbs 19:18).

Requisites for Teshubah

The Hinnuk includes *teshubah* as a mizvah[19] in the Torah under the scriptural command, "When a man or woman shall commit any sin that men commit, to commit a trespass against the Lord, and that soul be guilty; then they shall confess their sin which they have done" (Numbers 5:6, 7). In thus formulating the mizvah in terms of a confession of sin before God, the Hinnuk follows the specific construction of the commandment by Maimonides.[20] Nahmanides, however, derives the mizvah of *teshubah* from the scriptural verse, "And thou shalt return unto the Lord thy God . . . with all thy heart and with all thy soul" (Deuteronomy 30:2), from which he infers that one would comply with the precept even if oral confession were lacking.

The requisites for *teshubah* are determined by the Halakah.[21] The repentant must comply with the following conditions: He must forsake his iniquitous ways and remove the sinful thoughts and desires from his mind and heart; he must manifest regret and remorse, confess his sins and ask God's forgiveness; finally he must resolve to sin no more. Thus, while *teshubah* is essentially passive, involving an internalized process that will effect a radical change in a man's character and his outlook upon life, its active aspect is, in the view of the Hinnuk and Maimonides, the oral confession. However, this transformation from sinner to repentant must also reflect itself demonstratively in deeds. The law insists, for example, that the repentant sinner may not qualify as a witness until he has proven his sincere change of heart by withstanding a temptation equal to the one to which he had previously succumbed, and under similar circumstances.[22] Only then can he be reinstated in the community and his legal disabilities removed.

While *teshubah* generally effects atonement "for such sins as man commits in his relationship with God," [23] its efficacy is limited in instances where he sinned against his fellowman. There *teshubah* is of no avail until he has first made adequate restitution and begged his forgiveness.[24]

Teshubah in Jewish Tradition

Following upon historical example, Jewish tradition has designated certain days for introspection and repentance. These are the Ten Days of Repentance, which correspond to the concluding days of Moses' intercession on Mount Sinai in behalf of the people of Israel, seeking God's forgiveness for their grievous sin in worshipping the golden calf.[25] The Ten Days of Repentance begin with Rosh Hashanah and reach their climax with Yom Kippur, the day upon which God finally granted His pardon.[26]

The *shofar* is blown on Rosh Hashanah in order to rouse us to repentance. "The sound of the *shofar* is broken, intimating that everyone should break the power of his evil inclination and repent of his evil deeds."[27] In explaining the significance of Rosh Hashanah as a day of judgment, the Hinnuk writes: "It is out of kindness toward His creatures that God remembers them and reviews their deeds on this day, year after year, so that their sins may not become too numerous. Being few, God, who is abundant in kindness, will tend to be charitable and will overlook them. Thus it will be possible to atone for them. For were He not to judge them for a long time, their sins would become so numerous that the world would, God forbid, be doomed to destruction. This day therefore assures the world of survival."[28]

Yom Kippur is to be set aside wholly for fasting, confession, and repentance, so that the very day of Yom Kippur itself effects atonement. The Hinnuk explains, "After God, blessed be He, appointed this day as a day of atonement, it became hallowed and it received from Him the power to confer merit so that the day itself aids in the atonement."[29] In the time of the Temple, sacrifices were offered as a means of atonement on Yom Kippur. "Today, however," the Hinnuk points out,[30] "since because of our sins we have no Temple, nor a high priest officiating in his priestly garments, and no sacrifices, it has become traditional for all Israel to perform the divine service on this day with prayer and supplication, as it is written, 'we will offer the prayer of our lips in place of the sacrifice of bullocks.'" (Hosea 14:3).[31] In essence it is *teshubah* which is the decisive factor in achieving atonement on Yom Kippur.[32]

Though it is expected that a man should always be disposed to repent of his misdeeds and evil ways,[33] repentance is required by law at specific times. The Mishnah prescribes that one who is about to be given the death penalty must be directed to repent, "for everyone that makes his confession has a share in the world to come."[34] The implication quite evidently is that the repentance which precedes his death atones not only for his present sin, but for all previous transgressions

as well.[35] By extension of this tannaitic principle the Talmud concludes that every man, when he feels that death is near, must also
make his confession and pray for forgiveness of the sins which he
committed in his lifetime.[36]

Teshubah, a Factor in Law

Repentance is not only defined by the Halakah, but it appears that
it also conditions the Halakah under given circumstances. This can be
inferred from the Hinnuk's discussion of the commandment prohibiting
the court from rendering a conviction in capital cases on the sole basis
of presumption or circumstantial evidence.[37] The reason, he states, is
in order to prevent a miscarriage of justice. The law in actual application affords the court an opportunity to give the defendant the benefit
of the doubt by invoking devious legalities in order to acquit him. The
Hinnuk presumes a moral justification for this kind of procedure by
maintaining that "God wishes us to seek every possible merit in favor
of the defendant, for perhaps he has repented and regrets the wrong
that he has done, and he will henceforth promote the welfare of
society." [38]

On first thought it is difficult to accept the Hinnuk's justification of
procedures calculated to bring about an acquittal on the ground that
the accused has repented of his crime, particularly in view of the clear
duty of the court to render impartial judgment and to see to it that
the guilty party pays his debt to society. The Hinnuk's rationale becomes more plausible when we consider that, from the perspective of
the Halakah, imposing the death penalty involves two considerations:[39]
a) the protection of society by ridding it of a menace, as it is stated in
the Torah, "And thou shalt put the evil away from the midst of thee"
(Deuteronomy 19:19); b) personal atonement (kaparah), the death
penalty being the only means left for the criminal to obtain pardon for
his grave crime. It follows therefore that in a situation where the evidence or the circumstances are such that the court cannot or, in consonance with the law as strictly interpreted, need not carry out the
death penalty, the question of atonement is no longer its responsibility.
It becomes a matter for the individual himself. The only responsibility
left to the court is to protect society. In this case, therefore, where it

has reason to believe that the defendant has repented and will henceforth promote the welfare of society, the court can in good faith favor an acquittal. The concept of *teshubah* appears to be in this instance a motivating factor in determining the law.

THE IMPERATIVE OF THE LAW

The commandments are grounded in the primary postulate of the existence of a Divine Being. They constitute the expressed will of God as revealed to man. It is this fundamental belief that imparts to the Torah laws their distinctively theonomous character. The concept of a divine imperative underlying the mizvot, frequently invoked by the Sages,[40] is enunciated by the Hinnuk in setting forth the object of the appointment of judges and officers to enforce observance of the commandments of the Torah. "They shall compel those who deviate from the path of truth to return to it, and exhort the people to do that which is proper and restrain them from things that are indecent and improper. They are to take all necessary measures against transgressors so that the positive as well as the prohibitive commandments of the Torah shall not be subject to the belief and private opinion of every man." [41]

The Law Is Mandatory

Though the commandments are given to man for his benefit, they have an objective validity and sanction independent of his subjective judgment and will. One is not free to reject any of the mizvot but is duty-bound to observe them, subject to the penalties prescribed by the Law. This is evident, as the Hinnuk indicates, in the court's responsibility to punish transgressors,[42] but more particularly in the power that the court has to coerce one into complying with a positive commandment, even of a distinctly religious nature. The Hinnuk underscores this fact in his exposition of the mizvah to eat the meat of the Passover sacrifice, where he points out that the court may compel a person to comply with the commandment, noting that this is "an important principle with respect to the entire Torah." [43] The rationale of this principle is advanced by Maimonides, who explains that coercion in such instances is warranted because it serves to counteract a man's evil inclination, giving free rein to his truer nature which bids him comply with the divine command.[44] Judaism thus believes man by nature to be in accord with divine law, experiencing his essential freedom in submission to and in harmony with the divine will.[45]

Many of the mizvot have clearly discernible utilitarian objectives. An element of social and personal benefit may surely be said to inhere in those commandments which direct man in relation to his fellowman and society, and to a degree in religious precepts as well, insofar as they develop and refine certain facets of his ethical and spiritual nature. However, apart from these considerations, Judaism views the mizvot as categorical and mandatory. Compliance with the commandment is not subject to individual prerogative. Neither is it contingent upon one's preemptive assumption of punishment or voluntary renunciation of reward.[46] The Jew is not morally free to act counter to God's expressed will. He is bound by the eternal imperative of the covenant at Sinai. "There is not a single mizvah written in the Torah," say the Sages, "in connection with which forty-eight covenants were not made." [47]

The Hinnuk deduces the aforestated concept from the halakic principle that every law must be derived from two distinct scriptural admonitions; one to define the commandment and the other to define the penalty. The principle is enunciated by the Sages in the dictum, "The Torah does not indicate a punishment without having expressed a warning," [48] which the Hinnuk takes to mean that "God would not pronounce the punishment due for transgression of a commandment without first making known to us that it is His will that we refrain from the act that is subject to the stated punishment." [49]

The implication of this, according to the Hinnuk, is as follows: "If we had no explicit prohibitive command from God but were merely told that one who commits a certain act will suffer a given penalty, it might be inferred that whoever wishes to accept the penalty and is not concerned about the punishment that he will suffer is free to transgress the commandment and he will not thereby be going counter to the will and the command of God. The matter of observing the commandments would then assume the character of a business transaction; as if to say, whoever wishes to transgress, let him forfeit a stated amount or offer to bear his punishment and then proceed with the deed. The commandments were certainly not meant to be taken this way, but rather that for our own benefit God forbade us certain things and informed us of the punishment that will befall us immediately with regard to some of them. However, apart from this and of gravest concern is the violation of God's will." [50] The mizvot are thus to be conceived as imperatives issuing from God which, though they be absolute, are yet not arbitrary, since they are in consonance with the free nature of man when in harmony with the divine will.

The imperative of the Law, as the Hinnuk conceives it, is a notion universally enunciated by the Sages and later authorities. Thus, commenting on the verse "And God spoke all these words" (Exodus 20:1), by which Scripture prefaces the Ten Commandments, the *Mekilta* notes that the Deity is referred to as *'elohim,* meaning "God who is judge, exacting punishment." [51] Rashi, evidently expounding the *Mekilta,* explains this further in his commentary on the verse as follows: "Since there are chapters in the Torah that if a person observes the commands therein he will receive a reward and if he does not observe them he will not receive punishment on their account, one might think that the Ten Commandments are also of such a character, and that no punishment will follow upon the infringement of them; therefore Scripture expressly states, 'God spoke,' God Who is judge, exacting punishment." [52]

Israel Bound by the Law

Jewish tradition moreover describes the revelation at Sinai in terms which imply that the people of Israel, once committed to the eternal covenant with God, were unconditionally bound by the Law. On the scriptural verse, "And Moses brought forth the people out of the camp towards God, and they placed themselves at the nether part of the mountain" (Exodus 19:17), the Rabbis comment: "This teaches us that the Holy One, blessed be He, arched the mountain over them as a cask, and said to them, 'If you will accept the Torah it is well, and if not, there will your burial place be.' " [53] The lesson is succinctly drawn by Rabbi Judah Low of Prague, a sixteenth-century talmudist and philosopher, who states: "This matter requires great deliberation, inasmuch as the people had already said, 'We will do and we will hearken'; why, therefore, did He have to arch the mountain over them as a cask? But the reason is that the acceptance of the Torah is mandatory. For had they only accepted the Torah voluntarily they would think that the matter is subject to their own disposition." [54]

Another scriptural verse, "For I am the Lord that brought you up out of the land of Egypt to be your God" (Leviticus 11:45), elicits the following comment by the Rabbis: "It is on this condition that I have brought you up out of the land of Egypt, namely that you should accept upon yourselves the yoke of the commandments; 'to be your God'—against your will." [55] Even more pointed is the *Sifra,* which quotes Rabbi Eleazar ben Azariah as stating: "Whence do we know that one should not say, 'I have no desire to eat swine's flesh, or I do not want to enter into a forbidden marriage,' but one should say, 'I would indeed like it but what can I do since my Father in heaven has imposed this decree upon me?' Because Scripture states: 'I have separated you from the peoples that you should be mine,' that one should keep aloof from sin and take upon himself the yoke of the kingdom of heaven." [56]

It is the obligatory aspect of the mizvah that imparts the greater merit in the scale of divine service, as evidenced by the halakic ruling, "Greater is the merit of the one who performs the commandments when he is bound by the divine command, than the one who performs them though not bound by divine command." [57] The reason, as one of the early Tosafist commentators explains, is precisely "because he is commanded, and he accepts the authority of the commandments upon himself." [58]

Divine Sanction

The Rabbis are fully aware of the decisive implications of this view which invests every law of whatever nature with divine sanction. Commenting upon the scriptural verse, "If any one sin and commit a trespass against the Lord, and deal falsely with his neighbor . . ." (Leviticus 5:21), the Rabbis state, "A man will not deal falsely with his neighbor until he first denies God . . . And a man will not commit a sin unless he has denied the One who commanded its prohibition." [59]

The divine will remains ultimately the final arbiter of man's religious, as well as his moral and social, conduct.

In his discussion of the rational motivations and utilitarian purposes of some of the commandments, Saadiah takes pains to emphasize that "the chief reason for the fulfillment of these principal precepts and their derivatives and whatever is connected with them is the fact that they represent the command of our Lord." [60] Similarly, Maimonides concludes the *Book of Knowledge* in his Code on this theme. Whoever serves God out of love, says Maimonides, occupies himself with the study of the Law and the fulfillment of commandments, impelled by no external motive whatsoever, neither by fear of calamity nor by the desire to obtain material benefits. He notes several rabbinic utterances to this effect. "The text, 'Happy is the man that feareth the Lord, that delighteth greatly in His commandments (Psalms 112:1), has been explained by the Sages: 'In His commandments—not in the reward for His commandments.' [61] So, too, the greatest Sages were wont specifically to exhort those among their disciples who were understanding and intelligent, 'Be not like servants who minister to their master upon the condition of receiving a reward,' [62] but only because he is the master it is right to serve him; that is, serve him out of love." [63]

The mizvot, as we have seen from the Hinnuk's exposition, are designed to assure the spiritual, moral, and physical welfare of man and the preservation of a peaceful society. Some play an important part in the life of the Jewish people as a whole, in reflecting their history, in cultivating their religious beliefs, and in fostering Israel's national aspirations and destiny. Their ultimate objective however is to enable man to fulfill the will of God. The religious ideal envisioned by the Torah is thus not a mere compliance with its commands, but the acceptance of the mizvot as divine imperatives for man. There is thus indicated a higher purpose to the mizvot. Even social and ethical laws are given a spiritual motivation and placed within the framework of religious faith. The mizvot are the means by which God can be served. They not only effect a better relationship between man and man, but they confirm the covenant between man and God.

CHAPTER ELEVEN

PERSPECTIVES ON THE MIZVOT

ETHICAL-RELIGIOUS ASPECTS OF THE MIZVOT

In evaluating the Hinnuk's perspective on the mizvot, we find a major emphasis on the ethical and humanistic aspects of the mizvot, in their dual function of promoting the well-being of the individual and society.[1] Espousing a form of ethical idealism that holds moral action to be directed toward the improvement of the individual, the Hinnuk conceives of the divine laws of the Torah as serving to develop man's moral and spiritual nature, thereby rendering him worthy of God's beneficence. The welfare of humanity, expressed particularly in the principle of *yishub ha-'olam,* is, as we have seen, similarly a prime objective of the commandments.

Consideration of Diverse Elements

Apart from consideration of the patently rational elements and effects of a given mizvah, the Hinnuk also considers certain emotional impulses, which are at times key factors in determining its meaning, as in his appraisal of the laws which hold a woman to be unclean in her menstrual period and following childbirth.[2] He likewise takes note of the psychological impress of a mizvah on a man's character and mode of thought, as in his discussion of the effects of the specific laws pertaining to the Passover offerings.[3]

There is an evident disposition on the part of the Hinnuk to view the mizvot symbolically, highlighting in particular their religious and nationalistic aspects. A striking example is his midrashic exposition of the prohibition of eating the sinew of the thigh vein,[4] wherein he reflects upon its eschatological meaning and the deeper symbolism of the mizvah with respect to the historical fate and destiny of the Jewish people. This is in marked contrast to the literalism of Maimonides in this instance who, while surely aware of the midrashic allusions regarding the mizvah, nevertheless chooses to disregard them.[5] A further example is to be found in their divergent approaches to the meaning of the laws of Passover. While both view these mizvot initially in the role assigned to them in the Bible, as evoking a remembrance of Israel's deliverance from Egyptian bondage, Maimonides proceeds to stress the moral lesson "that man ought to remember his evil days in his days of prosperity," so that he will learn humility and gratitude to God, thus investing the Passover theme with a universal, ethical character.[6] The Hinnuk, on the other hand, emphasizes the special significance of the Passover festival for the Jewish people, relative to its religious beliefs and national aspirations, underscoring its exclusive message to Israel regarding its freedom, its nobility, and its status as a kingdom of priests and a holy nation.[7]

Unlike Maimonides, the Hinnuk addresses himself not only to those who are learned in philosophy, but to everyone who desires to study the mizvot and is inclined to inquire into their meaning and purpose. The Hinnuk's method affords him a flexible approach, so that within a broad philosophical frame he can consider differing views, unhampered by limiting, doctrinaire constraints.[8] He may, in one instance, incline to the rationalism of Maimonides, and in another instance follow Nahmanides in revealing some hidden, mystical strain, without completely yielding to the sharp rationalism of the former or the abstruse mysticism of the latter. By tempering the two, and by a judicious use of rabbinic dicta, he artfully weaves the varied and often divergent opinions of both of these expositors of the biblical commandments into a tapestry of thought distinctively his own.

Application of Ethical Principle

A notable aspect of the Hinnuk's exposition of the mizvot is his application of the underlying ethical principle to situations where the commandment is legally inapplicable, or in such instances where it is no longer in force in our day. Thus, as we have seen, the Hinnuk interprets the commandment to reward the Hebrew servant with a gift at the termination of his servitude, which was legally binding only in the time of the Temple when the Jubilee law was in force, as imposing a moral obligation upon an employer to grant severance pay to his employee in all times. He deems it reasonable that the mizvah, which calls for assuming this obligation "out of kindness," should at least apply morally, since one ought to share with his worker that "which God has blessed him." [9] Likewise, in his discussion of the commandment to love the stranger,[10] which in its strict meaning applies but to a Jewish proselyte, he enters into the spirit of the mizvah and draws from it the lesson that we should have compassion and extend aid to a stranger who finds himself in an alien land and far removed from his own family. The prohibition against pairing diverse kinds of animals together for work is understood by the Hinnuk to reflect a concern lest joining them, in disregard of their natural inclinations and physical disparity, would cause the animals pain and anguish. The underlying ethical principle, the Hinnuk believes, applies equally to human situations.[11]

Similarly, the law which obliges a man, who falsely accuses his bride of unchastity, to keep her as his wife all his days is taken by the Hinnuk to apply today, despite the fact that presently fines are legally unenforceable.[12] In this instance he does not deem retaining the wronged woman as a wife a fine, but a mizvah, the obligation that the defamer bears out of a purely humanitarian consideration. In like manner, in the case of one who has violated a maiden, whom he then must marry and never divorce, the Hinnuk draws the same distinction between an imposed penalty, which would be unenforceable, and a duty that he is bound to assume as a mizvah.[13]

Preserving the Harmony of Nature

The Hinnuk does not subscribe to the historical approach to certain of the mizvot. Thus, he specifically rejects Maimonides' contention that the reason for the scriptural prohibition of cooking meat and milk together is because it was once an idolatrous rite or a heathen custom practiced during their festivals.[14] "This reason," he states, "does not satisfy me." [15] The Hinnuk relates the mizvah to the general prohibition of interfering with God's prescription of the powers of things in nature, and thus disturbing the harmony of man's physical nature and of the cosmic order.

The thesis that man must live in harmony with nature, which the Hinnuk develops with regard to several of the commandments,[16] is of contemporary relevance, in view of the present universal concern for maintaining the complex ecological balance in nature, which has been demonstrated to be of profound importance to the well-being and the very survival of mankind. "At the beginning of Creation," the Hinnuk states,[17] "God endowed everything in the world with its own nature, to fulfill its function in a good and proper manner for the benefit of mankind which He created." It behooves man, therefore, to refrain from activities that would counter the will of God that "everything be conducted in accordance with the law of nature established at the beginning of Creation." [18]

THE MYSTICAL SYMBOLISM OF THE KABBALAH

In his exposition of many of the commandments, evidently following the lead of Nahmanides, the Hinnuk intimates that a true and full understanding of the reason for the mizvah requires probing at a deeper level of meaning, which is possible only by recourse to the wisdom of the Kabbalah.

Esoteric Meaning of Mizvot

The Hinnuk was evidently well acquainted with kabbalistic writings,[19] since he refers several times to traditions held by the Kabbalists regarding the reasons for certain commandments. His references indicate that he held this esoteric study in very high esteem. Thus, after presenting his reason for the commandment to prepare the lamps for kindling in the Sanctuary, he states, "I believe that the Kabbalists possess notable wisdom and wondrous secrets on these matters." [20] He makes a similar statement about the wonderful secrets of the Kabbalists regarding the *lulab* and the other species commanded for Sukkot.[21] Again, in his discussion of sacrifices, he remarks, "Were it not for the help of the Kabbalists, we would be completely at a loss as to their meanings. Let us pay them homage for having opened our eyes in these matters." [22]

The Hinnuk's references to the Kabbalah relate in the main to individual details of a commandment for which, as he explains, it is not his policy to attempt to ascribe reasons. Accordingly, regarding the golden altar and other holy vessels of the Sanctuary, he writes, "I have heard that the Kabbalists have wondrous reasons and deep secrets concerning every one of the details." [23]

Notwithstanding his great regard for the Kabbalah, the Hinnuk does not generally propose kabbalistic concepts although, as he states in the commandment on levirate marriage, he is aware that "a proper and true reason" concerning the commandment is known to the Kabbalists. [24] This reluctance to cite kabbalistic reasons is probably due to the fact, as he himself intimates, [25] that his purpose is to make the mizvot intelligible to everyone, and he therefore does not wish to enter into abstruse discussions.

While the Hinnuk is, consequently, not explicit as to the wisdom he believes to be stored up in kabbalistic lore on the esoteric meanings of the mizvot, it is, however, reflected in his conception of some of the mizvot. Thus, in his discussion of the Sabbatical year and the seven-fold cycle of Sabbaticals, [26] he develops the mystical import of the number *seven* as it pertains to several of the mizvot. Another instance is his explanation of the reasons for the dietary laws, in which he considers the psycho-physical effect of diet upon man, a view maintained in particular by the Jewish mystics, which prefigures certain aspects of present day psychosomatic research. [27]

Mystical Doctrine and the Halakah

In extolling the kabbalistic conception of the mizvot, the Hinnuk sensed the integral relationship that exists in Kabbalah between mystical doctrine and the established norms of the Halakah. For, apart from its preoccupation with the noumenal character of the Law, it is the mizvah, the dynamic impact of its practical observance, which is the very core of the mystical ideology of the Kabbalah. [28] Jewish mystics were especially inclined to the pursuit of *ta'amei ha-mizvot* because they believed that the mizvot have esoteric meanings and possess latent, mystical power, which when unlocked and set free renders man capable of affecting transcendental realms. In its world of '*Azilut,* or divine emanation, the Kabbalah conceives of a mystical bond between man and the creative power of God.

In the Kabbalah the exposition of the mizvot takes the form of a mystical symbolism, which is essentially the application of theosophic doctrine that is an inherent part of the highly structured, obscure world of kabbalistic thought. The mizvot are viewed not only as affecting man directly, whether physically, ethically or spiritually, but as the means of maintaining, through some mystical process, the harmony of the universe, and of effecting a reciprocal influence between upper and nether forces in worlds of mystical reality. The search for the reasons of the commandments in the kabbalistic system focuses initially upon their explicit role in perfecting man's moral and spiritual nature, and concludes in an attempt to fathom their transexperiential character and their mysterious, undulating effect upon the entire cosmos. Thus R. Hayyim Vital, in his exposition of the mizvot in accordance with the kabbalistic tradition of the Lurianic school and, in particular, its doctrine of *tikkun,* or restitution, delineates their primary effects. The mizvot, he notes,[29] remedy the defects in the celestial worlds caused by man's transgressions, thereby bringing about a return of the divine light, and they effect unity and harmony in the world, whereby man becomes a partner with God in his work of creation.[30]

The Hinnuk evidently subscribed to the kabbalistic view regarding the profound symbolical import of a mizvah and the correlation of its symbolic and halakic elements.

The influence of kabbalistic thought upon the Hinnuk, while not overtly manifest in his exposition of the commandments, is yet, as we have indicated, subtly discernible in individual instances where the Hinnuk refers to secrets of the Law possessed by the Kabbalists. His great regard for the wisdom of the Kabbalah was undoubtedly inspired by Nahmanides, whose mystical allusions in his commentary on the Bible gave rise to a number of kabbalistic commentaries and treatises. While it was primarily Nahmanides' work that later served as guide to a mystical exposition of the mizvot,[31] it is interesting to note that the

Sefer ha-Hinnuk had a significant, though limited, influence within the mystical school as well.[32]

META-HALAKIC ASPECTS OF THE MIZVOT

Halakic and Philosophic Elements

In addition to the traditional forms of scriptural exegesis and inter- pretation, the Hinnuk often uses the basic halakic elements of a mizvah as building blocks for his exposition of the mizvah and in formulation of its rationale. Thus, for example, in the course of his discussion of the Sabbatical year,[33] he indicates that the law serves to inculcate a firm belief in God's creation of the world, a principle of belief which is similarly imparted by the Sabbath. The relationship between the Sab- bath and the Sabbatical year is, however, not only conceptual, but is evidently based as well upon the congruity of texts[34] and the scriptural reference to both as "a Sabbath unto the Lord," an expression found in the Bible only with respect to the Sabbath and the Sabbatical year.[35] In its essential, halakic elements, namely abandonment of the produce of the seventh year and the remission of debts, the Hinnuk views the Sabbatical year as teaching, in addition, a belief in divine mastery of the world, and as developing a generous nature, promoting honesty, and fostering trust in God.

The method of exposition alluded to is accordingly pursued by the Hinnuk along a wider spectrum and the Halakah judiciously employed in his investigation of the purpose of the mizvot. In thus endeavoring to integrate the halakic and philosophic elements of the mizvot within the same system and conceptual frame, while nonetheless retaining the independent status of the Halakah, the Hinnuk succeeded in impart- ing a character of organic unity to the mizvot of the Torah.

The relationship between the halakic and philosophic realms, as thus explored by the Hinnuk, bears further investigation.[36] Such investigation should be directed especially along analytical, typologi- cal, and analogical lines of scriptural inquiry, since Scripture itself, as Ibn Ezra points out, is the primary source for a comprehension of the purpose of the mizvot. "The wise man," he writes, "whose eyes are opened by God, is able to know from the words of the Torah the reason of all the commandments." [37]

Jewish tradition holds Scripture to be spiritually charged, and the biblical narrative permeated with moral values and religious doctrine.[38] It would be instructive to examine the narrative context of certain laws for a clue to their meaning. The direction will most likely be indicated by the Sages in their midrashic exposition of passages in the Bible, as in the prohibition of the sinew of the thigh vein (Genesis 32:25-33).[39] Some significance may attach to the appearance of a mizvah, either in association with, precedent to, or subsequent to a recorded event. A case in point is Israel's encampment at Marah and the mizvot imparted to the people on that occasion (Exodus 15:22-26).[40]

Application of Halakic Methodology

Application of the methodology of Halakah and its exegetical forms, such as the principle of *semukim*, or collocation, logical deduction, and lexicographical analysis, to the philosophical investigation of mizvot would open yet another line of inquiry.[41] The significance that is accorded in the Halakah to the contiguity of texts,[42] the juxtaposition of verses, and the proximity of chapters or sections of the Bible may be taken account of in probing for the meaning of the laws as well. Indeed the Rabbis appear to follow a similar course in certain instances. According to the *Baraita,* for example, the scriptural source for the section of *Malkiot* included in the 'Amidah on Rosh Hashanah is derived solely from the juxtaposition of the verses, "I am the Lord your God" (Leviticus 23:22), and "In the seventh month" (Leviticus 23:24). Here, proclaiming the kingship of God on the New Year was evidently the underlying consideration in the exposition of the Sages.[43] Similarly, the inclusion of a reference to "true proselytes" in the prayer for the righteous, in the thirteenth benediction of the *Shemoneh 'Esreh,* is on the strength of the proximity of scriptural verses (Leviticus 19:32, 33).[44]

We may, likewise, probe for a rational connection between seemingly unrelated laws which are collocated, or follow a specific order in the Torah. Such instances abound in Halakah. The Rabbis, for example, expound the twenty-fifth chapter of Leviticus, by presuming that a logical sequence is implicit in the scriptural order of the laws, beginning with the prohibition against trading with seventh-year produce and concluding with the prohibition of idols.[45] In another instance they find a justification for the death penalty in the case of a rebellious son, and also draw a moral lesson on the wages of sin, from the juxtaposition of laws dealing with a woman captive in war, a rebellious son and the exposed corpse of a criminal (Deuteronomy 21:10-23).[46] The Rabbis, likewise, see an illustration of the cumulative effects of a mizvah and the rewards of virtue in the succession of laws which follow the command to spare the mother bird when taking a nest (Deuteronomy 22:6).[47] Similarly, the Rabbis note the logical sequence in Scripture's enumeration of the following laws: "Ye shall not steal, neither shall ye deal falsely, neither lie one to another. And ye shall not swear by My name falsely" (Leviticus 19:11, 12). They are moved to comment, "If you steal, you will in the end come to deny it, then you will lie, and ultimately you will swear falsely."[48] Elsewhere, they interpret the juxtaposition of the Sabbath and the festive seasons (Leviticus, chapter 23) as teaching that the observance or desecration of the Festivals is comparable to the observance or the desecration of the Sabbath.[49]

The causal and legal relationships presumed to exist between commandments in the realm of Halakah may be indicative as well of like relationships in respect of their underlying purpose. Thus, a relationship of a halakic nature is noted in the Talmud[50] between the command to spare the mother bird (Deuteronomy 22:6, 7), and the prohibition of slaughtering an animal together with its young (Leviticus 22:28). On the question whether the latter prohibition applies only to the female parent or to both the male and the female, R. Hananiah is of the opinion that it applies to both, while the Rabbis, comparing it to the case of the mother bird, maintain that the prohibition applies only to the female parent.[51] The comparison between the two mizvot, drawn by the Rabbis along halakic lines, suggests a parallel comparison along ideational lines. Such a relationship is, in fact, noted by the religious philosophers in their quest for the purpose of the two commandments. In the opinion of Nahmanides,[52] which is shared by the

Hinnuk,[53] they are related not only in a general abhorrence of cruelty to animals, but particularly in their common purpose of preserving the species, wherein the female has the determining role. Maimonides relates the two in that they both betoken a recognition of "the love and tenderness of the mother for the young," in consequence of which one is duty-bound to refrain from thus causing grief to animals.[54]

Juxtaposition of Laws in the Bible

Recourse to the halakic method, particularly in regard to the juxtaposition of laws in Scripture, in the investigation of the meaning of mizvot, which as we have seen is discernible in rabbinic literature, is equally evident in the works of such philosophers and exegetes as Maimonides, Abraham Ibn Ezra, Nahmanides, Ralbag, Abrabanel, and others. Ibn Ezra sets forth the guiding principle as follows. "Every law or mizvah stands by itself. Nevertheless, if we can find a reason to account for the fact that one law is joined with another, or one mizvah is close to another, we shall strive to do so to the best of our ability. If we cannot do so, we shall consider this inability as a lack of understanding on our part." [55]

Ibn Ezra proceeds to search for a common thread of reason that would tie together certain mizvot that are juxtaposed in Scripture, even when they are apparently totally dissimilar. An example of the latter is his explanation of the proximity of the command to love one's neighbor and the prohibition of mixed breeding of cattle (Leviticus 19:18, 19). In this case he believes the unifying factor to be the element of kedushah, which precludes harming one's fellowman, as well as altering the nature of God's creation.[56]

Nahmanides, likewise, finds a logical sequence in the cluster of mizvot in sidrah Kedoshim (Leviticus 19:17, 18), which culminates with the command, "Thou shalt love thy neighbor as thyself." He explains it as follows. "Scripture states: Do not hate your brother in your heart when he wrongs you, but rebuke him, lest you bear sin by harboring hatred in your heart and not informing him of the matter. For when you rebuke him, he may excuse himself or confess and repent of his sin, and you will forgive him. After this comes the admonishment not to take vengeance or bear a grudge on account of what he did to you, for it is possible that one may not hate another and yet continue to brood upon the wrong done him. He is therefore admonished to blot out all thoughts of the other's iniquity. Only then does Scripture command him to love his neighbor as himself." [57]

Precisely this kind of scriptural exposition is the basis for Maimonides' radical notion that the prohibition of cooking meat and milk together stems from the fact that it was associated with idolatrous practice. In his discussion of the law in the *Moreh Nebukim*,[58] he states, "I find a support for this view in the circumstance that the Law mentions the prohibition twice [59] after the commandment given concerning the Festivals, 'three times in the year all thy males shall appear before the Lord God' (Exodus 23:17, 34:23), as if to say, 'When you come before Me on your Festivals do not seethe your food in the manner as the heathen used to do.' This I consider the best reason for the prohibition." [60]

Another striking indication of this approach is the exposition by Ibn Ezra and Maimonides of the biblical verse prohibiting one from rounding the corners of the head and marring the corners of the beard (Leviticus 19:27). Ibn Ezra is of the opinion that this verse is to be joined with the verse following it, which forbids cutting the flesh or imprinting any marks upon it, both verses to be understood as prohibiting heathen practices in connection with the dead.[61] Maimonides explains the prohibitions by reason of the fact that they were "the custom of idolatrous priests." [62] While Maimonides does not explicitly correlate the verses, it is nevertheless apparent that exactly such a correlation underlies his assumption that the laws in both instances derive from the same root, namely the prohibition of idolatrous practices. Indeed, this is the conclusion arrived at by R. Joseph Karo in his defense of Maimonides' position on ascribing a reason for these mizvot. "It appears to me," he writes, "that the reason given for them by Maimonides is not his own, but rather one that he believed to be intimated in the Torah, since he found these commandments preceded and followed by prohibitions directed against the customs of idolatry." [63]

Maimonides goes even further in his endeavor to establish relationships between laws in order to ascertain their reasons by including a form of *gezerah shavah,* the principal of scriptural exposition employed in Halakah, which consists of drawing an analogy between two laws strictly on the basis of verbal congruities in the texts. Thus, in pondering the reason for the severe prohibition regarding the eating of blood, Maimonides theorizes that such a barbaric practice was part of the idolatrous rites of the heathens when they sought communion with the spirits.[64] He asserts that the Bible itself draws attention to the connection between eating blood and idolatry by employing a similar expression only in these two instances. The Bible emphasizes the former prohibition with the statement, "I will set My face against the soul that eateth blood" (Leviticus 17:10). The same language is used in reference to one who worships the idol Moloch, "I will set My face against that man" (Leviticus 20:5). He therefore concludes that the reason for the prohibition is because it leads to idolatry.

Ethical Dimension of Halakah

A further line of inquiry along this range of tenuous contact between the halakic and philosophic aspects of the mizvot may be most instructive. There is, in the final analysis, an inner ethical core in Halakah which is, at times, the purposive factor in determining the law, even where the Rabbis may presume to base the law upon strictly legal principles. A case in point is the law that a woman may not be coerced into a levirate marriage with a man who is afflicted with a disease which would preclude normal conjugal relations.[65] The Rabbis derive this law through the principle of proximity of texts, since the law of *yibum*, or levirate marriage, follows directly after the law forbidding the muzzling of an animal to prevent it from eating while working (Deuteronomy 25:4, 5). It is apparent, however, that the determining factor in this instance is the underlying humanitarian consideration, which is the same in the case of the *yebamah* as in the case of the dumb animal. We have herewith indicated an adroit adaptation of a halakic principle in response to a situation warranting an ethical sensitivity and resourcefulness on the part of the Halakah.

The Halakah affords several more such instances with regard to the biblical injunction of levirate marriage and *halizah,* where the Sages evidently sought to ensure the woman's freedom and facilitate her remarriage with a man of her own choosing.[66] In these and in similar cases, the Rabbis base their rulings on the ground of the Torah's moral concern, citing the verse, "Her ways are ways of pleasantness, and all her paths are peace" (Proverbs 3:17).[67]

The admissible extent of such exposition, and whether halakic implications may be drawn from reasons when offered,[68] is apparently at the basis of the controversy between R. Simeon and R. Judah as to whether "we expound the reason of Scripture," that is, whether or not the reason for a law is to be adduced for its legal interpretation. In the law prohibiting one from taking a widow's garment as a pledge (Deuteronomy 24:17), R. Simeon takes the presumed reason for the law into account in delineating the scope of its applicability, maintaining that it applies only to a poor widow, because only in her case would the creditor be obliged to return the pledge daily and by his frequent visits subject her to disrepute among her neighbors. R. Judah does not take the reason into account and therefore holds the law to apply generally to all widows, rich and poor alike.[69] At issue thus is the question whether certain limitations or modifications of a law, which are not indicated in the scriptural text, may be deduced from its apparent reason.[70]

It should be noted, however, that while certain considerations may condition or even prompt a halakic decision, it must ultimately be grounded in Scripture and the Oral Tradition. Nevertheless, in the above and other analogous instances, the Halakah invokes patently ethical principles and moral grounds in determining the Law. Investigation of related areas of a meta-halakic character, as well as a closer examination of the reasons, both general and specific, intimated by Scripture itself, for certain commandments, should prove revealing, and may provide a better understanding of the meaning of the mizvot.[71]

Thus, in tracing the lines of confluence between the halakic and the ideational or philosophical elements of the mizvot, the Hinnuk succeeded in sketching the outline and configuration of a philosophy of the mizvot of the Torah.

CHAPTER TWELVE

CONCLUSION: THE CONTINUING QUEST

In subjecting the mizvah to a process of ratiocination it is presumed that God's will is not arbitrary and, while divinely ordained, the mizvah is not without reason. But, even as we assume a divine reason underlying the mizvot, on what do we base our presumption that it is to be identified with what our reason appears to persuade us, or that it is comprehensible at all by the categories of human reason?

The traditional approach to *ta'amei ha-mizvot* is presently confronted by radically changed conceptions and modes of thought.[1] The traditional approach was predicated upon two philosophical premises: the presumption of divine purpose in creation of the world, at least with respect to its inner structure, and the presumption of a metaphysical link between human reason and a cosmic Intelligence. It is from this perspective that the medieval philosophers endeavored to ascertain the reasons for the divine commandments. But these premises are no longer universally acknowledged. The world is no longer viewed as purposeful, and in modern science nature is thought of as a rational structure, not in a teleological, but in a causative sense. Nor is man deemed, as in the classic, Aristotelian tradition, to have access, through the mediacy of the Active Intellect, to Divine wisdom.

THE COMMITMENT OF FAITH

In the last analysis, if the commandments are not to be perceived merely as the products of an evolutional, historic process, or as a system of law fashioned by man, we must view them as a divinely revealed Law, and take our stand finally upon a commitment of faith and the acceptance of revealed truth in accord with the scriptural directive, "The secret things belong unto the Lord our God; but the things that are revealed belong unto us and to our children forever, that we may do all the words of this law" (Deuteronomy 29:28).[2]

As to the apparent, revealed purpose of the mizvot, the Torah affirms that God gives meaning to man's existence and to life's activities when they are centered upon serving the Creator. It is the mizvah, within the bounds of *Halakah*, that creates this reality, since man cannot relate to God through abstract faith alone, nor can there be an act of service to God unless it is divinely ordained.[3]

Suspension of Judgment

Judaism demands such a commitment of faith and, consequently, a suspension of judgment as to ultimate purposes or reasons of the mizvot, in the realization that the wisdom and the will of God are inscrutable, and God's decrees are beyond the capacity of man to fathom. Man's finite reason must, in the end, retreat before the unfathomable mystery of Divinity.[4]

Thus, there is in the mizvah a dialectical tension which arises, on the one hand, from an apparent rationale that commends itself to reason and, on the other, from an inner dogmatism that pervades it as a divine decree. While the Hinnuk, along with the medieval philosophers, moved intellectually within the traditional, Maimonidean frame of thought that conceived of God as having created man and the world in a rational, purposeful manner, and as having imparted laws to man for a specifically ordained purpose in accord with his own nature, he was nonetheless cognizant of this dialectical tension. It is evident that, for the Hinnuk, the validity and the ultimate purpose of the mizvot are independent of their ascribed reasons.[5]

THE HINNUK'S EDUCATIVE METHOD

The Hinnuk was mindful, as well, of the danger inherent in a rationale of mizvot, lest by rendering them subject to rational assent, it deprive them of their heteronomous character, weakening their force and undermining one's commitment to their observance.[6] He justifies his investigation of the reasons for the commandments by invoking what he believed to be a greater and more immediate threat, namely the complete abandonment of the mizvot. The Hinnuk expresses a deep concern for the continued observance of the divine precepts in a time of religious doubt and waning loyalty to the Torah.[7] His avowed intention, in view of their prevalent neglect, therefore, is to persuade the young people of his day that there is reason and purpose to the laws of the Torah. "Let the mizvot not be for them, at the very outset, like a closed book," he states, "lest they spurn them in their youth and abandon them forever." [8]

Ultimately, the mizvot rest upon the foundation of faith in their divine origin. The Hinnuk recognizes, however, man's inherent need to utilize his reason, with which God endowed him, to strive to understand the divine laws. While the higher purpose underlying the mizvot is beyond the reach of man's intellect, and the reasons contemplated, unless indicated in the Torah, remain purely speculative, whatever understanding of the laws he attains will, nonetheless, render their observance a more meaningful experience. Learning about the meaning of mizvot will result in greater insight and a reassurance of faith, which in turn will lead to the acceptance of those mizvot whose reason eludes him.

The Hinnuk's approach is thus pragmatic and pedagogically oriented. The reasons he offers for the mizvot are designed to assuage a feeling of doubt as to their purposefulness and to satisfy a natural desire for knowledge and enlightenment. For the youth, in particular, the reasons are meant to serve as tenuous strands binding them to the mizvot through a period of youthful questioning, until such time when they will be able to apprehend their deeper meanings and begin to weave stronger bonds.[9]

It may be noted that Maimonides' venture into this field of inquiry and his decision to devote to it a considerable portion of the *Moreh Nebukim*,[10] which he wrote for the perplexed of his time, was evidently prompted by a similar concern, occasioned by a climate of religious doubt. Apprehensive about embarking upon his philosophical quest, Maimonides states in his Introduction that his work is "for the sake of heaven," and consonant with the guiding principle followed by the Sages, "It is time to do something for the Lord, for they make void Thy law" (Psalms 119:126). Judah Halevi, likewise, deemed it necessary to advance reasons, even for what he termed the "divine (revealed) laws," noting that such a course is to be preferred "to abandoning them to evil opinions and to doubts." [11]

The method which the Hinnuk followed, as indicated above, was essentially educative. In order to elicit a firmer commitment to the mizvot, which he took to be the pivots of Judaism, the Hinnuk endeavored to train the people in their observance. Believing, moreover, that observance of the Torah laws would be promoted and enhanced by a greater perception of their significance, he sought to educate them as to their relevant meanings and purposes.

MIZVOT IN THE CONTEMPORARY AGE

The Hinnuk, consequently, pointed the way to an ongoing investigation of the mizvot, and a periodic restatement of their meanings, so as to make them intelligible to each successive age. In this respect the Hinnuk addresses himself with equal cogency to our contemporary age, although there may be differences in impulse and perspective.

Where genuine piety prevails and a simplicity of faith, unruffled by doubt, there is in all likelihood no need felt to seek the reasons of the Torah laws. That they represent the will of God, "royal decrees" not to be questioned, is reason enough for them to be observed. This is the attitude of *temimut,* an ingenuous, unsophisticated faith in God and a wholehearted acceptance of His commands, in the tradition of *na 'aseh ve-nishma',* "All that the Lord hath spoken we will do and we will hearken" (Exodus 24:7).[11a] On the other hand, where there is a lack of concern with matters of religious faith, this enterprise can be of no more than historical, sociological, or psychological interest. As for those who are caught up in the crisis of faith, the demand is more likely for a demonstration of the very validity and sanction of the commandments.

The quest for *ta'amei ha-mizvot,* in terms of their root-meanings, is of vital import for those who, starting from the premise of faith, are by nature and inclination given to intellectual inquiry or, being subject to the impact of contemporary and often alien currents of thought, are either in search of greater certainty and truth, or are fundamentally in quest of their Jewish identity. In the latter instances, however, the quest cannot be merely for a rationale of mizvot in any narrow or limited sense, but rather for a philosophy of mizvot as the basis for a philosophy of Judaism, more precisely a Jewish ideology, rooted in Jewish tradition and the eternal verities and values of Torah, and grounded in the *Halakah*. In effect, this is the direction charted by the Hinnuk, who proceeded with his exposition of the mizvot and his inquiry into their root-meanings from the firm foundation of Jewish Law, as derived from biblical and rabbinic tradition, thereby developing a philosophy of mizvot within the framework of *Halakah* and Jewish religious thought.

The Dimension of Kedushah

The revelation of Torah fashioned for Judaism a religious norm, determined by the definitive principles and delineated laws of the Halakah, yet addressing itself to the human condition. Within the existential reality created by the *Halakah,* the mizvot represent a divine blueprint for the ideal temporal life, to be realized by adapting human existence to the ideal concepts of the Torah. In ordering his life according to the mizvot, while gratifying his human needs, the Jew lives within the dimension of *kedushah,* his life sanctified and consecrated in the service of God, and filled with meaning and a sense of divine purpose.

The manner in which mizvot pervade the life of man, elevating and ennobling virtually every human endeavor, is vividly depicted by the Sages in a midrashic exegesis and parable.[12]

"It is written, 'Light is sown for the righteous, and gladness for the upright in heart' (Psalms 97:11) . . . God sowed the Torah and the mizvot for Israel, so that they would inherit the life of the World to Come. He left nothing in the world concerning which He did not give a mizvah . . . This may be illustrated by one who was cast into the water. The helmsman stretches out a rope and says to him, 'Take hold of this rope and do not let go, because if you let go, you will lose your life.' Even thus said the Holy One, blessed be He, to Israel: As long as you hold fast to the mizvot, it will be said of you, 'But ye that did cleave unto the Lord your God are alive every one of you this day'

(Deuteronomy 4:4) . . . It is also written, 'And be holy unto your God' (Numbers 15:40). When you observe the commandments, you are holy, and the fear of you lies upon the idolaters. But if you part from the commandments and commit sins, you forthwith become profaned."

A Philosophy To Live By

From this perspective, a philosophy of mizvot can have profound significance in the contemporary age for the Jew who, in common with modern man, seeks a philosophy to live by as he strives to meet the challenge of life, indeed at times to preserve his essential humanity in a confused and threatening world. It represents the Jewish philosophy of life as lived within the divinely structured world of the Halakah, a God-centered, kedushah-oriented life, capable of transforming a mundane existence into one of beauty and transcendent sublimity.

The meaning of mizvot thus resolves itself finally into a consideration, primarily, of their effects within the realm of human experience, and their role in shaping the distinctive world of Halakah brought into being by divine revelation.

THE CONTINUING QUEST FOR THE MEANING OF MIZVOT

A Meaning for Every Age

Jewish thinkers have, understandably, felt free to develop their individual conception of the mizvot, each one seeking a comprehension of the laws, initially in accord with his own perspective and philosophy, but also one that would provide them with meaning for his own day. The literary history of ta'amei ha-mizvot, beginning with the midrashic expositions of the Sages, reflects a variety of conceptions and a multiplicity of approaches.[13] To the extent that it was grounded in authentic tradition, each conception could lay claim to the truth, in accord with the dictum of the Rabbis, "These and these are the words of the living God."[14] The common denominator is the quest for a sustained thread of purpose and meaning to the divine commandments that would impart to them a vital relevance in each generation.

That the mizvot can be viewed from different perspectives and can have meaning on several levels, a conception of mizvot which, the Hinnuk believed,[15] was already held by the Sages, would appear to be indicated by the biblical characterization of the Sabbath. The Sabbath, as recorded in the Ten Commandments in Exodus, chapter 20, and introduced by the word *zakor*, "remember", is described as having been ordained by God in remembrance of Creation, while in the parallel version of the Ten Commandments in Deuteronomy, chapter 5, and introduced by the word *shamor*, "observe," it is said to be a reminder of Egyptian bondage and the redemption of Israel. The Rabbis reconcile the two versions by declaring that "*zakor* and *shamor* were spoken by God in one utterance." [16] The Sabbath, undoubtedly, has profound, but diverse meanings and varied significance for the Jewish people and for humanity. As a divine law it is eternal, but at times it is its theological and philosophical meaning that needs to be stressed, at other times its national and personal significance has to be emphasized. In the one divine utterance God encompassed, as it were, every meaning as it would unfold in the course of time.

This is true not only of the Sabbath, but of all the mizvot.[17] The Hinnuk assumed the possibility of more than one reason for a mizvah. We may presume that a divine Intelligence would have manifold purposes to be served by a mizvah, that would become manifest in the course of time as the complex skein of life unfolds.

The divine commandments are everlastingly binding upon all generations, but every generation may seek an understanding and an appreciation of the laws, given the knowledge and experience that it uniquely represents. The capability for deeper insights and greater perception has surely been enhanced by the intellectual and scientific resources that are presently at man's disposal.

The search for meaning certainly does not presume that the Torah laws need justification from the outside world, nor does it imply that they are to be measured by any contemporary scale of values. Divinely ordained, they are possessed of an eternal relevance, being in accord, ultimately, with a world of values independent of time and place.

A purposeful evaluation of the mizvot, while responsive to the prevailing intellectual, moral and spiritual climate, must primarily reveal the timeless values, and the uniquely Jewish ideals which they embody. One must needs take into particular account the role of mizvot in preserving Israel throughout its history, and its current function in determining the quality of Jewish life and in maintaining the singular identity and character of the Jewish people.

The mizvot nowadays have special meaning in relation to the dynamics of Jewish life and thought, and the religious and national interests and personal concerns of the Jew as Jew and as human being: in strengthening his faith, in cementing ties with the Jewish people and the Land of Israel, and in forging bonds of brotherhood with his fellowman.

The quest for the meaning of the mizvot is thus a continuing, progressive process. The Hinnuk cites the statement of the Rabbis in the Midrash "Things which were not revealed to Moses were revealed to Rabbi Akiba and his colleagues." [18] The Midrash alluded to by the Hinnuk adds, "Things which are hidden in this world are destined to be revealed in the world to come," quoting the prophecy in Isaiah 42:16, "And I will cause the blind to walk in a way that they have not known; in paths that they have not known will I lead them; I will make darkness light before them, and crooked places plain." The determining factors in this new revelation concerning the meaning of mizvot to Rabbi Akiba and his colleagues and to generations in the distant future are the fresh insights and perceptions that God affords man from the cumulative store of knowledge of the ages, together with the new vistas of knowledge that constantly open before him. [19]

The Torah Has Seventy Faces

"It is well known to us, the people who received the mizvot," the Hinnuk states, [20] "that there are seventy ways of expounding the Torah" (literally, "the Torah has seventy faces"). Like a multi-faceted jewel, each mizvah in the Torah reflects a new glow of interpretive meaning with every turn, a new brilliance in every age, its refracted light changing in hue and intensity, while always emanating from the same divine source.

EXCURSUS

THE SEFER HA-HINNUK

I. Authorship

Although a tradition of long standing ascribes the *Sefer ha-Hinnuk* to Rabbi Aaron ha-Levi of Barcelona, the noted thirteenth-century, Spanish talmudist, authorship of the book has nevertheless been in doubt.[1] The early manuscripts do not indicate the name of the author, and apart from noting the title of the book,[2] the author does not in any way reveal his identity other than to say that he is "a Jew of Barcelona of the house of Levi."[3] However, the first printed edition which appeared in 1523, carried the following inscription on the title page: *"Sefer ha-Hinnuk,* written by Rabbi Aaron."[4] It is not clear, however, on what basis the author's name is given there as Rabbi Aaron.[5] The first to suggest that the *Sefer ha-Hinnuk* is the work of Rabbi Aaron ha-Levi was Gedalyah ibn Yahya,[6] author of a history of halakic literature written in 1549.

It will be noted that for a period of about two hundred years, from the time the book was written until the appearance of the first printed edition, there is no mention of the author. It would seem, therefore, that unless the references in the first printed edition, as well as that of Gedalyah ibn Yahya, reflect a well-rooted tradition as to the author's identity, the view that Rabbi Aaron ha-Levi of Barcelona is the author of the *Sefer ha-Hinnuk* is based upon conjecture. Notwithstanding, this view gained currency and itself became an accepted tradition among rabbinic scholars.[7] Its authenticity was finally questioned by Azulai,[8] who points to certain difficulties, especially the fact that the *Sefer ha-Hinnuk* is, in several instances, at variance with opinions and decisions expressed by Rabbi Aaron ha-Levi in his known works.[9] Furthermore, the author's reluctance to identify himself in his Introduction to the

Sefer ha-Hinnuk is in marked contrast to the manner in which Rabbi Aaron ha-Levi records his genealogy in the Introduction to his book, *Bedek Habayit*.[10]

The evidence in favor of the tradition that the *Sefer ha-Hinnuk* was written by Rabbi Aaron ha-Levi of Barcelona is thus, at best, inconclusive.[11] Indeed, there is mounting evidence that the author of the *Sefer ha-Hinnuk* was of the period following Rabbi Aaron ha-Levi, and that he was more likely a disciple of Rabbi Solomon ben Adret[12] and perhaps of Rabbi Aaron ha-Levi as well.

Another problem posed by the book, further beclouding the author's identity, is the date of its composition. In a discussion of the Sabbatical year,[13] the *Sefer ha-Hinnuk* indicates the forthcoming Sabbatical year to be 5017 according to Rashi, and 5018 according to Rabbi Hananel, or 1257 and 1258 respectively. If the Sabbatical dates are to be considered as indicative, then the book must have been written in the lifetime of Nahmanides. This, it is believed, presents a difficulty, since the *Sefer ha-Hinnuk* consistently refers to him as to one already deceased.[14] It has been suggested,[15] therefore, that the text should be emended to read 5067 and 5068, corresponding to 1307 and 1308. The date of composition is, thus, taken to be within the Sabbatical cycle preceding 1308. A later date is precluded since one of the manuscripts[16] of the book is itself dated as of the year 1313.[17]

The above dating of the work may provide a possible clue to its anonymity, since it would place its composition at the time of an intense renewal of opposition to the study of philosophy, in particular the philosophical writings of Maimonides. The controversy between the Maimonists and the anti-Maimonists greatly agitated the Jewish communities of Spain and France in the thirteenth century, leading to the denunciation of Maimonides' works and culminating in the ban on philosophical and scientific study issued by Rabbi Solomon ben Adret (Rashba)[18] and the scholars of Barcelona in 1305. It was precisely Maimonides' rationalistic method, which had prompted the Hinnuk's own investigation of a rationale for the mizvot, that figured prominently in the anti-Maimonidean controversy. A desire to avoid dissension and a direct confrontation with his contemporaries and possible personal embroilment in the controversy may have been a factor, and surely would have provided ample reason for the author to seek anonymity. The apologetic tone of the work would tend to reinforce this view.

Nonetheless, it appears unlikely that the author of the *Sefer ha-Hinnuk* really sought complete anonymity. He reveals as many pertinent facts about himself, his times and his views, as any author would be expected to reveal in such a work.[19] Indeed, in his Epilogue to Leviticus, after giving the name of the book and indicating his purpose in writing it, the author makes the following statement: "I ask but one thing . . . that God accept my small offering . . . and if I have done this but to have my name remembered and to enhance my fame, may He not continue to be gracious unto me, nor seek my welfare." The author would hardly have felt it necessary to offer such an apologia if he were intent upon keeping his name forever unknown.

Often the guise of anonymity was but an affectation on the part of an author, and only thinly veiled his identity. This may have been prompted either by modesty,[20] or by the author's desire that a certain work, especially in the case of a popular treatise, shall not be the criterion in a judgment of his true scholarly stature.[21] It may, therefore, be that for the above reasons the Hinnuk did not wish to attach his name directly to his work, but resorted, instead, to veiled hints and allusions. These may have been sufficient to have identified him for his contemporaries.

Yet the question persists: How is it that the name of the author of the *Sefer ha-Hinnuk* has not clearly come down to us, and that we are still uncertain of his identity? The answer may perhaps lie in the persecutions which the Jews in the time of the Hinnuk suffered,[22] and the pogroms that engulfed many Jewish communities in Spain in the 14th century. Unfortunately, some great works by Jewish authors were either completely lost to posterity or lapsed into anonymity as a result of persecutions and expulsions.[23] The latter may well have been the fate of the *Sefer ha-Hinnuk*.

II. Sources

The Hinnuk acknowledges the works of three great predecessors as his prime sources.[24] In his Prefatory Letter, he states: "The greater part of this book is gathered from the books of the pillars of the earth,

renowned for their greatness and wisdom among all nations, Rabbi
Isaac Alfasi and Rabbi Moses ben Maimon, may they be remembered
for good—to them is justly due the preeminence, the glory and the
honor in this treatise—and to the third in this three-fold cord of wisdom, understanding and knowledge, Rabbi Moses ben Nahman, of
blessed memory. . . ."

While Rabbi Isaac Alfasi is mentioned in the Prefatory Letter as
one of the two preeminent sources, he is, nonetheless, referred to directly only a few times in the book.[25] The author's dependence, primarily, upon Maimonides is amply evident and freely acknowledged.[26]
In his description of the commandments, the author follows Maimonides' *Sefer ha-Mizvot*.[27] In discussing the specific laws relating to
each of the commandments, he generally follows the *Mishneh Torah*
of Maimonides, quoting it either directly or in paraphrased form, with
slight variations and interpolations of his own. In the section on the
reasons for the commandments the author was influenced by Maimonides' views as set forth in his *Guide of the Perplexed* as well as in
the *Mishneh Torah*,[28] and by Nahmanides' *Commentary on the
Torah*.[29]

The Hinnuk's third major source is Nahmanides, with particular
reference to his *Sefer ha-Mizvot*,[30] known as *Hassagot ha-Ramban* and
his *Commentary on the Torah*.[31] The Hinnuk generally cites the differences of opinion between Maimonides and Nahmanides on which
commandments are to be reckoned in the *Taryag* classification. In this
regard, as already noted, he invariably follows Maimonides.[32] "We will
follow the king's highway," the Hinnuk states, "turning neither to the
right nor to the left." [33] This he proceeds to do even where he is inclined to favor a contrary view.[34] In one instance, however, he deletes
a commandment included by Maimonides,[35] substituting another for
it.[36] In another instance he follows Nahmanides rather than Maimonides regarding the biblical source for a commandment.[37] Halakic decisions are generally rendered in accord with the position of Maimonides, though on several points of law he accepts the view of
Nahmanides.[38]

In addition to the above and the basic biblical and talmudic
sources,[39] as well as the halakic and aggadic Midrashim,[40] the Hinnuk

makes reference to works of the Gaonim. The *Halakot Gedolot* is referred to relative to Nahmanides' defense of it against Maimonides' critique.[41] R. Hai Gaon is mentioned specifically,[42] and reference is also made to Rabbeinu Hananel ben Hushi'el of Kairawan.[43] Later authorities cited are: Rashi,[44] Rabbeinu Tam,[45] Rabbi Abraham ben David of Posquieres,[46] and Rabbi Moses of Coucy.[47] There are frequent references to unnamed contemporary scholars and teachers.[48] Though respectful of his sources, the Hinnuk does not hestitate to dispute their opinions or to present his own views.

NOTES TO INTRODUCTION

1. See Maimonides' exposition of the meaning of the term *lishmah* in his *Mishneh Torah*, Hilkot Teshubah 10:5. Cf. *Berakot* 17a, *Sotah* 22b and parallel talmudic sources.
2. The Rabbis note that the plural form "and laws" (*ve-ha-Torot*) alludes to the Written Law and the Oral Law, both of which were given by God to Israel at Sinai. See *Sifra* and Rashi ad loc.
3. See Dr. Joseph B. Soloveitchik's article, "The Lonely Man of Faith" in *Tradition,* Summer 1965.
4. Cf. Alexander Altmann, *Was Ist Judische Theologie?* (Frankfurt am Main 1933); Gershom G. Scholem, *Major Trends in Jewish Mysticism,* Schoken Books, New York, 1972, p. 28f.
5. See Dr. Samuel Belkin's study on the Jewish philosophy of man as expressed in rabbinic tradition in *In His Image,* Abelard-Schuman 1960. Note in particular his statement regarding the relationship between Jewish theology and Halakah on p. 16.

NOTES TO CHAPTER ONE

THE QUEST FOR THE MEANING OF MIZVOT

1. The Bible does not provide any definitive criteria to distinguish between חק and משפט .
2. Ibid. Cf. *Shabbat* 87b and Tosafot ad. loc.
3. The *Mekilta* cites as proof-text Lev. 18:30, taking the phrase "abominable hukot" as referring to the forbidden sexual relations mentioned in that section. Cf. *Mekilta,* Exod. 15:26.
4. See *Sanhedrin* 56b, where the Rabbis state that ten mizvot were given to the Israelites at Marah: the seven Noahian laws and three additional laws, namely, the administration of civil law, the Sabbath and honoring parents. In his commentary on Exod. 15:25, Rashi indicates the three additional laws to have been the Sabbath, the administration of civil law, and the red heifer. Cf. Rashi, Exod. 24:3, where he mentions also honoring parents (cf. Rashi, Deut. 5:16) and again includes the red heifer, although no mention of the latter is made either in the *Mekilta* or in the

Talmud. The suggestion has been made that this is due to a misreading of an abbreviation in Rashi; see B. Epstein, *Torah Temimah,* Exod. 15:25. It will be noted, however, that even Nahmanides already quoted Rashi as given. A plausible explanation is that the inclusion of the red heifer was on the reasoned assumption that *hok* refers to the red heifer, since the Rabbis generally cite it as the classic example of a *hok.* Cf. the commentaries *Mizrahi,* by R. Eliyahu Mizrahi, and *Gur Aryeh* by Maharal of Prague, ad. loc.

5. Yoma 67b.

6. An alternative reading includes, "and the peoples of the world repudiate." Cf. R. Hananel, who also records this reading, but has *yezer ha-ra',* the evil inclination, instead of Satan. Rashi notes that Satan refers to *yezer ha-ra'.* Cf. *Baba Batra* 16a, "Resh Lakish said: Satan, the evil prompter (*yezer ha-ra'*), and the Angel of Death are all one."

7. Cf. R. Hananel and *Tosafot Yeshanim,* ibid., for the variant laws which they list under *hukim.*

8. The same exposition of the verse is given in the *Sifra,* 140:9, which includes among the *hukim* the rite of the red heifer. Cf. *Midrash Tanhuma,* Parashat Hukat, VII.

9. Lev. 18:4; cf. Rashi, *Yoma* 67b. Cf. also Malbim, *Perush ha-Torah ve-ha-Mizvah,* Deut. 6:20; Radak, Perush to I Kings 2:3.

10. See Deut. 10:13, "To keep for thy good the commandments of the Lord, and His statutes, which I command thee this day." Cf. Deut. 5:30, Lev. 18:5. On the latter, however, see *Sifra* and *Targum Onkelos* ad. loc.

11. See M. *Makkot* III, 16, "The Holy One, blessed be He, was minded to grant merit to Israel; therefore he multiplied for them the Law and commandments." See also *Genesis Rabbah,* 44:1, "The commandments were given for the purpose of refining men through them." Cf. *Leviticus Rabbah* 30:12.

12. *Kiddushin* 31a, *Baba Kamma* 38a, *'Aboda Zara* 3a; cf. Maimonides, *Moreh Nebukim* III, 17, 26. The theonomous nature of the commandments is also suggested in the statement of the Rabbis that God arched the mountain over the Israelites and said to them, "If you accept the Torah, well and good; if not here will be your grave." See *Shabbat* 88a; cf. Rashi, Exod. 19:17.

13. *Sifra,* Lev. 20:26; cf. Rashi, ibid. See Maimonides, *Shemonah Perakim,* VI, who cites this passage relative to the observance of *hukim.*

14. Whether or not the Sages were inclined to look for *ta'amei ha-mizvot,* or to favor a search for the reasons of the commandments, is a question explored in a closer analysis of the midrashic and talmudic sources cited by the Hinnuk in his consideration of this problem. See chapter V.

15. Cf. *Leviticus Rabbah* 30:9 ff. The citron, palm-branch, myrtle and willow are viewed symbolically as representing God and the people of Israel.

16. *Niddah* 31b.
17. M. *Pesahim* X,5. See Bertenoro ibid. The reasons must be explicated, namely their portrayal of the bitterness of Egyptian bondage, divine protection and the redemption of Israel.
18. See *'Arakin* 16b; *Leviticus Rabbah* 16:2 ff. See chapt. X.
19. Rashi, Exod. 21:6; cf. *Kiddushin* 22b.
20. Ibid.
21. *Mekilta*, Exod. 21:37; 22:6; Rashi, Exod. 21:37; *Baba Kamma* 79b; cf. Rashi, ibid.
22. *Rosh Hashanah* 16a.
23. On the subject of *ta'amei ha-mizvot* in the literature of the classical and medieval period, see I. Heinemann, *Ta'amei ha-Mizvot be-Sifrut Yisra'el* (Jerusalem, 1949), vol. I. Heinemann does not include a full discussion of the views of Nahmanides, Rashi, and the Tosafists, nor does he discuss the Hinnuk, the primary subject of our study.
24. See H. A. Wolfson, *Philo* (Harvard University Press, 1947), vol. II, p. 200 ff. for an analysis of Philo's treatment of the laws; Samuel Belkin, *Philo and the Oral Law* (Harvard University Press, 1940), p. 11-17, for a study of Philo in relation to the allegorists and the literalists.
25. See *Emunot ve-De'ot* III, 1-3. Cf. A. Altmann, *Saadya Gaon, The Book of Doctrines and Beliefs* (Oxford, 1946), p. 96, n. 4.
26. Ibid. V, 8; cf. Treatise VII (variant version), chapt. 5.
27. The philosophical ground of Maimonides' position will be discussed at the end of this chapter. We shall deal here mainly with his general perspective on the question of *ta'amei ha-mizvot*.
28. *Moreh Nebukim*, III, 26.
29. Ibid. See Maimonides' assertion at the end of his *Sefer ha-Mizvot* (Mizvat Lo' Ta'aseh 365) that God concealed the reasons of most of the precepts because the people would not comprehend them.
30. Ibid. III, 31.
31. Ibid. III, 26, cf. Me'ilah 8:8, where Maimonides gives the following definition, והמשפטים הן המצות שטעמן גלוי וטובת עשייתן בעולם הזה ידועה, והחוקים הן והמצות שאין טעמן ידוע. ...
32. Chapter VI.
33. The inclusion of forbidden relations among the *hukim* is at variance with its classification by the Rabbis in the Talmud, *Yoma* 67b. Cf. the marginal gloss and the commentary of Maharsha, *Hidushei 'Aggadot*, ibid. It is however in accord with the *Mekilta* on Exod. 15:25, 26. Saadiah, Halevi, and Nahmanides also evidently follow the *Mekilta* in this regard; see *Emunot ve-De'ot* III, 2; *Kuzari* III, 11. It is noteworthy, however, that Saadiah distinguishes between incestuous and adulterous relations, classifying the latter among rational laws and the former among the revealed laws. We would suggest that this distinction may provide the basis for a reconciliation of the apparently contradictory texts and differing classifications with regard to forbidden relations.

34. Cf. *Moreh Nebukim* III, 28 where Maimonides cites as *hukim* the prohibitions of wearing garments containing wool and linen, of sowing diverse seeds, boiling meat and milk together, the commandment of covering the blood of slaughtered beasts and birds, the rite of breaking the neck of a heifer in expiation of an untraced murder, and the law concerning the first born of an ass. Cf. also ibid. III, 32 where, on the basis of the rabbinic tradition as to the laws imparted at Marah, he likewise regards the Sabbath as a *hok*. In Me'ilah 8:8 he includes among *hukim* the prohibition of eating swine's flesh. He further notes that all sacrifices are to be considered in this category as well.

35. In Me'ilah, ibid., Maimonides calls further attention to the special significance of the *hukim*, noting that they are mentioned first in the scriptural verse, "Ye shall therefore keep My statutes and Mine ordinances, which if a man do he shall live by them" (Lev. 18:5).

36. *Moreh Nebukim* III, 12.

37. Ibid. III, 27. Maimonides' grading of the laws in this manner and his assertion that the rational laws are precedent to the revealed laws is anticipated by Halevi. Cf. *Kuzari* II, 48.

38. Cf. Aristotle, *Nicomachean Ethics*, Book X. Cf. *Moreh Nebukim* III, 27, 54.

39. Cf. Ibid. II, 40; cf. H. A. Wolfson, *Philo*, II, p. 310 ff.

40. Ibid. III, 28.

41. *Moreh Nebukim*, Part III, chapters 35-49.

42. Ibid. III, 49.

43. Ibid. III, 32, 46. Maimonides explains the sacrifices as being a general mode of worship with which the Israelites were familiar, and which the Torah found necessary to continue in order to effect the transition from idolatrous worship to the service of God. This is not to be misconstrued as suggesting that the Torah generally acquiesced in the retention of certain rites and cultic practices, tacitly accepting them because the people were accustomed to such practices. Maimonides invokes this reason only with regard to sacrifices, although he was aware of other practices that were universally known and observed, and even notes certain similarities in these instances. Cf. ibid. III, 43. An exception is the law of levirate marriage, concerning which Maimonides states, "It was a custom in force before the Law was given, and the Law perpetuated it." See ibid. III, 49. On this question, see I. Heinemann, op. cit., Vol. I, p. 93 f.

44. Cf. ibid. III, 26, 28, 45, 47. For a further explanation, see end of this chapter.

45. Cf. ibid. III, 43, where he expresses this view with regard to the aggadic interpretation of the four species on Sukkot; for other examples, see III, 45, 47.

46. The term *hok* appears for some to have a limited meaning, signifying, as in the case of the red heifer, an irrational or supra-rational law. It is in

this sense that Rashi and, to a degree, Maimonides understand the term as traditionally applied. It also admits of a wider meaning, judging from the classification of others, such as Judah Halevi, as signifying revealed laws of a broadly religious nature. See *Kuzari* III, 11.

47. Perush, Gen. 26:5; cf. Exod. 15:26, Lev. 19:19, Num. 19:2: As examples of the class of laws designated as *hukim* he cites the prohibition of wearing a mixture of wool and linen, of causing cattle of diverse kind to gender, of sowing diverse seed, of eating swine's flesh and the law of the red heifer. Cf. Rashi's commentary on the verses previously cited and also on Prov. 25:2.

48. *Berakot* 33b. Cf. Rashi, *Megillah* 25a, "They are decrees of the King to impose His yoke upon us, to make known that we are His servants and the keepers of His commandments."

49. See Tosafot, *Megillah* 25a, citing the eminent Tosafist, R. Elhanan.

50. See Kalir's *piyut* for the second day of Passover, whose opening words are: מה אילו פלאי נסיך. For support of Kalir's assumption, see *Deut. Rabbah* 6:1.

51. A notable exception among the Tosafists is Rabbi Samuel ben Meir (Rashbam), Rashi's grandson and a famed exegete, whose interpretation of Scripture is basically along rationalistic lines. Rashbam applies this same method of interpretation to the mizvot, advancing moral and hygienic reasons for some generally designated as *hukim*. Cf. Rashbam's interpretation of Rabban Gamliel's statement, quoted in M. *Pesahim* X, 5, concerning the three mizvot of *pesah, mazah, maror*. Cf. Bertenoro, ibid. Cf. Rashbam's commentary to Exod. 23:19; Lev. 11:3; 23:43. Particularly indicative of his rationalist view of the mizvot are his comments on Gen. 26:5. Apart from intellectual considerations, Rashbam appears to have been motivated by a need to respond to questions raised by apostates. See his commentary to Lev. 11:34; 19:19.

Another Tosafist who sought to give reasons for the mizvot was R. Joseph of Orleans, a disciple of the renowned Tosafist, R. Jacob Tam, and author of *Bekor Shor*, a commentary along the lines of Rashbam. He was similarly inclined in order to refute the arguments of apostates and Christians with whom he was engaged in disputations. See E. E. Urbach, *Ba'ale ha-Tosafot* (Jerusalem 1955), p. 115 f.

52. *Perush ha-Torah*, Deut. 22:6.

53. Ibid. Lev. 19:19. Nahmanides cites as proof-text the verse, "Every word of God is tried" (Prov. 30:5).

54. Ibid. Lev. 18:6.

55. Ibid. Gen. 26:5; cf. end of *Tosefta, Kiddushin*.

56. Ibid. Lev. 18:4.

57. Ibid. Lev. 26:15.

58. Ibid. Lev. 18:6.

59. The distinction drawn herein between Rashi's view of the *hukim* as supra-rational and that of Nahmanides as meta-rational, though a fine one, serves us to distinguish between a conception of the *hukim* as entirely beyond the ken of human reason, and a conception of these commandments as being of a recondite nature, whose reasons, while abstruse, are yet accessible to the select few.

60. Cf. especially Rashi's commentary on Prov. 25:2, where he notes that the restriction of searching for reasons applies to the *hukim*, and he equates it with a similar restriction against speculation regarding the secrets of the divine chariot and creation.

61. In explaining the scriptural verse, "These are the animals which ye may eat among all the beasts that are on the earth" (Leviticus 11:2), Rashi states, "The word *hayyah* denotes life. It is used here to express the idea that, because the people of Israel cleave to God and deserve to remain in life, He therefore separated them from what is unclean and imposed commandments upon them, whilst to the heathen nations He prohibited nought. This will be understood by a parable of the physician, who in visiting the sick permits the incurable to eat whatever he chooses, whilst to the patient who may recover he gives directions as to what he may eat and may not eat, as will be found in the *Midrash* of Rabbi Tanhuma." Rashi is here echoing the view of the Rabbis that there is a reason for these commandments which is intimated by Scripture and is furthermore capable of being rationally apprehended.

   Presumption of a rationale for certain mizvot on the part of the Tosafists is also evident in their commentary, where they cite the same midrashic parable as to the reason why reptiles and creatures that swarm are forbidden to Israel. See commentary of the Tosafists on Exod. 21:1. The source given for the parable cited is *Exod. Rabbah* 30:18. Cf. *Hullin* 101b, where Rashi and Tosafot tacitly accept the statement of the Baraita that Scripture records the prohibition of the sinew of the thigh vein (Gen. 32:33) in connection with Jacob's encounter in order to indicate the reason for the commandment. Cf. chapter XII, n. 19.

62. Among the precepts which the Rabbis traditionally take to be *hukim*, Nahmanides mentions in his commentary the laws of *Shemitah* and *Yobel* (Lev. 25:18), sacrifices (Deut. 11:32), forbidden foods (ibid.), the law of the red heifer (Lev. 26:15, Num. 19:2), forbidden sexual relations (Lev. 18:6), the rite of breaking the neck of a heifer in expiation of a murder (Deut. 21:4), and the rite of the scapegoat (Lev. 16:8). As to the latter, he differentiates between sacrifices which are offerings to God and the rite of the scapegoat, for which the idolaters taunt us for what they believe to be a mimicking of their rites. Cf. Nahmanides' sermon, "Torat ha-Shem Temimah," *Kitbei Ramban*, ed. C. B. Chavel, (Jerusalem, 1963), Vol. I, p. 165.

63. In the verse, "Because that Abraham hearkened to My voice and kept My charge, My commandments, My statutes and My laws" (Gen. 26:5), he takes *hukotai* to denote the ethical principles of justice, righteousness, mercy, and compassion which Abraham charged his children and household to keep in emulation of the ways of God. In another instance, however, in a rather strict construction of the rabbinic designation of a *hok*, he includes the prohibition of wearing a garment made of a mixture of wool and linen (sha'atnez) but not the prohibition of mixing diverse species, contending that the Sages mention only the former as a *hok*, since in the case of animals and other species the reason is apparent that it is forbidden because God had commanded each species to reproduce itself after its own kind. See Perush, Lev. 19:19.
64. Perush, Exod. 15:25.
65. Ibid. Lev. 1:9. For a discussion of the controversy, see chapter IX.
66. Ibid. Lev. 19:23.
67. Ibid. Exod. 13:16.
68. Ibid.
69. Ibid. 20:13; 15:25.
70. Ibid. Lev. 1:9.
71. Ibid. 25:2.
72. Ibid. 22:32.
73. Cf. *Moreh Nebukim* I, 2, "On account of this gift of intellect man was addressed by God and received His commandments, as it is said, 'And the Lord God commanded' Adam' (Gen. 2:16), for no commandments are given to the brute creation or to those who are devoid of understanding."
74. Cf. ibid., III, 25; 32-33.
75. Ibid., III, 51
76. Ibid. II, 39.
77. Me'ilah 8:8. "It is proper for a man to reflect upon the laws of the holy Torah and know their purpose to the extent of his ability."
78. Ibid. III, 31.
79. See ibid. III, 32. Maimonides notes that, according to tradition, the first laws given to the Israelites at Marah were, significantly, the Sabbath and civil laws, thus imparting to the people the truth of Creation and the basic principles of justice. Cf. also Temurah 4:13.
80. See Maimonides' *Iggeret Teiman*.
81. *Moreh Nebukim* III, 35; cf. ibid., III, 26, 28.
82. Ibid., III, 45.
83. Ibid., III, 46. In this instance he nevertheless cites a reason suggested by others.
84. Ibid., III, 47.
85. Ibid.

86. *De Migratione Abrahami* 16:89-94.
87. *Emunot ve-De'ot,* Treatise VII (Variant Version), chapter 5.
88. *Moreh Nebukim* III, 26.
89. See *Sefer Minhot Kena'ot* by R. Abba Mari ben Mosheh of Lunel, later of Montpellier, Letters XX, LXXXI, (Pressburg, 1838; republished in New York, 1958), p. 59-61, 152-154. See also Rashba's letter to the Rabbis of Provence, printed in part in *Seder R. Amram ha-Shalem,* ed. by A. L. Frumkin (Jerusalem, 1912), p. 78. On the Hinnuk's possible relationship to the controversy, see Excursus I.
90. *Tur,* Yoreh De'ah, 181.
91. *Bet Yosef,* Yoreh De'ah 181. In support of this explanation he cites Maimonides' own statement of his view at the end of Me'ilah, Temurah and Mikva'ot. Cf. Maimonides, *Moreh Nebukim* III, 26; Saadiah, op. cit., III, 2; Halevi, *Kuzari* III, 7.
92. Ritba, *Sefer ha-Zikaron,* Hakdamah.
93. Nahmanides' influence is greatly evident in the exegesis of Rabbeinu Bahya ben Asher and Shem Tob Ibn Gaon. A marked feature of the period seems to be the feeling of being caught up in a crosscurrent of Maimonidean and Nahmanidean thought. This is particularly evident among the later scholars of the period, as exemplified by Ritba. His treatise, *Sefer ha-Zikaron,* ostensibly a defense of Maimonides against the strictures of Nahmanides in the latter's commentary on the Bible, nevertheless adds up to an endorsement, by and large, of the Nahmanidean position. Cf. *Sefer ha-Zikaron,* Parshat Vayikra and Parshat Hukat.

NOTES TO CHAPTER TWO

THE TARYAG MIZVOT

1. The term *TaRYaG,* formed by the Hebrew letters תרי"ג with a numerical value of six hundred and thirteen, is frequently used in rabbinical literature to designate the accepted number of divine commandments that are derived from Scripture.
2. *Makkot* 23b. See Rashi, ibid., for the symbolic meaning of the numerical totals of the positive and negative commandments; cf. Nahmanides at the end of his monograph on *Taryag Mizvot, Kitbei Ramban,* ed. by C. D. Chavel (Jerusalem, 1964) Vol. II, p. 548. For the 248 members of the body see M. *'Oholot* I, 8; *Bekorot* 45a. Cf. *Shulhan 'Aruk, 'Orah Hayyim* 61:3 for a reference to the symbolism of this number in connection with the *Shema'.* See a study of its midrashic source by S. K. Mirsky, "Mekorot ha-Halakah be-Midrashim," *Talpiot,* Vol. I, Hoberet 2, (New York, 1944). For the symbolic significance of the negative com-

mandments as they coincide with specific days of the year, see Menahem ha-Babli, *Ta'amei ha-Mizvot*, Lo' Ta'aseh 1.

3. In the *Mekilta* on Exodus 20:2 Rabbi Simon ben Eleazar states: "If the children of Noah could not fulfill seven commandments, how much less will they be able to fulfill six hundred and thirteen." Cf. *Sifre* on Deut. 12:23. It would seem that the Talmud was thus recording Rabbi Simlai's further exposition of the tradition. Cf., however, E. E. Urbach, *The Sages: Their Concepts and Beliefs* (Jerusalem, 1969), p. 302, who maintains that this statement is a later interpolation. Cf. H. A. Rabinowitz, *Taryag*, (Jerusalem, 1967) p. 33 f.

For additional references in the talmudic and midrashic literature, see *Shabbat* 87a, *Yebamot* 47b, *Nedarim* 25a, *Shebuot* 29a, *Genesis Rabbah* 24:5, *Exodus Rabbah* 32:1, 33:8, *Numbers Rabbah* 13:15, 14:22 and 18:17, *Canticles Rabbah* 1:13, and *Tanhuma Ki Teze'* 2.

4. See Maimonides' Hakdamah to *Sefer ha-Mizvot*, critical text ed. by Ch. Heller (Jerusalem, New York 1946) p. 4. התורה ספר שיכללם המצות שכל
אשר נתן לנו הא-ל יתעלה הם תרי"ג מצות.
See also his Hakdamah to the *Mishneh Torah*: ומנין מצות התורה הנוהגות לדורות שש מאות ושלש עשרה מצות.
Cf. Me'iri, *Bet ha-Behirah, Sotah* 3a, who also stresses that the number 613 stands uncontested.

While Nahmanides accepts the system of *taryag mizvot* in fact, he nevertheless questions the tradition on two counts: first, whether it is in reality the universally accepted view of the Sages; second, whether the number six hundred and thirteen is to be taken literally as stemming from Sinai. See his *Hassagot*, Shoresh 1, and at the end of the *Hassagot*. Among others who voiced doubt concerning the tradition were Judah Ibn Bal'am in his commentary on Deut. 30:2 and Ibn Ezra in his *Yesod Mora'*, Chapter 2. Cf. Bahya Ibn Pakuda, Hakdamah to *Sefer Hobot ha-Lebabot*, who states that the *taryag mizvot* refer to "duties of the limbs," or practical duties, exclusive of the "duties of the heart."

5. Liturgical poems enumerating the commandments were composed by the early Paitanim. These poems, known as *'Azharot*, were incorporated in the synagogue liturgy, to be recited especially on Shabuot. The oldest is believed to be of the eighth century. Among those who wrote such *'Azharot* were Natronai Gaon, Saadiah Gaon, and Solomon Ibn Gabirol. Saadiah lists the mizvot under each of the Ten Commandments. Cf. Rashi, Exod. 24:12. A similar classification is made by Nahmanides in his *Taryag Mizvot*. This method of classification of the laws of the Torah was first adopted by Philo in his *De Decalogo* and in his *De Specialibus Legibus*. See H. A. Wolfson, *Philo* II, p. 201. That the Ten Commandments subsume all of the divine commandments is possibly intimated in the Jerusalem Talmud, *Shekalim* VI, 1, and in the Midrash. See *Numbers Rabbah*, 13:16; cf. *Canticles Rabbah* to Cant. 5:14.

6. In his Hakdamah the author enumerates 265 positive commandments and 348 negative commandments.

7. Maimonides' enumeration of the *taryag mizvot* is also appended to the *Mishneh Torah*, and a classification of the commandments for the purpose of philosophical inquiry appears, as well, in the *Moreh Nebukim*, Part III. For a bibliographical study of the scholarship on the *Sefer ha-Mizvot* see Jacob I. Dienstag, *En ha-Mizvot*, (New York, 1968).

8. See Hakdamah; see also Shoresh I. A defense of the *Halakot Gedolot* is made by Nahmanides in his *Hassagot*. He draws attention to the fact that the *Halakot Gedolot's* version of Rabbi Simlai's statement differs significantly from that of Maimonides. The accepted reading of the passage in *Makkot* 23b is, "six hundred and thirteen precepts were communicated to Moses." Maimonides takes the reading to be, "were communicated to Moses at Sinai." The same is to be found in the *She'eltot*, Parshat Vezot ha-Beraka, She'elta 166 and in *'Ein Ya'akob*, *Makkot*, ibid. The addition of the word בסיני strengthens the argument of Maimonides. Nahmanides draws attention to the Halakot Gedolot's version of Rabbi Simlai's statement which reads "were commanded unto Israel." This would, of course, make it quite proper to include rabbinical as well as biblical laws. See Nahmanides' *Hassagot*, Shoresh I. In this connection it is of interest, however, that the Rome Ms. of the *Halakot Gedolot* has an altogether different reading; namely, "were received by Israel on Mount Sinai." See Hakdamah in *Halakot Gedolot*, Rome Ms., ed. J. Hildesheimer, (Berlin, 1888). Cf. end of Hakdamah in the printed edition which also reads "on Sinai." This reading, which conforms to that of Maimonides, would weaken the point of Nahmanides' defense. See Ch. Heller's critical text of the *Sefer ha-Mizvot*, op. cit., Shoresh I, note 1, for the variant readings. Notwithstanding his defense of the *Halakot Gedolot*, Nahmanides supports the basic position of Maimonides.

9. Differing views are in fact recorded in the Talmud as well regarding certain mizvot, as to whether they are mandatory on scriptural authority. See *Sotah* 3a. Cf. Tosafot, ibid, who cites additional instances in the Talmud. Me'iri explains that this does not affect the total number which remains uniformly 613, since in any case where one mizvah is excluded another is included in its place. Cf. op. cit. For the variant commandments of Nahmanides, Semag, Semak, and Sefer Haredim, see B. Bencher, *Sefer Mizvot Hashem* (Warsaw, 1870).

10. As a preface to his discussion of the six hundred and thirteen commandments in the *Sefer ha-Mizvot*, Maimonides presents in the first part of the book the Fourteen Roots, or Principles, which determine the inclusion or the exclusion of given commandments within the accepted number. These principles are established by Maimonides on the basis of rabbinic tradition, and are developed by him in considerable detail and with incisive logic.

11. For a full discussion of the authorship of the *Sefer ha-Hinnuk* see Excursus I.

12. See Mizvah 507: "As for me, I will set the words of Rabbi Moses ben Maimon, of blessed memory, before my eyes and draw from his well,

because he is responsible for this preoccupation with a reckoning of the mizvot on my part, as well as all who followed him." For a discussion of the Hinnuk's sources, see Excursus II.

13. It should be noted that Maimonides' influence initially was primarily through his *Mishneh Torah* rather than his *Sefer ha-Mizvot* since the latter work, originally written in Arabic, did not at first reach as wide a circle of scholars. The Semag, for example, who in his Hakdamah acknowledges Maimonides' profound scholarship as "enlightening the eyes of Israel" and "strengthening many in Torah through his books which were widely disseminated in the lands of Edom and Ishmael," and whose *Sefer Mizvot Gadol* contains passages that are transcribed verbatim from the *Mishneh Torah*, apparently had no access to the *Sefer ha-Mizvot*. See Ch. Heller, op. cit., Foreword, p. 2, who indicates that the Rokeah, 'Or Zarua', Ritba, Me'iri, Semag, and possibly Rabad, were among the early scholars who did not see the *Sefer ha-Mizvot*.

14. See the Hinnuk's preface to Seder u-Minyan ha-Mizvot.

15. See Maimonides' Hakdamah to his *Sefer ha-Mizvot*, wherein he also notes that it would differ from his major compendium in tracing the law to its biblical and rabbinical sources.

16. An earlier division of the commandments is already drawn in the Mishnah as it distinguishes between mizvot that govern the relationship "between man and God" and "between man and his fellow-man." See M. *Yoma* VIII, 9. For a discussion of the scriptural designation of *hukim* and *mishpatim* as defined by the Jewish sages and philosophers, see chapter I.

17. The Hinnuk refers to the *taryag mizvot* and their division into 248 affirmative and 365 prohibitive commandments as a firm rabbinical tradition. See Hakdamah.   ועתה דע לך לפי מה שקיבלנו מחכמינו זכרונם

לברכה ומפירושיהם כי חשבון המצות הנוהגות לדורות שנכללו בספר
התורה שנתן לנו השם יתעלה עולה תרי"ג מצות ... ואותן שציוה לעשות
עולה חשבונן רמ"ח, ושלא לעשות עולה שס"ה.

18. This altered arrangement was first adopted in the Frankfurt edition of 1783.

19. See Iggeret ha-Mehaber and Hakdamah.

20. The classification of mizvot according to their application is of mishnaic origin. The Mishnah in *Hullin* V:1, for example, states: "The law of 'It and its young' is binding both in the Land of Israel and outside the Land, both during the time of the Temple and after the time of the Temple." In *Kiddushin* 1:7, the Mishnah states: "All the obligations . . . on men and women." Cf. also M. *Hullin* VI:1, VII:1, X:1, XI:1, XII:1, M. *Kiddushin* I:8, 9.

21. Cf. Maimonides' categories of mizvot, given in his *Sefer ha-Mizvot* at the end of the section on the Positive Commandments, where Maimonides

is apparently only suggestive, citing only *f*, *h*, and *k* of the first grouping and *a* of the next. For additional classifications see ibid. Shoresh IX and *Moreh Nebukim* III, 35.

22. Epilogue to Leviticus. והנני עודני בא להזכירך... שאין הכוונה רק לחנך

הנערים ולתת אל לבם כי יש במצות תועלות רבות גלויות לכל אדם באשר יוכלון הבין בילדותם, ועל כן קראתי שם הספר חינוך.

23. Cf. Prov. 22:6. An alternative translation of the title would be *The Book of Training*.

24. See Mizvah 330; cf. Mizvah 419.

25. Mizvah 117; cf. Hakdamah.

26. Hakdamah and throughout the mizvot; cf. Mizvah 497. In the epilogue to Leviticus, he intimates that he prepared the book while in exile. It is therefore possible that the Hinnuk wrote and sent his discussions of the commandments as individual studies to his son in place of his own personal instruction; see Mizvah 111. The practice of directing a written treatise to a son or disciple was a common literary device. Maimonides, for example, wrote his *Guide of the Perplexed* for his disciple, Joseph ibn Aknin. Ibn Caspi wrote his commentary on the *Guide* for his own son; see his Hakdamah to *Sefer 'Amudei Kesef* and *Maskiot Kesef*.

27. In listing the weekly scriptural portions, he considers as separate divisions Ve'eleh ha-Mishpatim (Exod. 21:1-22:23) and 'Im Kesef Talveh (Exod. 22:4-24:18), while Nizabim and Vayelek are considered together. Our present division uniformly combines 'Im Kesef Talveh with Ve'eleh ha-Mishpatim to form the scriptural reading for one Sabbath. Nizabim and Vayelek are separate portions, though they may in some years be read together in one Sabbath. See *Midrash Tanhuma* (ed. S. Buber, Wilna 1885) which includes only Nizabim, indicating that Vayelek was not to be considered as a separate portion. In the Palestinian triennial cycle 'Im Kesef Talveh is the beginning of a new *Seder*. Cf. *Tanhuma* where it is the subject of a new lecture and also the *Mekilta de Rab Yishma'el* where it constitutes a separate division. It is also the reading for Hol ha-Mo'ed Pesah. See J. Mann, *The Bible as Read and Preached in the Old Synagogue*, (Cincinnati, 1940), pp. 420, 475. Cf. *Menorat ha-Ma'or* by R. Israel Ibn Al-Nakawa, ed. by H. G. Enelow, (New York 1931) Part III, p. 326.

28. He mentions also a two-year cycle and a three-year cycle, emphasizing however that the annual cycle has been generally accepted in most Jewish communities. In Mizvah 603 he writes: "In all places in Israel they read the Torah in one year, or at least in two or three years." In the Hakdamah, however, he states it more definitely: "According to what we have heard, the majority of Israel today follows the custom of reading all of it in one year." The annual cycle is known to have been prevalent in Babylonia, while in Palestine a triennial and possibly a three-and-a-half-year cycle prevailed. See *Megillah* 21a, 29b, 31b, and other citations by

P. Finfer, *Masorat ha-Torah ve-ha-Nebi'im* (Wilna, 1906). See J. Mann, op. cit., Vol. 1, p. 4-6. See Maimonides, Tefillah 13:1, who also refers only to an annual and triennial cycle. The Hinnuk's reference to a two-year cycle is, therefore, of singular significance.

29. Hakdamah. See *Baba Kamma* 82a. Cf. Nahmanides' Hakdamah to his Perush ha-Torah.

   Some similarity is to be noted in this regard between the *Sefer ha-Hinnuk* and the *She'eltot*, a compendium of halakic discourses by R. Ahai Gaon, and the *Sefer ha-Mizvot* of Hefez ben Yazliah, a book on the commandments written about the tenth century. In both of these works the laws are arranged in the order of the scriptural readings on the Sabbath in the synagogue. In the latter work the commandments are further grouped into the two divisions of affirmative and prohibitive commandments.

   On the origin and the structure of the *She'eltot*, see S. K. Mirsky, Introduction, *She'eltot de Rab Ahai Gaon*, Vol. 1, (Jerusalem 1959). On the *Sefer ha-Mizvot* of Hefez ben Yazliah, see B. Halper, *Introduction to a Volume of the Book of Precepts*, (Philadelphia 1915). Maimonides has occasion to refer to the work in his *Sefer ha-Mizvot* in connection with his critique of the *Halakot Gedolot*, since Hefez ben Yazliah also questioned the latter's enumeration of the commandments. See Maimonides' Hakdamah to the *Sefer ha-Mizvot* and Shoresh XIV. The work is also cited by Bahya in the Hakdamah to his *Sefer Hobot ha-Lebabot*. Whether or not the Hinnuk was familiar with the work is not known.

30. The Hinnuk uses the term *shoresh ha-mizvah* in his discussion of every commandment, a term already employed, with varying connotations, by Bahya, Maimonides and Nahmanides. Cf. Nahmanides, *Perush ha-Torah*, Exod. 13:16 for his use of it in a discussion of the mizvah of *tefillin*. Maimonides, *Moreh Nebukim* III, 51, speaks of "those who are not trained to investigate *sharashei ha-Torah*." The term is frequently employed by Bahya in connection with the need to investigate the root-principles of faith and the mizvot. See Bahya ibn Pakuda, Hakdamah to *Sefer Hobot ha-Lebabot;* cf. also his preface to *Sha'ar ha-Yihud*, ibid.

31. For the Hinnuk's primary sources for this fourfold division, see Excursus II.

32. This is intimated by the author himself; see Mizvah 333; see also Mizvot 58, 92, 330, 472.

33. Its prominence in halakic literature has come about primarily as a result of the halakic commentaries that have been written on it, especially the *Minhat Hinnuk* written in 1869 by Joseph ben Moses Babad of Tarnopol.

34. See, in particular, his epilogue to Leviticus; cf. Mizvah 611.

35. For a further discussion of this subject see Chapter XI.

NOTES TO CHAPTER THREE

THE DIVINE PURPOSE

1. Hinnuk's Hakdamah. This fact is already noted by Judah Halevi. See the *Kuzari* I, 4: "I believe in all that is written in the Torah and all the other books of the Israelites which are undisputed, because they are generally accepted as everlasting and have been revealed before a vast multitude." Cf. ibid., I, 8, 86, 88. This is also intimated by Saadiah. See *Emunot ve-De 'ot*, Introductory Treatise, chapt. 6.

2. Hakdamah.

3. See Ibn Ezra, *Perush ha-Torah*, Exod. 19:9; Maimonides, *Mishneh Torah*, Yesodei ha-Torah 8:1, 2. Halevi likewise appears to tend to this view. See Kuzari I, 49, 87, 91; II, 2.

4. Nahmanides, *Perush ha-Torah*, Exod. 19:9.

5. Hakdamah.

6. Ibid. This is, likewise, set forth by Halevi who states: "The approach to God is only possible through the medium of God's commandments, and there is no knowledge of the commandments of God except by way of prophecy, not by means of speculation and reasoning." See *Kuzari* III, 53. Cf. ibid. IV, 15.

7. Hakdamah; cf. Mizvah 73. Cf. Nahmanides, *Taryag Mizvot*, at end; cf. also the Hakdamah to his *Perush ha-Torah*.

8. See Prologue to Deuteronomy where he cites this as reason for the fact that the mizvot contained therein were not written previously in the Torah. On the question of the validity of interpretation based upon the confluence or proximity of biblical texts, see *Yebamot* 4a; *Berakot* 10a; *Mekilta*, Exod. 15:9; *Midrash*, Psalms 3; *Sifre*, Num. 9:1, 25:1. See also S. K. Mirsky, "Midot ha-Parshanut ha-Mikra' it," *Sura*, (Jerusalem 1954) pp. 398-406. For a full discussion see chapter XI.

9. Mizvah 77, with reference to the many laws relating to judicial procedure that are derived from the single verse in Exod. 23:2. Cf. Mizvah 95.

10. Cf. *'Otiot de Rabbi Akiba*; *Numbers Rabbah*, 13:15.

11. Cf. Prov. 8:22; *Rosh Hashanah* 21b; *Genesis Rabbah* 17:5, See Nahmanides, Hakdamah, *Perush ha-Torah*, who states that all knowledge was imparted to Moses and is revealed in the Torah either explicitly or by intimation.

12. Mizvah 77; cf. *Genesis Rabbah* 1:2; M. *Abot* III, 14.

13. Hakdamah.

14. Ibid; cf. *Moreh Nebukim* III, 13, 25. Cf. Saadiah, op. cit., I, 4.

15. Ibid. Cf. Mizvah 291, "God created the world absolutely perfect."

16. Cf. Mizvot 257, 374. See Mizvah 180. כי עיקר היותו בעולם אינו רק להבין במושכלות ולעבוד בוראו,

17. Hakdamah.
18. See Mizvah 73.
19. Cf. H. A. Wolfson, *Crescas' Critique of Aristotle*, Prop. 11, n. 4, p. 604, (Cambridge, 1929); cf. also I. Epstein "The Conception of the Commandments of the Torah in Aaron Halevi's Sefer ha-Hinnuk," in *Essays Presented to Dr. J. H. Hertz*, (London 1942), p. 151, n. 17.
20. Cf. Bahya, op. cit., III, 2, 3.
21. Cf. *Moreh Nebukim* III, 54.
22. Mizvah 296, "Man was created to serve his Creator." Cf. M. *Kiddushin* IV, 14; Saadiah, op. cit., X, 15; Bahya, op. cit., II, Introduction; Halevi, *Kuzari* II, 5; III, 50; Maimonides, *Moreh Nebukim* III, 27.
23. See op. cit., IV, Exordium; VII, 1; IX, 1. Cf. Ibn Gabirol's opening statement in his *Tikkun Midot ha-Nefesh*, and Bahya, op. cit., II, 5, both of whom likewise assert that man is the purpose and the crown of creation.
24. Op. cit., I, 4.
25. Ibid., III, Exordium.
26. *Moreh Nebukim* III, 13; cf. ibid. 17; I, 69.
27. Ibid., III, 13.
28. Part III, chapt. 25; cf. Maimonides' Hakdamah to Seder Zer 'aim, Part VI.
29. See *Sefer Shamayim Hadashim* VI, 4. Cf. J. Guttmann, *Philosophies of Judaism*, (New York, 1966) p. 196, 197.
30. Hakdamah. This question is anticipated, by implication, in the tradition recorded in the Midrash that God offered the Torah to the other nations, but they refused it exclaiming, "We have no desire for the knowledge of Thy ways, give your Torah to Israel." See *Exodus Rabbah* 27:8. Apparently the Hinnuk is not content with this explanation, since he does not refer to the Midrash.
31. *Moreh Nebukim* II, 25.
32. *Perush ha-Torah*, Exod. 20:1. Ibn Ezra takes the question to be intimated in the scriptural verse, "When thy son asketh thee in time to come, saying: 'What mean the testimonies and the statutes and the ordinances which the Lord our God hath commanded you?' " Ibn Ezra notes, "He means to say, 'Why are we obliged to keep the commandments of God any more than the rest of mankind? Have we not all one Creator?' "
33. What, if anything, prompted the apologetic turn in the formulation of the question can only be conjectured. In this connection, it is interesting to note that Obadiah Sforno, the sixteenth-century exegete, reflecting the humanistic spirit of his age, poses the question in the same manner, and resolves it by indicating that the selection of Israel does not imply a lesser regard for the rest of mankind. He writes, "All of mankind is precious to Me . . . even as our Sages have said, 'Man is beloved since he was created in the image of God.' " Israel was chosen to be "a kingdom

of priests and a holy nation" with the implicit duty "to teach the rest of mankind to call upon the name of God and to serve Him." See his *Perush* to Exod. 19:5, 6. See Heinemann, op. cit., Vol. II, p. 2, who notes that Moses Mendelssohn develops a similar view on the basis of Sforno's exegesis of the biblical passage.

34. The Noahian laws are: to establish courts of law; not to blaspheme; not to worship idols; not to commit adultery; not to murder; not to rob; not to eat flesh cut from a living animal. For the Hinnuk's exposition of these laws, see chapter VII.

35. Hakdamah.

36. Mizvah 347.

37. Ibid.

38. Ibid.

39. *Kuzari* I, 26, 27.

40. Cf. ibid., I, 102, where Halevi has the King exclaim: "Would it not have been better or more commensurate with divine wisdom if all mankind had been guided in the true path?"

41. Ibid. I, 101-103; cf. ibid. II, 14; III, 17.

42. See *Kuzari* 2:10, with respect to the special qualities of certain countries in plants, metals, etc., which is similarly stated in the Hinnuk's Hakdamah, and may indicate a possible influence by Halevi upon the Hinnuk. See also Nahmanides, *Perush ha-Torah*, Lev. 18:25, particularly on the interdependence of the people and the Land of Israel.

43. See *Midrash Tehillim* 24:3. "The Holy One, blessed be He . . . created the nations, and chose for Himself the Levites; He created the Levites, and chose for Himself the priests; He created the lands, and took to Himself the Land of Israel as a heave-offering from all the other lands." Cf. *Mekilta* on Exod. 12:1 (Parashah I, 4).

44. *Kuzari* I, 27. Cf. Ibn Ezra, *Perush ha-Torah*, Exod. 20:1.

45. Ibid., II, 56; Cf. ibid., III, 10.

46. Mizvah 357. Cf. *Mekilta*, Exod. 12:12; *Shabbat* 156a; Tosafot ibid. and *Niddah* 16b; cf. also *Kuzari* III, 17.

47. Mizvah 344.

48. Mizvah 533.

49. Ibid.

50. Mizvah 42. The same thought is expressed by Maimonides: "Cruelty and arrogance are to be found only among idolaters who worship idols, but the children of our father Abraham, the people of Israel, whom the Holy One, blessed be He has influenced with the goodness of the Torah and commanded them righteous statutes and laws, are above all merciful." See *Mishneh Torah*, 'Abadim 9:8.

51. Mizvah 360.

52. Exod. 19:6. Several commandments relating to the Passover are thus

intended to impress upon the people not only their new-found freedom, but also this status of nobility. See Mizvot 7 and 16; cf. Maimonides, *Moreh Nebukim* III, 46.

53. Mizvah 379. Cf. Mizvot 96, 612.
54. Hakdamah.
55. Ibid.
56. Mizvah 306. Cf. *Nedarim* 32a; Rashi Exod. 3:12; Maimonides, *Moreh Nebukim,* III, 43.
57. Mizvah 13, cf. Mizvah 14. Cf. Saadiah op. cit., III, 7, "Our nation of the children of Israel is a nation only by virtue of its laws."
58. Cf. *Zebahim* 22b.
59. Mizvah 13.
60. Mizvah 14; cf. Mizvah 17.
61. Cf. Saadiah, op. cit., III, 10, at end of chapter.
62. Hakdamah. As to a conception of the world to come, the Hinnuk supplies us with only a few random and broad strokes. The reward in the world to come will reflect the degree of perfection and worthiness of the righteous. Each will attain to the level that he is deserving of, there being an infinite number of levels. See Mizvah 311. Cf. Maimonides, Teshubah 8:2, 8.
63. Ibid.
64. See *Berakot* 5a. Cf. *Baba Batra* 15b; *Yoma* 86a; *Sanhedrin* 101a; Jer. *Sanhedrin* X, 27c; *Yalkut,* Exod. 339; Ibid., Deut. 850. Cf. Nahmanides, *Sha'ar ha-Gemul.*
65. Mizvah 170. For a discussion of the suffering of the righteous in this general vein of the Hinnuk, cf. Nahmanides, op. cit. above.
66. See Mizvot 169, 241.
67. See Mizvah 264.
68. Hakdamah. Cf. Maimonides, Teshubah 8:1.
69. Hakdamah. Cf. Maimonides, ibid 9:1.
70. Hakdamah, cf. Maimonides, ibid., 9:2.
71. Mizvah 3. See Midrash, *Genesis Rabbah* 77:2; cf. Nahmanides, *Perush ha-Torah* 32:26.
72. Mizvah 503.
73. Mizvah 497. Cf. Maimonides *Perush ha-Mishnayot, Sanhedrin* X, 1, Principle 12.
74. This is indicated in his interpretation of the verse, "If thou shalt keep all this commandment to do it . . . then shalt thou add three cities more for thee" (Deut. 19:9). Following the view of the Sages, he takes this to refer to "the time of the king Messiah." See Mizvah 520. Cf. *Sifre,* Deut. 19:9. See Rashi and Nahmanides ad loc. Cf. Maimonides, Rozeah 8:23.
75. Hakdamah.
76. See *Berakot* 34b; *Pesahim* 68a; *Sanhedrin* 99a; *Shabbat* 63a, 151b. An-

other reading, in *Sanhedrin* 91b, has "the oppression of the exiles." See
Maimonides, Melakim 12:1, 2 and Teshubah 9:2.

77. *Perush ha-Torah*, Deut. 30:6. Cf. the divergent views of Maimonides
and Rabad on the nature of the Messianic era in Melakim 12:1. Rabad
alludes to a fundamental change in the character of life in the world in
Messianic times.

78. Hakdamah.

79. Melakim 12:4; see also Teshubah 9:2; *Perush ha-Mishnayot, Sanhedrin*
X, 1.

80. Mizvah 3.

NOTES TO CHAPTER FOUR

THE PREAMBLE OF FAITH

1. See M. *Sanhedrin* X, 1; cf. M. *Berakot* I, 5; M. *Pe'ah* I, 1.

2. See S. Schechter, "The Dogmas of Judaism," *Studies in Judaism*, (Philadelphia, 1896), p. 160; cf. Abrabanel, *Rosh 'Amanah*, Chapter XXIII.

3. *De Opificio Mundi* 61, 170-172; *De Specialibus Legibus* I, 327-63; *De
Decalogo* 4, 15; *De Vita Mosis* II, 3, 14. See H. A. Wolfson, *Philo* I,
p. 164 ff. Philo enumerates eight essential beliefs taught in the Bible.

4. Cf. Saadiah, *Emunot ve-De'ot*, who states in his Introductory Treatise,
chapter 2, "My soul was stirred on account of our people, the children of
Israel. For I saw in this age of mine many believers whose belief was not
pure and whose convictions were not sound."

5. *Kuzari*, III, 17; cf. D. Kaufman, *Studies in Hebrew Literature of the
Middle Ages*, (Jerusalem, 1965), p. 212f.

6. Cf. R. Isaac Abrabanel, op. cit., chapter I: הראשון אשר התחיל בהנחת
עיקרים ויסודות התורה האלקית הוא הרב הגדול הרמב״ם.
Cf. Maimonides' concluding remarks in his commentary on the Mishnah,
Berakot IX, 5, as to the importance he attaches to a study of religious
beliefs. כי יקר בעיני ללמד עיקר מעיקרי הדת והאמונה יותר מכל
אשר אלמדהו.
See N. M. Adler, Hakdamah to his *Netinah la-Ger*, a commentary on
Targum Onkelos, who suggests that Maimonides' Thirteen Principles of
Faith were anticipated by Onkelos, who endeavored to incorporate them
in his Targum.

7. *Perush ha-Mishnayot*, op cit. Maimonides terms them *yesodot*, "fundamental principles." Cf. Yesodei Ha-Torah 1:1, where he introduces the
first basic principle, namely the existence of the Creator, with the words
yesod ha-yesodot. Maimonides, however, also refers to the articles of faith
in his Mishnah Commentary as *'ikarei datenu* and again in the *Moreh
Nebukim*, III, 51, he makes reference to *'ikarei ha-dat*. See Abrabanel,

op. cit., chapter VI, for his explanation of the distinctive meanings of *yesod* and *'ikar* as employed by Maimonides in this context.

8. Maimonides makes this evident when, upon concluding his thirteen articles, he states: "When a man will affirm his belief in these principles of faith and his conviction of them is well established, he then enters into the community of Israel, and it is incumbent upon us to love him, to have compassion upon him, and to do for him all that God commanded us to do for one another in the way of affection and brotherliness. And even though he be guilty of transgressions by reason of desire or his having been overcome by his baser nature, he will receive punishment according to his sins, but he will have a portion in the World to Come." Similarly, Halevi's intention in formulating principles of belief was evidently to provide the basis for a definition of an Israelite worthy of receiving the "divine essence." See op. cit. III, 17.

9. They are presented by the Hinnuk in a brief statement of beliefs in the Hakdamah. Our analysis is based upon this, and upon references and intimations by the Hinnuk in the course of his discussion of the commandments.

10. Hakdamah. The term *'ikar*, root, has in rabbinical literature the meaning essence, reality, main object, chief; see M. Jastrow *A Dictionary of the Targumim, the Talmud and Midrashic Literature*, (London-New York 1903). It occurs often in the Talmud in this sense, as in *Shabbat* 2b, *Sanhedrin* 87a, *Berakot* 12b. In later Hebrew literature, especially in medieval Jewish philosophy, it acquired the meaning of root-principle of faith. Maimonides was probably the first to use the term in this technical sense. See *Perush ha-Mishnayot, Sanhedrin* X, 1; *Moreh Nebukim* III, 51; cf. *Mishneh Torah*, Yesodei ha-Torah 1:6; De'ot 2:3; 'Abodat Kokabim 1:3; Teshubah 5:3; 'Issurei Bi'ah 14:2. Rashi, Lev. 26:15; *Sifra* ibid., 2:18. See D. Neumark, *Toledot ha-'Ikarim be-Yisra'el*, Vol. 1, pp. 1-5.

11. Hakdamah.

12. Mizvah 25.

13. Mizvah 418. Cf. Maimonides, *Sefer ha-Mizvot*, Mizvat 'Aseh 3; Yesodei ha-Torah 2:2. Since the Hinnuk does not qualify the term 'wisdom,' we may infer that it means all wisdom which leads to a knowledge of God.

14. Yesodei ha-Torah 1:1. See also ibid. 1:6, and Minyan ha-Mizvot. Cf. Nahmanides, *Hassagot, Sefer ha-Mizvot*, Mizvat 'Aseh 1.

15. Ibid., 1:6.

16. *Moreh Nebukim*, II, 33. Cf. *Ta'amei ha-Mizvot* by David Ibn Zimra, Mizvah 1.   ולכן כתב ... לידע שיש שם מצוי ראשון ולא כתב להאמין כי עיקר המצוה היא הידיעה כי מלבד האמונה צריך מופת וראיה שכליות כי השכל והדת שני מאורות.

See Ch. Heller's critical edition of Maimonides' *Sefer ha-Mizvot*, op. cit., Mizvat 'Aseh 1, n. 1.

17. For Maimonides the term *la-da'at* has still another connotation. See

Moreh Nebukim III, 24, where he discusses it in connection with the problem of divine trials. In that context he takes it as meaning to demonstrate to others.

It has further been suggested that in view of Maimonides' contention that knowledge, more specifically the communion with God gained through knowledge, is a necessary, preliminary condition for the immortality of the soul, these principles are, hence, to be understood as the essential minimum of religious and metaphysical knowledge that one must acquire to qualify for the World to Come. See J. Guttman, *Philosophies of Judaism*, (New York, 1964) p. 178f. See also A. Hyman, "Maimonides' Thirteen Principles," in *Jewish Medieval and Renaissance Studies*, ed. by A. Altmann, (Cambridge, Mass., 1967) p. 140f.

18. See Maimonides' *Perush ha-Mishnayot*, op. cit., Yesod 1. The term *le-ha'amin* appears in the Hebrew translation but not in the Arabic original. See D. Neumark, op. cit., Vol. 2, p. 127. See *Sefer ha-Mizvot* Mizvat 'Aseh 1. See Ch. Heller, ibid., who notes that in the Arabic original of the *Sefer ha-Mizvot* the term is *'i'tikad* which, though translated into Hebrew "to believe" (*le-ha'amin*), also has the connotation "to know" (*la-da'at*), as in the title of the book by Saadiah, *Kitab Al-'Amanat wa'l-I'tikadat*, which is translated in the Hebrew as *Sefer 'Emunot ve-De'ot*. Cf. Alexander Altmann, *Saadya Gaon: Book of Doctrines and Beliefs*, p. 29, in *Three Jewish Philosophers*, (New York, Philadelphia, 1960). Altmann contends that the term *'I'tikad*, as used by Saadiah and Maimonides, denotes belief based on reason. Cf. also S. Rawidowicz, "Maimonides Studies" I, p. 132ff., in *Metsudah*, London 1943.

19. Mizvah 25. Cf. Bahya ibn Pakuda, *Sefer Hobot ha-Lebabot*, Hakdamah; *Sefer Mizvot Gadol* of R. Moses of Coucy, Mizvat 'Aseh 1, 2; see the commentary of the *Berit Mosheh*, ibid.

20. Mizvah 25. Cf. Maimonides, *Moreh Nebukim*, I, 50, on the nature of belief as "that which is apprehended by the soul." Cf. Nahmanides, *Perush ha-Torah*, Exod. 20:1. The Hinnuk more probably follows Nahmanides' lead, both in the explanation of the verse, as well as in the conception of the belief that it implies.

21. Op. cit., Introductory Treatise, chapter 6. Cf. S. Guttmann, op. cit., p. 64ff.

22. Op. cit., I, 2; cf. ibid., 3, 4.

23. See *Perush ha-Torah*, Exod. 20:2.

24. Op. cit., I, 3.

25. Mizvah 25.

26. It is of interest to note that Bahya, similarly, asserts that this is his objective. At the end of his Hakdamah, he states: "My aim is to bring to light the root-principles of our religion that are deeply fixed in the lucid intellect, and the pivot-principles of our Torah which are latent in

our souls." The Hinnuk thus adopted an intermediate position between Maimonides and those religious philosophers who maintain that a belief in God is based essentially not on philosophical speculation but on faith and prophetic tradition. Cf. *Kuzari*, I, 13, 65; V, 14, 16.

27. Yesodei ha-Torah, 1:11; cf., ibid., 1:7.
28. Ibid., 1:1, 2; cf. Teshubah, 3:7.
29. In the *Guide*, in order to obviate the notion that God acts without purpose, Maimonides interposes the attribute of wisdom relative to creation. "Creation was not the exclusive result of His will; but His wisdom, which we are unable to comprehend, made the actual existence of the universe necessary." *Moreh Nebukim* III, 25. Cf. Saadiah, op. cit., I, 4.
30. *Moreh Nebukim*, I, 71.
31. See Yesodei ha-Torah, 1:11.
32. *Moreh Nebukim*, II, 16; cf. ibid., II, 13-25.
33. *Kuzari*, I, 67.
34. Ibid., I, 65. This is remarkably paralleled in Maimonides' discussions in the *Guide*. Cf. *Moreh Nebukim*, II, 15, 16. Another instance of parallelism in this connection is the admission on the part of both Maimonides and Halevi of the possibility of accommodating Scripture to a theory of eternity, had such a course been necessary. Cf. *Moreh Nebukim*, II, 25 and *Kuzari*, I, 67, at the end. However, see Maimonides' *Mishneh Torah*, Teshubah, 3:7, where the commentaries, such as *Kesef Mishneh* and *Lehem Mishneh*, interpret Maimonides as clearly condemning those who maintain a belief in the eternity of the universe. On Maimonides' understanding of Aristotle's conception of the eternity of the universe, see H. A. Wolfson, "The Platonic, Aristotelian and Stoic Theories of Creation in Halevi and Maimonides," in *Essays Presented to J. H. Hertz*, (London 1943) pp. 427-42. Cf. *Moreh Nebukim*, II, 22; *Kuzari*, I, 1, IV, 25.
35. *Moreh Nebukim*, II, 13; cf. ibid., 25.
36. See Yesodei ha-Torah, I, 7; cf. ibid., I, 5.
37. Mizvah 25. The Hinnuk uses the term *kofer ba-'ikar*, which we have taken to mean a denial of God's existence. In the *Mishneh Torah*, Yesodei ha-Torah, I, 6, Maimonides employs the same term in this very context. See the explanation of *Kesef Mishneh*. This is the meaning given to the term in early rabbinical literature. Cf. *Sifra*, Leviticus 25:14, *Baba Batra* 16b, *Sanhedrin* 38b. It later took on the meaning of denying a fundamental principle of faith. See note 10, this chapter. Cf. Maimonides, *Perush Ha-Mishnayot, Sanhedrin* X, 1, following Principle 13.
38. Hakdamah. Hebrew: *Le-ha'amin ki hu' 'ehad beli shum shituf ba'olam.*
39. Op. cit.; cf. Yesodei ha-Torah, 1:7; Teshubah, 3:7; *Moreh Nebukim*, I, 1; *Kuzari*, II, 2.
40. Cf. Bahya, op. cit., Preface to Sha'ar ha-Yihud, "In using the word

shema' the text refers not to hearing with the ear, but to inward belief . . .
Whenever the term 'hear' is used in this way, it is intended to express
nothing else but believing and accepting."

41. Mizvah 417. Cf. Nahmanides, *Perush ha-Torah*, Deut. 6:4, who notes
that *shema'* follows the Ten Commandments in the Bible to emphasize
that God's unity, implied in the first of the Ten Commandments, is a
root-principle of faith, and whoever denies it is *kofer ba-'ikar*.

42. *Sanhedrin* 63a, *Sukkah* 45b. Cf. *Exodus Rabbah* 42:2; The term *shituf*
is used by the Hinnuk again with respect to God's attributes in Mizvah
74.

43. See Tosafot, *Sanhedrin* 63a. The term is used in this sense by Bahya; cf.
op. cit., I, 2; III, 4. See also Abraham ibn Ezra, *Perush ha-Torah*, Exod.
20:1, at end; Saadiah, op. cit., Introductory Treatise, Chapter VI.

44. *Moreh Nebukim*, I, 35; see also ibid., I, 60. In the latter reference, however, Efodi and Shem Tob take the passage to have a different meaning.

45. Shebu'ot 11:2.

46. Spanish Jewry in the time of the Hinnuk may have been troubled by this
doctrine to a greater degree than were the Jews living in the religious
climate which prevailed for Maimonides. See, however, Maimonides'
Ma'amar Tehiyat ha-Metim I, wherein he notes the need for rejecting
such notions as dualism and the Trinity.

47. Mizvot 25, 417.

48. Iggeret. Cf. Bahya, op. cit., Hakdamah.

49. *Sefer ha-Mizvot*, Mizvot 'Aseh 1, 2. Cf. Maimonides' *Minyan ha-Mizvot*.
The later treatises which enumerate the commandments, such as *Sefer
Mizvot Gadol* and *Sefer Mizvot Katan*, generally follow Maimonides in
this respect.

50. *Hassagot, Sefer ha-Mizvot*, Mizvat 'Aseh 1.

51. Ibid. Cf. *Mekilta*, 20:3, which Nahmanides cites. Cf., however, *Makkot*
23b, which Maimonides cites in his own support.

52. See *Hassagot*, op. cit., Mizvat Lo' Ta'aseh 5, and *Perush ha-Torah*, Exod.
20:2. Ibn Ezra is also equivocal in this matter. In his *Perush ha-Torah*,
Exod. 20:1, he likewise questions inclusion of the belief in God's existence among the Ten Commandments, while in the *Yesod Mora'*, chapter
VII, he includes it in the *Taryag Mizvot*.

53. See *'Or Adonai*, Introduction. ‏ולזה טעה טעות מפורסם מי שמנה במצות‎
‏עשה להאמין מציאות הא־ל יתברך. וזה כי המצוה (מן) המצטרף ולא יצוייר‎
‏מִצְוָה בזולת מְצַוֶּה ידוע.‎

The very same point is already made by Ibn Ezra in his *Perush ha-Torah*,
Deut. 5:16. ‏הישר בעיני שמלת אנכי איננה מהעשרה כי ׳דבור אנכי הוא‎
‏המצוה.‎

Cf. Abrabanel's logical presentation of the point at issue in *Rosh
'Amanah*, Chapter IV.

54. Crescas, op. cit., ibid. See H. A. Wolfson, *Crescas' Critique of Aristotle*,
(Cambridge, 1929), p. 319.

55. See Mizvah 433, where the Hinnuk discusses prayer and divine worship as acknowledgment and awareness of the omnipotence and the providence of God.

56. Cf. Maimonides, *Perush ha-Mishnayot, Sanhedrin* X, 1, Principle III; *Moreh Nebukim*, I, 35; II, Introduction, Propositions 10, 16; II, 1. See Wolfson, op. cit., p. 664.

57. Mizvah 25.

58. See *Hobot ha-Lebabot* I, 9, 10.

59. Exod. 20:4; Deut. 4:15; Lev. 19:4; Isaiah 46:5.

60. This is the reason offered by Prof. H. A. Wolfson, who concludes, "The scriptural principle of the unlikeness of God is thus raised to the philosophic principle of the incorporeality and hence also simplicity of God." Wolfson, *Philo*, II, p. 98. See also I. Twersky, *Rabad of Posquieres*, (Cambridge, Mass., 1962) p. 285. Prof. Twersky calls attention to this with regard to the famous polemic between Rabad and Maimonides on the question of divine incorporeality.

61. *Moreh Nebukim*, I, 55. Cf. Saadiah, *Emunot ve-De'ot*, II, 1; Judah Halevi, *Kuzari*, I, 89.

62. Yesodei ha-Torah, 1:7.

63. Ad loc.

64. Mizvah 74.

65. Mizvah 25.

66. *Moreh Nebukim*, I, 51-60; cf. *Kuzari*, II, 2.

67. The attributes, according to Bahya, are of two classes, active and essential. The active attributes are such as are ascribed to God by reason of His actions and effects upon man. We must resort to them in order to realize His existence and thus be able to serve Him. Indeed, Scripture resorts to them, for had it limited itself to abstract metaphysical or philosophical terms, the average person would not have been able to understand, and would have found it impossible to worship Him. The wise will strip away the materialistic ascriptions and apprehend the truth. The essential attributes are existence, unity, and eternity. These attributes are one in meaning, each implying the other, and, in reality, are negative attributes, signifying only a denial of their contraries. See *Hobot ha-Lebabot* I, 10. The distinction between active and essential attributes is already intimated by Saadiah; cf. op. cit., II, 4, 13. Cf. also *Kuzari* II, 2.

68. Cf. Maimonides, *Moreh Nebukim*, I, 59: "God cannot be the object of human comprehension, none but He himself comprehends what He is." See *Kuzari* IV, 3, 16. Halevi contends that while God's essence is impossible of rational comprehension, His presence is nevertheless real, as evidenced through revelation and the historical experience of the people of Israel.

69. *De Posteritate Caini*, 48, 167; *Quod Deus Sit Immutabilis*, 13, 62. See Wolfson, *Philo*, II, pp. 111, 119, 150.

70. *De Mutatione Nominum* 2, 7, 9. Cf. Maimonides, *Moreh Nebukim* I, 54.

71. Hakdamah.

72. Ibid.; Mizvah 159. By the term *nefesh* the Hinnuk obviously means the rational soul, to which he refers elsewhere variously as נפש השכלית, נפש המשכלת, נפש השכל, in contrast to נפש חיונית , the animal soul. See Mizvah 148; cf. Mizvot 120, 179, 362, 550. The Hinnuk also terms the rational faculty of the soul as נפש המדברת (Mizvah 231), הנפש החכמה (Mizvah 313), and נפש יודעת ומשכלת (Mizvah 33). On the nature of the soul, and its immortality cf. Maimonides, *Moreh Nebukim* I, 41; *Shemonah Perakim* I; Yesodei ha-Torah, 4:9; Teshubah, 8:3.

73. Hakdamah.

74. See Maimonides, *Perush ha-Mishnayot, Sanhedrin* X, 1; Cf. *Moreh Nebukim*, II, 27; III, 22; Teshubah, chapter VIII; cf. *Kuzari* III, 20.

75. Hakdamah. Cf. Ibn Ezra, *Perush ha-Torah*, Deut. 32:39.

76. Hakdamah. Cf. Nahmanides, *Perush ha-Torah*, Exod. 6:2; Saadiah, op. cit., III, 10, and IX.

77. Hakdamah.

78. Mizvah 311. In this conception of the personal immortality of the human soul Jewish religious philosophy, whose traditional position is herein stated by the Hinnuk, departs radically from the Aristotelian position which denies individuality to the soul in its immortal state.

79. Hakdamah.

80. Mizvah 545; see also Mizvah 169.

81. See Mizvot 169, 249, 255, 294, 400, 405, 433, 545.

82. Mizvah 169. Cf. Maimonides, *Moreh Nebukim*, III, 17, for his discussion of four ancient theories concerning divine providence which are rejected by him. The Hinnuk's second class is the equivalent of Maimonides' third theory. The third class partly approximates the first theory, while the first class is not included by Maimonides.

83. Ibid.

84. Cf. *Moreh Nebukim*, III, 17, where Maimonides states, "I hold that divine providence is related and closely connected with the intellect." Cf. ibid. III, 51; *Kuzari* II, 24.

85. Mizvah 357.

86. Passover *Haggadah*. Cf. *Mekilta*, Exod. 12:12.

87. Op. cit. Cf. *Moreh Nebukim*, III, 16, 17; *Mishneh Torah*, Teshubah, chapter 5.

88. Mizvah 21.

89. Mizvah 132.

90. Cf. Nahmanides, *Perush ha-Torah*, ibid., who draws attention to the fact

that the miracle was deliberately hidden by God, but offers a different explanation for it.

91. See *Perush ha-Mishnayot, Abot* V, 6.
92. See *Moreh Nebukim*, II, 29.
93. Mizvah 545.
94. Mizvah 87.
95. Mizvah 169; see also Mizvah 241. Cf. *Berakot* 5a, 60b; Nahmanides, *Sefer Torat ha-Adam*, Sha'ar ha-Gemul, at the beginning.
96. See *Sanhedrin* 64b; cf. *Mo'ed Katan* 28a.
97. Mizvah 424.
98. *'Abodah Zarah* 3a; cf. *Hullin* 142a.
99. Hakdamah. Cf. Maimonides, *Perush ha-Mishnayot, Sanhedrin* X, 1; *Mishneh Torah*, Teshubah, chapter 9.
100. Cf. *Kiddushin* 39b, 40b; *Ta'anit* 11a.
101. Op. cit.; cf. Teshubah 8:1, 9:1.
102. Hakdamah.
103. Ibid. Cf. Saadiah, op. cit., Introductory Treatise, 6; III, 6.
104. *Perush ha-Torah*, Exod. 20:7.
105. See *Horayot* 8a, *Makkot* 24a.
106. *Moreh Nebukim*, II, 33; cf. Yesodei ha-Torah 8:1, 2. Cf. *Moreh Nebukim*, II, 32; *Shemonah Perakim*, VII.
107. Mizvah 516.
108. Ibid.; see also Mizvah 424. Cf. *Nedarim* 38a, *Sanhedrin* 11a; *Kuzari* I, 103; Maimonides, Yesodei ha-Torah 7:1; *Moreh Nebukim*, II, 32.
109. Mizvah 424. Cf. Maimonides, Yesodei ha-Torah 7:4.
110. Hakdamah.
111. On the Rabbinic tradition regarding the Sinaitic experience see *Makkot* 24a; *Mekilta*, Exod. 14:2, 20:16. On Saadiah's view of tradition as a source of religious knowledge, see op. cit., Introductory Treatise, 5, 6; cf. III, 6. Cf. J. Guttmann, op. cit., p. 64.
112. *Kuzari*, I, 87; cf. ibid., I, 91, 95; II, 2.
113. *Perush ha-Torah*, Exod. 19:9. Cf. Yesodei ha-Torah 8:1, 2, where Maimonides cites the verse, "That the people may hear when I speak with thee, and may also believe thee forever" (Exod. 19:9). Cf. *Mekilta*, ibid. The same proof-text alluded to by Maimonides, Ibn Ezra, and the Hinnuk is already cited by Saadiah as indicating the authentication of revelation on the testimony of the people. Cf. op. cit., Introduction.
114. Hakdamah. See *Kuzari*, III, 53; cf. Saadiah, op. cit., III, 6.
115. Hakdamah.
116. Ibid. On these problems see *Baba Batra* 123b; Rashi, Exod. 6:18, 12:15, 40; Nahmanides, *Perush ha-Torah*, Exod. 12:40; R. Moses of Coucy, *Sefer Mizvot Gadol*, Hakdamah.
117. See *Sefer ha-Ikkarim*, I, 1-4.

118. Hakdamah, and Mizvot 3, 497, 503, 520.
119. Hakdamah.
120. *Sefer ha-Ikkarim*, I, 4. Albo bases his contention upon the statement in *Sanhedrin* 99a, "Israel has no Messiah; they consumed (enjoyed) him in the days of Hezekiah." Ibid., I, 1. Cf. Abrabanel, op. cit., chapter 14, for another explanation of this statement, which incidentally is immediately refuted in the Talmud itself by citing a prediction for the coming of the Messiah in the prophecy of Zechariah, long after the time of Hezekiah. See Maimonides' own admonition (Melakim 12:2), reflecting a traditional concern about undue preoccupation with the subject.
121. M. *Sanhedrin*, X, 1.
122. *Sanhedrin* 91b; cf. Rashi, Exod. 15:1.
123. Cf. Maimonides, *Perush ha-Mishnayot, Sanhedrin*, X, 1; *Mishneh Torah*, Teshubah, 8:2, 8, and note Rabad's *Hassagot*, ad loc. See Maimonides' exposition of his view, affirming a belief in bodily resurrection, in his essay, *Ma'amar Tehiyyat ha-Metim*. Cf. Saadiah, op. cit., chapter VII. Cf. Albo, op. cit., I, 23; IV, 30, 31.
124. Prof. Wolfson states that Philo throughout his writings makes no direct or indirect reference to resurrection apart from immortality. See Wolfson, op. cit. I, p. 404. It is noteworthy that in the three doctrines, already mentioned as having been omitted by the Hinnuk, namely, incorporeality, the coming of the Messiah, and resurrection, the position of the Hinnuk appears to parallel that of Philo.
125. Cf. *Moreh Nebukim*, II, 32-35; Yesodei ha-Torah, chapters 7-9; Mamrim, 1:1, 2. One who denies the divine origin of either the Written Law or the Oral Law is considered by Maimonides to be a *"kofer ba-Torah."* See Teshubah, 3:8; cf. *Kesef Mishneh*, ibid.
126. Mizvah 454; cf. Mizvah 455. Cf. also Maimonides, *Sefer ha-Mizvot*, Mizvot Lo' Ta'aseh, 313, 314; Yesodei ha-Torah, 9:1. Cf. Saadiah, III, 7.
127. Mizvot 25, 417. Similarly, the love of God and the fear of God are also mandatory commandments. (Mizvot 418, 432).
128. Mizvah 516.
129. Mizvah 26.
130. Mizvah 387.
131. See R. David ibn Zimra, *Sefer Mezudat David, Ta'amei Mizvot le-Rad-baz*, Mizvah 107. שאני סובר שאין לשום עיקרים לתורתינו הקדושה, לפי
שכולה עיקר ושורש, שאינה כשאר הדתות והנמוסיות שצריכים עקרים על מה
שיסמיכו. ואפילו סיפורי תורתינו הקדושה הנראים לכאורה שאינם עיקר, יש
להם סוד גדול מה שלא יוכל שכל האנושי להשיגו ולא הלשון להגידו.
With regard to the wisdom inherent in the Torah, Maimonides writes, in Principle VIII of his Thirteen Principles, "Every statement of the Torah is full of wisdom and mystery for one who understands it. Its ultimate wisdom has never been comprehended."
132. *Rosh 'Amanah*, chapter XXIII.

133. Certain of the beliefs, to be sure, are mentioned by Maimonides in his *Moreh Nebukim*, Part I, chapter 35. However, this does not constitute a definitive summary of belief, nor are all the principles mentioned. This can equally be said of his *Sefer ha-Mizvot* and the *Mishneh Torah*. While the propositions concerning God's existence and His unity are listed in the *Sefer ha-Mizvot* as specific commandments, as also the prohibition against the worship of any other being, none are therein designated as principles of faith. In the *Mishneh Torah* Maimonides does discuss all of the principles, with the exception of resurrection of the dead, in Yesodei Ha-Torah (1:1-12; 7:1-6; 9:1), Teshubah (3:6-8; 8:1; 9:1, 2), 'Abodah Zarah (1:3; 2:1), and 'Issurei Bi'ah (14:2). They are, however, interspersed among the various *halakot*, often referred to only obliquely and, with the exception of the principles regarding God's existence, His unity, and the denial of idolatry, they are not definitively characterized as *'ikarim*.

Indeed, it has been suggested that, in view of Maimonides' statement ('Issurei Bi'ah 14:2) that the "principles of faith" which must be communicated to a would-be proselyte are the unity of God and the prohibition of idolatry, it may be concluded that Maimonides retreated from his position in the Thirteen Principles. See S. Adler, "Tenets of Faith," in *Kobez 'al-Yad*, p. 92. It should be pointed out, in this connection, however, that Maimonides significantly adds the phrase, "and they should expatiate on this subject." Cf. *Magid Mishneh*, ibid. It would appear that, at least as regards his *Sefer ha-Mizvot* and the *Mishneh Torah*, in view of the nature of these works, Maimonides' later works are inconclusive on the question of a formalized credo of faith. However, see A. Hyman, "Maimonides' Thirteen Principles," op. cit., who endeavors to show that Maimonides does enumerate his principles in the *Guide* as well as in his legal works, the *Sefer ha-Mizvot* and the *Mishneh Torah*.

134. This is precisely the reason advanced by Radbaz for designating his root-principles as שרשי האמונה rather than שרשי הדת. See Radbaz op. cit., ibid.

135. Abrabanel draws attention to this fact with regard to Maimonides. In his *Ro'sh 'Amanah*, chapter VI, he states: "You will also perceive that the principles and doctrines which are outlined by the great Master are not only principles of faith or religious doctrines. The Master intended them as the Principles of Judaism that classify one who believes in them as being of the people of Israel, and with respect to which the Mishnah states, 'All Israelites have a share in the World to Come.' It is as if he had stated that those principles are the foundations upon which everyone who is called an Israelite can build and establish his spiritual inheritance in the World to Come." It may be noted that Judah Halevi appears to have had a similar objective; see *Kuzari* III, 17.

136. Cf. Hatam Sofer, *Responsa*, Yoreh De'ah, no. 356. The author, R. Moses

Sofer, an eminent, halakic authority of the early 19th century, distinguishes between the one fundamental principle of faith in the Torah and the Prophets, without which the structure of Judaism cannot stand, and other instances of belief which are to be accepted as truths taught therein. Thus, he considers the coming of the Messiah and Israel's redemption in the latter category, but nevertheless views them as clearly taught in Scripture and, hence, their denial would constitute a denial of the Torah itself.

137. See D. Neumark, *Toledot ha-'Ikkarim be-Yisra'el*; S. Schechter, "The Dogmas of Judaism," op. cit. See also Neumark's historical study, "The Principles of Judaism," in *Essays in Jewish Philosophy*, (Central Conference of American Rabbis, 1929).

138. Cf. R. Saul Berlin, *Besamim Ro'sh*, p. 331. The Talmud records a striking statement by the Rabbis on what appears to be formulations of religious doctrine, based upon selective mizvot, in successive periods by King David and the prophets Isaiah, Micah, and Habakkuk. See *Makkot* 24a; cf. the commentaries of Rashi and Maharsha', ibid.

NOTES TO CHAPTER FIVE

A RATIONALE OF MIZVOT

1. See Chapter I.
2. *Moreh Nebukim* III, 26-49.
3. See, for example, 'Abodah Zarah 12:1, 7, 11, 13; Me'ilah 8:8; Temurah 4:13; see J. Leiner, "Halakah ve-'Agadah Besofei ha-Sefarim she-be-Mishneh Torah le-ha-Rambam," *Talpiot*, vol. VII, 1 (New York, 1958).
4. Mizvot 159, 545.
5. *Numbers Rabbah* 19:3.
6. On the enigma of the red heifer, whose ashes purified the unclean and defiled the clean, see *Numbers Rabbah* 19:5.
7. *Numbers Rabbah* 19:6. Cf. Recanati, *Perush ha-Torah*, Parashat Hukat, who maintains that the law of the red heifer is comprehendible by all, with the exception of the paradox noted which was intelligible only to Moses.
8. *Pesahim*, 119a. Cf. *Sanhedrin* 102a for a similar comment by the Rabbis on the verse in I Kings 11:29.
9. See Isaiah 23:18.
10. See Maimonides' interpretation of the verse in *Moreh Nebukim*, III, Hakdamah, Cf. Bahya ben Asher, *Midrash Rabbeinu Bahya*, Introduction to Genesis I.
11. M. *Pesahim*, X, 5; note particuarly Rashbam and Bertenoro ad loc.

12. *Rosh Hashanah* 16a. For further instances, see chapter I.
13. Cf. *Baba' Mezia'* 115a; *Kiddushin* 68b; *Sotah* 8a, *Sanhedrin* 16b, 21a. The author of the *Shulhan 'Aruk* takes this as ascribing reasons for mizvot; see *Bet Yosef, Yoreh De'ah* 181.
14. See I. Heinemann, op. cit., vol. I, p. 35.
15. Cf. Mizvah 159.
16. M. *Berakot* V, 3; M. *Megillah* IV, 9.
17. Mizvah 545.
18. Apparently in the sixteenth benediction, which is the last of the intermediate benedictions in the Shemoneh Esreh. This is indicated by Rabbah's statement in the Talmud. See also Rashi, *Megillah* 25a; Maimonides, *Perush ha-Mishnayot*, M. *Berakot* V, 3.
19. *Berakot* 33b, *Megillah* 25a. See the comparable opinions cited in Jer. M. *Berakot* V, 3; Jer. M. *Megillah* IV, 10.
20. Rashi, *Megillah* 25a; cf. Rashi, *Berakot* 33b. Cf. *Aggadot Maharsha'*, *Berakot* 33b.
21. See Rashi, *Berakot* 33b. On this meaning of the term *middot*, cf. *Gittin* 76a, and Rashi, ad loc.
22. *Perush ha-Mishnayot*, ibid.; *Mishneh Torah*, Tefillah, 9:7.
23. *Moreh Nebukim*, III, 48; cf. ibid., 28.
24. Ibid., III, 48. Saadiah, likewise, deems this law to be an instance of "pity on animals." See *Emunot ve-De'ot* V, 6.
25. *Deut. Rabbah* 6:1.
26. See *Perush ha-Mishnayot*, M. *Berakot* V, 3: אבל היא מצוה מקובלת אין לפי שהטעם אינו צד רחמניות and similarly in M. *Megillah* IV, 9: לה טעם. מהשם יתברך באמרו לא תקח האם על הבנים אבל היא גזירת הכתוב.
27. Tefillah, 9:7. The *Lehem Mishneh*, ad loc., understands Maimonides to favor the second view advanced in the Talmud. See *Tosafot Yom Tob*, M. *Berakot* V, 3, who notes Maimonides' contradictory views. Cf. M. *Bekorot* IV, 9, where *Tosafot Yom Tob* cites other apparent contradictions, venturing the opinion that in some instances Maimonides changed his views in his several works.
28. Mizvah 545; cf. Mizvah 169. See *Kol Bo*, chapt. 111, who states that while the Torah permits the slaughter of animals for food, it nevertheless commands sparing the mother bird and prohibits the slaughter of an animal together with its young, the reason being to prevent decimation of the species. Similarly, Bahya ben Asher, op. cit., in his commentary on Deut. 22:7, also takes the object of the mizvah to be the preservation of the species. Cf. *Moreh Nebukim*, III, 17, on the nature of divine providence.
29. Mizvah 294. In the view of Nahmanides, which is shared by the Hinnuk, the two commandments, to let the mother bird go and not to slaughter an animal together with its young, have the common purpose of perpetuating the species, in addition to an abhorrence of cruelty to animals. See

Nahmanides, *Perush ha-Torah*, Deut. 22:6. Maimonides relates the two in that man is prohibited from causing grief to animals. See *Moreh Nebukim*, III, 48.

30. Cf. Maimonides, Tefillah 9:7; Nahmanides, ibid.
31. Mizvah 545. Cf. Maimonides, *Moreh Nebukim*, I, 54, 57; *Kuzari*, II, 2.
32. Mizvah 545. In support of the Hinnuk's contention that the mizvah is not to be viewed as a special manifestation of divine mercy, we may further note that the Rabbis have understood the mizvah to be limited in its application. The Mishnah states, for example, that the law does not apply in the case of birds that are either consecrated, captive, or unclean. See M. *Hullin* XII, 1, 2; see ibid., XII, 3 for further restrictions of the area in which the law is operative.
33. See Abraham Buchner, *Ha-Moreh le-Zedakah* (Warsaw, 1838), for a further discussion of this problem. Buchner notes that since the Mishnah itself does not state the basis of its objection to the form of the prayer, while the Talmud offers the views of two Amoraim, one of whom appears to forbid giving reasons for the commandments and the other does not, it therefore cannot be said that the prohibition attributed to the former is universally accepted in Judaism.

   A radically different view is advanced by S. D. Luzzatto. In his opinion the Mishnah has no bearing whatever on the mizvah of *shiluah ha-ken*. It is, he believes, but a prayer invoking God's pity on the community of Israel, which is metaphorically likened to a bird fleeing its nest, and the prayer is deemed improper because the metaphor may not be understood by the congregation. See Luzzatto, *Yesodei ha-Torah* (Jerusalem 1947), p. 35, n. 6.
34. Mizvah 159.
35. *Sanhedrin* 21b; cf. *Exodus Rabbah* 6:1.
36. Deut. 17:16, 17; cf. I Kings 10:29, 11:4.
37. Mizvot 73, 159. Cf. Maimonides, *Moreh Nebukim*, III, 26; *Sefer ha-Mizvot*, Mizvat Lo' Ta'aseh, 365.
38. Mizvah 159.
39. Ibid., III, 26.
40. Temurah 4:13; cf. Me'ilah 8:8. Maimonides' statement is cited by the Hinnuk; see Mizvah 352.
41. *Perush ha-Torah*, Deut. 22:6. Nahmanides refers here to the law of the red heifer.
42. Mizvah 104.
43. *Moreh Nebukim*, III, 26; cf. ibid. III, 41; see also *Mishneh Torah*, Temurah 4:13.
44. Mizvah 117. Cf. Hinnuk's Epilogue to Leviticus.
45. Cf. Me'ilah 8:8, where Maimonides also intimates this.
46. *Rosh ha-Shanah* 21b.

47. Mizvah 159.
48. Me'ilah 8:8; cf. *Moreh Nebukim*, III, 49; *Sefer ha-Mizvot*, Mizvat Lo' Ta'aseh, 365.
49. *Emunot ve-De'ot*, III, 2.
50. *Perush ha-Torah*, Exod. 20:1.
51. Mizvah 452.
52. Cf. *Yalkut Shim'oni*, 'Emor 23. "I have commanded you many mizvot in order to make you worthy of My favor."
53. Mizvah 95.
54. Cf. Lev. 20:25.
55. Mizvah 545. The Hinnuk points out that this is a recurring theme in the Bible, as in Deut. 6:24, 10:13.
56. Ibid.
57. *Perush ha-Torah*, Deut. 22:6, quoted by the Hinnuk.
58. *Genesis Rabbah* 44:1; *Leviticus Rabbah* 13:3. Cf. *Midrash Tanhuma*, Parashat Shemini 7. Maimonides also quotes this Midrash but interprets it in a different way. See *Moreh Nebukim*, III, 26. Additional verses cited are Psalms 12:7; Proverbs 30:5; cf. II Samuel 22:31.
59. M. *Nedarim*, 9:1. R. Nissim explains Rabbi Zadok's statement to mean: They say to him, "If you had known that he who vows is disrespectful of God, would you have made your vow?" See his commentary, ad loc.; cf. Rashi and Bertenoro ad loc.
60. Ibid.
61. Cf. Job, 22:3.
62. Neilah prayer for the Day of Atonement, *'Atah Hibdalta 'Enosh*.
63. See *Moreh Nebukim*, III, 13.
64. This view is also expressed by Judah Halevi. In discoursing on the meaning of sacrifices, he states, "God, however, is most holy and far too exalted to find pleasure in their meat and drink. It is for their own benefit." The Sages take this to be implicit in Lev. 19:5, "And when ye offer a sacrifice of peace-offerings unto the Lord, ye shall offer it that ye may be accepted." See *Menahot* 110a, *Kuzari*, II , 26.
65. See Mizvah 545; cf. Nahmanides, *Perush ha-Torah*, Deut. 22:6.
66. Mizvah 166.
67. Mizvah 73.
68. Mizvot 159, 362.
69. *Yoma* 39a.
70. Mizvah 73.
71. Mizvot 147, 148. Cf. Maimonides, *Moreh Nebukim*, III, 28.
72. Mizvah 154.
73. Mizvah 159. Cf. Maimonides, *Shemonah Perakim*, I.
74. Mizvah 73.
75. See *Moreh Nebukim*, III, 12. In discussing the class of evils which man

causes to himself by his own action, he states: "This class of evils origi-
nates in man's vices, such as excessive desire for eating, drinking and
love, indulgence in these things in undue measure, or in improper manner, or partaking of bad food. This course brings diseases and afflictions
upon body and soul alike. The sufferings of the body in consequence of
these evils are well known; those of the soul are twofold. First, such evils
of the soul as are the necessary consequence of changes in the body,
insofar as the soul is a force residing in the body; it has therefore been
said that the properties of the soul depend on the condition of the body.
Secondly, the soul, when accustomed to superfluous things, acquires a
strong habit of desiring things which are neither necessary for the preservation of the individual nor for that of the species."

76. *Perush ha-Torah*, Lev. 17:11. Cf. Mizvah 148.
77. Derashat Torat ha-Shem Temimah, *Kitbei Ramban*, ed. C. B. Chavel,
    (Jerusalem, 1963), p. 166.
78. *Perush ha-Torah*, ibid. Cf. Nahmanides' *Perush* to Lev. 17:11, where he
    elucidates further: ‏כי הנאכל ישוב בגוף האוכל והיו לבשר אחד, ואם‎
    ‏יאכל אדם נפש כל בשר והוא יתחבר והיו לאחדים בלב, תהיה עובי‎
    ‏וגסות בנפש האדם ותשוב קרוב לטבע הנפש הבהמית אשר בנאכל.‎
79. *Perush ha-Torah*, Deut. 14:3.
80. *Ta'amei ha-Mizvot*, Mizvah 185.
81. *Emunot ve-De'ot*, V, 1.
82. Mizvah 16.
83. In discussing the effect of habit and custom on the development of moral
    virtue, Aristotle states, "Our moral dispositions are formed as a result of
    the corresponding activities." See *The Nicomachean Ethics*, II, 1, trans.
    by H. Rackham, The Loeb Classical Library.
84. De'ot, 1:7. Cf. *Shemonah Perakim*, IV; *Moreh Nebukim*, II, 31.
85. M. *Makkot*, III, 16.
86. Mizvah 16; cf. Maimonides, *Moreh Nebukim*, III, 51.
87. Mizvah 99.
88. Mizvah 16, cf. *Pesahim* 50b, *Sotah* 22b.
89. Mizvah 16.
90. Mizvah 491. Cf. *Yoma* 86b.
91. Mizvah 159; cf. Mizvah 73.

NOTES TO CHAPTER SIX

MAN'S ETHICAL DUTIES

1. It is noteworthy that the tractate *Abot*, which is a Mishnaic treatise on
   ethics, begins with an account of the Oral Tradition that is traced back
   to the divine revelation at Sinai. This is taken to be an indication that the

moral and ethical teachings in this tractate are not the result of mere speculation by the Sages of the Mishnah, but were revealed at Sinai. See M. *Abot* I, 1 and especially the commentary of R. Obadiah of Bertenoro, ibid.

2. Mizvah 430.
3. Mizvah 66. This reason, the Hinnuk points out, was already intimated by Rabbi Akiba in his reply to the question put to him by a skeptic, "If your God loves the poor, why does He not provide for them?" See *Baba Batra* 10a.
4. Mizvah 430.
5. See *Sotah* 14a; *Exod. Rabbah* 26:2; *Sifra*, Lev. 19:2; *Sifre*, Deut. 10:12.
6. *Shabbat* 133b.
7. Mizvah 611; see also Mizvah 74.
8. *Mekilta* to Exod. 15:2.
9. *Sefer Ha-Mizvot*; Mizvat 'Aseh 8; cf. De'ot 1:5, 6.
10. *Moreh Nebukim*, I, 54.
11. Ibid., III, 54.
12. De'ot 1:4; see also *Shemonah Perakim*, IV. Cf. Aristotle, *Nicomachean Ethics*, Book II.
13. Mizvah 611; cf. Mizvah 178, *Mo'ed Katan* 5a.
14. Cf. Jer. *Hagigah* II, 1; *Tosefta, Hagigah* II; *Abot de-Rabbi Nathan* 28:10.
15. *Emunot ve-De'ot*, X, 17, 19.
16. *Hobot ha-Lebabot*, III, 4; IX, 7.
17. *Kuzari*, II, 50; III, 5.
18. Cf. also *Moreh Nebukim*, II, 39; *Perush ha-Mishnayot, Abot*, IV, 4.
19. De'ot, 1:7; see Gen. 18:19. Echoing Jewish tradition, Maimonides further draws the distinction between those who only follow the mean, which he also terms "the way of the wise," and those who depart somewhat from the exact mean and tend to the more desirable extreme, which he characterizes as "the virtue of saintliness." See op. cit., 1:4, 5.
20. Mizvah 248; cf. Mizvah 178, 313; Maimonides, *Moreh Nebukim*, III, 33.
21. Mizvah 248; cf. Mizvah 374. *Moreh Nebukim* III, 8.
22. Mizvah 95.
23. Mizvah 77.
24. *Genesis Rabbah* 44:1.
25. Mizvah 421. Cf. Mizvot 16, 386. See *Menahot* 43b, and Rashi ad loc., on the numerical value and the symbolic character of the fringes as a reminder of the 613 commandments. Cf. Maimonides, Mezuzah, 6:13.
26. Mizvah 421.
27. Mizvah 38. Cf. *Mekilta*, Exod. 20:14; Maimonides, *Sefer ha-Mizvot* Mizvat Lo'Ta'aseh 265; Gezelah ve-'Abedah, 1:9.
28. Mizvah 416. Cf. Maimonides, op. cit., Mizvat Lo' Ta'aseh 266; Gezelah ve-'Abedah 1:10, 11. See the *Mekilta*, ibid., where violation of this commandment is seen as leading to the transgression of other prohibitions.

29. Cf. Maimonides, Gezelah ve-'Abedah 1:12.
30. Mizvah 416. Cf. Ibn Ezra, Exod. 20:14.
31. Mizvah 374.
32. *Nazir* 19a, *Nedarim* 10a.
33. Nahmanides, *Perush ha-Torah*, Num. 6:14. The Hinnuk evidently also veers from the prosaic interpretation of Maimonides, who regards the object of Naziritism to be obvious. "It keeps away from wine that has ruined people in ancient and modern times." See *Moreh Nebukim*, III, 48. For Maimonides' approach to the question of asceticism generally, see op. cit., II, 36; III, 8.
34. *Ta'anit* 22b.
35. Mizvah 430.
36. See Exod. 20:5, 6; 34:6, 7; Deut. 5:9, 10.
37. Mizvah 216. Cf. Mizvot 218, 220, 222.
38. See *Shabbat* 63a.
39. *Sefer Ha-Mizvot*, Mizvat 'Aseh 197; Malveh ve-Loveh 1:1; Matnot 'Aniyim 10:7.
40. Mizvah 66.
41. *Moreh Nebukim* III, 39.
42. Ibid.
43. Mizvah 66. Cf. Mizvot 216, 591.
44. Mizvah 84.
45. Mizvah 330.
46. Mizvah 340.
47. Mizvah 477.
48. Mizvah 480.
49. Mizvah 451, 550. Cf. *Baba Mezia* 32a, *Shabbat* 128b; Cf. Maimonides, *Moreh Nebukim*, III, 17 on the prohibition of killing animals for sport.
50. Mizvah 294. Cf. Maimonides, op. cit., III, 48.
51. Mizvah 596.
52. Ibid.
53. Mizvah 550.
54. See *Moreh Nebukim*, III, 49.
55. *Perush Ha-Torah*, Deut. 22:10. Cf. S. D. Luzzatto, *Yesodei Ha-Torah*, (Jerusalem 1947), chapter 21, pp. 35, 36.
56. Mizvah 550.
57. Mizvah 451.
58. *Moreh Nebukim* III, 26.
59. Mizvah 186.
60. Mizvah 545. A somewhat different emphasis to the moral lesson conveyed by this commandment is given by S. D. Luzzatto, who maintains that it is intended to teach us to value compassion, in this instance that shown by the mother bird for its young when it does not pay heed to its own safety, and refrains from flying away, but remains to protect its

nest. Had the Torah permitted one to take advantage of the mother bird in such a situation, it would have meant that mercy and compassion are foolish traits, which are likely to result in harm to those who exhibit them. See op. cit., p. 36.

61. According to the Hinnuk, the reward indicated may be understood to be the promise of progeny, which can be regarded as a form of everlasting life for the individual in this world, "because children are the assurance of a man's existence and the perpetuation of his memory." Cf. *Deuteronomy Rabbah* 6:3.

62. M. *Hullin* XII, 5; cf. *Tosafot Yom Tob,* M. *Abot* II, 1.

63. See for example Maimonides' explanation of the law prohibiting the slaughter of an animal and its young on the same day. *Moreh Nebukim* III, 48. Maimonides stresses the pain caused under such circumstances, noting that the love and tenderness of the mother for her young are produced, not by the rational, but by the imaginative faculty, which is found in most living beings. The Hinnuk prefers in this instance to stress rather the importance of cultivating the quality of mercy. See Mizvah 294.

64. Cf. Aristotle, *Nicomachean Ethics,* Book X.

65. Mizvah 257; cf. Maimonides, Yesodei ha-Torah, 1:1, 2:2; *Moreh Nebukim,* II, 36; III, 8.

66. Mizvah 419; cf. Maimonides, Talmud Torah, 3:1; Teshubah, 10:2.

67. Mizvah 257.

68. Mizvah 434.

69. Mizvah 450.

70. Mizvah 450.

71. *Moreh Nebukim,* III, 54.

72. Mizvah 434.

73. Mizvah 491.

74. Mizvah 71.

75. Mizvah 498. Cf. Maimonides, *Moreh Nebukim* III, 50; Melakim 1:7.

76. See *Yebamot* 79a.

77. Mizvah 498. Cf. Maimonides, *Sefer ha-Mizvot,* Mizvat Lo' Ta'aseh 362; Melakim 1:4.

78. Mizvah 498.

79. Mizvah 491.

80. Ibid.

81. Maimonides tentatively suggests a method of renewal of *Semikah* in our day through the concerted authority of all of the Sages in the Land of Israel. See *Perush ha-Mishnayot, Sanhedrin* I, 1; Sanhedrin 4:11. On the strength of Maimonides' opinion, an attempt was made to reinstitute *Semikah* by the Rabbis of Safed in 1538 under the leadership of R. Jacob Berab. One of the first to be ordained was R. Joseph Karo, author of the

Shulhan 'Aruk. Due to the opposition of R. Levi Ibn Habib and others the attempt eventually proved abortive. Cf. Commentaries of Radbaz and *Lehem Mishneh,* ibid.

82. Cf. Gen. 18:25.
83. Cf. M. *Abot* I, 18. Cf. *Sifre,* Deut. 16:20.
84. Mizvah 49.
85. See *Sanhedrin* 7a.
86. See Num. 35:30; Deut. 17:6; 19:15; *Sifre,* ibid. See Mizvah 523 for the law with respect to the testimony of two witnesses and a list of the exceptions. Cf. Maimonides, 'Edut, 5:1, 2.
87. M. *Sanhedrin* IV; 1, 5; V; 1, 2; M. *Makkot* I, 10.
88. Mizvah 409.
89. Mizvah 76.
90. The testimony of two witnesses, though not absolutely conclusive proof, must be accepted as scripturally ordained, the Hinnuk notes, on the presumption that two qualified and worthy witnesses will not conspire to testify falsely. Cf. Maimonides, Yesodei ha-Torah, 7:7, "For thus, too, are we enjoined to decide a suit on the evidence of two competent witnesses, we rely on their qualification." Cf. ibid, 8:2.
91. Exod. 23:2.
92. See *Sanhedrin* 69a, *Rosh Hashanah* 26a. Cf. Mizvah 409.
92a. Mizvah 521, citing Deut. 19:13, 21; M. *Abot* III, 2.
93. Mizvah 77. Cf. M. *Abot* IV, 8, "Judge not alone, for none may judge alone save One."
94. See *Sanhedrin* 34a; Maimonides, Sanhedrin 10:2.
95. See *Mekilta,* Exod. 23:2; Maimonides, *Sefer Ha-Mizvot,* Mizvat Lo' Ta'aseh 283; Sanhedrin 10:1, 2. See M. M. Kasher, *Maimonides and the Mekilta of Rabbi Simeon ben Johai,* (New York 1943) p. 122, for the identity of the *Mekilta* cited by Maimonides in his *Sefer Ha-Mizvot,* and presumably by the Hinnuk as well. On this see Ch. Heller's edition of the *Sefer Ha-Mizvot,* ibid., n. 20.
96. *Sanhedrin* 17a.
97. Mizvah 77.
98. Sanhedrin 9:1.
99. This is intimated by the explanatory statement of the Talmud, *Sanhedrin* 17a. The key to the problem lies in the meaning of the phrase *"poterin 'oto",* generally taken to mean "he is freed." Another meaning suggested is that he is done away with forthwith. See B. Epstein, *Torah Temimah,* Exod. 23:2, n. 17 for references. This meaning is given to the phrase by Rashi, *Shebuot* 39a, in another context. However, cf. Tosafot, ibid.
100. See M. *Sanhedrin* IV, 1.
101. A similar view with respect to this law is expressed by an eminent nineteenth-century talmudist as follows: "There are always mitigating cir-

cumstances that may be cited in favor of the accused in an attempt to save him from the death penalty . . . In many places it is customary that the judges act in the capacity of advocates arguing in favor of the defendant. Hence, if this court was immediately convinced of his guilt and could find nothing in his favor, even in the remotest way, then it is an indication that this court is either not competent and their judgment is not valid, or that they rendered judgment in haste without due deliberation and inquiry into the facts and the evidence. See R. Zvi Hirsch Chayes, *Annotations, Sanhedrin* 17a.

102. Mizvah 77.
103. *Moreh Nebukim* III, 39.
104. Mizvah 78.
105. Ibid.
106. Cf. *Sanhedrin* 2a; Maimonides, *Sefer ha-Mizvot*, Mizvat 'Aseh 175; *Sanhedrin* 8:1.
107. Cf. *Sanhedrin* 88b.
108. See Mizvah 496. Cf. *Horayot* 2a; *Sifre*, Deut. 17:11; Nahmanides, *Perush Ha-Torah*, ibid.
109. Mizvah 78.
110. See Mizvah 496; cf. Maimonides, Mamrim 3:5, 6; 4:1.
111. M. *Sanhedrin* XI, 2; see *Sifre*, Deut. 17:12.

NOTES TO CHAPTER SEVEN

THE INDIVIDUAL AND SOCIETY

1. Mizvah 1. The phrase *yishub ha-'olam* means, literally, the inhabitation or settlement of the world and, more broadly, the betterment of the human condition in society.
2. Cf. M. *'Eduyot*, I, 13; M. *Gittin*, IV, 5. The Hinnuk does not indicate whether the commandment presently applies to a non-Jew. Cf. *Minhat Hinnuk*, ibid. On this question see *Sanhedrin* 59b; Tosafot, ibid.; *Yebamot* 62a; *Hagigah* 2b, Maharsha', ibid.; Maimonides, 'Ishut 15:6, *Mishneh Le-Melek*, Melakim 10:7.
3. See Mizvah 190; cf. Mizvah 209; Maimonides, *Moreh Nebukim* III, 49. On the exemption of women from the duty of procreation, see M. *Yebamot* VI, 6; ibid. 65b; Maimonides, 'Ishut 15:2. However, it is not deemed proper for a woman to remain unmarried. See *Shulhan 'Aruk*, 'Eben ha-'Ezer 1:13. On the laws of family purity, see Mizvah 166.
4. Mizvah 188. Cf. Mizvah 552, Mizvah 579. Cf. Maimonides 'Ishut 15:19, 20.
5. Mizvah 579.
6. Mizvah 582.

7. Mizvah 35. Cf. *Sanhedrin* 57b; Maimonides, Melakim 9:7.
8. Mizvah 579.
9. Ibid.
10. Mizvah 248.
11. Cf. *Sifre*, ibid; M. *Sanhedrin* VIII, 5; ibid, 72a.
12. Mizvah 248.
13. Mizvah 419. Scriptural exemption for the mother is deduced from Deut. 11:19, which limits the obligation as stated in Deut. 6:7, "And thou shalt teach them diligently unto thy children" as applying to the male parent. Cf. M. *Kiddushin* I, 7; ibid. 29b.
14. Mizvah 419; cf. Maimonides, Talmud Torah 1:6; 2:2.
15. Mizvah 419; cf. Maimonides, ibid. 1:13; M. *Sotah* III, 4; Tosafot, ibid. 21b; *Berakot* 17a.
16. Mizvah 421; cf. *Erubin* 96a; however, see *Shulhan 'Aruk*, 'Orah Hayyim 38:3. For discussion of the rule applying to women, see Mizvah 251; M. *Kiddushin* I, 7, 8; ibid. 34a, ff. The reason generally advanced for the rule that a woman is exempt from positive precepts for which there is a specific time is that a woman is not free to dispose of her time as she wishes. Cf. *Torah Temimah*, Exod. 13:9, n. 42, who cites Abudraham, Tosafot Rid, Ritba, *Malmed ha-Talmidim* (Parshat Lek Leka) by Jacob Anatoli, and *Kol Bo* (73), among the authoritative sources for this view.
17. Mizvah 188.
18. Mizvah 16.
19. Ma'akalot 'Asurot 17:28.
20. Ibid., 17:27. Cf. Shabbat 12:7, 24:11; *Yebamot* 114a.
21. See Genebah 1:10.
22. Such an opinion is advanced by Isidore Epstein, who believes that Maimonides is led to this view by what he characterizes as the educative aim of the Torah. See Epstein's essay, "The Distinctiveness of Maimonides' Halakhah," in the *Leo Jung Jubilee Volume* (New York, 1962) p. 66f.
23. Cf. Maimonides, 'Ebel 3:12; *Magid Mishneh*, Genebah 1:10.
24. Mizvah 33.
25. See *Berakot* 58a for the saying of Ben Zoma on the interdependence of all men.
26. *Sifra*, ad loc.
27. Mizvah 243.
28. Ibid.
29. 'Ebel 14:1. Cf. *Perush ha-Mishnayot* Pe'ah 1:1.
30. Cf. Maimonides, *Sefer ha-Mizvot*, Mizvat 'Aseh 206; De'ot 6:3.
31. Nahmanides, *Perush ha-Torah*, Lev. 19:18. He notes that Scripture reads *le-re'aka* and not, as would be expected, *'et re'aka;* the latter would have conveyed a more personal relationship.
32. Mizvah 243. Cf. M. H. Luzzatto, *Mesillat Yesharim*, chapt. XI.

33. Mizvah 243.
34. M. Jer. Hagigah 2:1. Cf. Maimonides, De'ot 6:3. The dignity of man is the concern of the Rabbis in such disparate situations, for example, as capital punishment and marriage. In the one case, we are duty-bound to choose the more merciful and dignified form of death for the criminal (*Sotah* 8b, *Sanhedrin* 45a, *Ketubot* 37b); in the other, it is forbidden to contract marriage before viewing the bride, lest he later find her to be ugly and come to hate her (*Kiddushin* 41a; Maimonides, 'Ishut 3:19). In both instances the Rabbis advance the principle of love of fellowman as the rationale for the law.
35. Lev. 19:18.
36. For R. Akiba the creation of man alone in the divine image is indicative of God's love for him. See *Abot* III, 14.
37. Mizvah 42.
38. Mizvot 344, 345, 346.
39. Mizvah 344; cf. Nahmanides, ibid.
40. Mizvah 43. See Exod. 21:7-11; Maimonides, 'Abadim 4:2, 7, 8.
41. Cf. Mizvot 230, 588.
42. M. *Shebuot* VII, 1.
43. *Baba Kamma'* 116b. Cf. Maimonides, Sekirut 9:4.
44. Mizvah 482; cf. *Minhat Hinnuk*, ibid.
45. Mizvah 74.
46. Ibid.; cf. *Makkot* 23a, *Hullin* 44b.
47. Mizvah 337.
48. Mizvah 68. Cf. *Baba Mezia* 75b; Rashi, Exod. 22:24; Maimonides, Mizvat Lo' Ta'aseh, 237.
49. Mizvah 235. See *Sifra'*, Lev. 19:16; M. *Abot* I, 6; *Shebuot* 30a. Cf. Maimonides, Mizvat 'Aseh 177.
50. Deut. 10:18; 24:17, 19, 20, 21; 26:12, 13; 27:19.
51. Mizvah 65, based upon Exod. 22:21. Cf. Maimonides, De'ot 6:10.
52. Mizvah 65.
53. Mizvah 331; Maimonides, De'ot 6:4.
54. Mizvot 216-223.
55. Mizvot 63, 64, 569; cf. Maimonides, Mizvat 'Aseh 207.
56. See Mizvah 431.
57. Mizvah 431.
58. Ibid.
59. Mizvah 431.
60. Cf. Mizvah 239.
61. Mizvah 206.
62. Mizvah 338; see also Mizvah 337. Cf. *Baba Mezia* 85b; *Sifra*, Lev. 25:17; Maimonides, Mizvat 'Aseh 251.
63. Mizvah 338.

64. Mizvah 239.
65. Cf. Nahmanides, ibid.
66. Mizvah 236; cf. Mizvot 74, 553. The Hinnuk includes slander (*lashon ha-ra'*) under the injunction of talebearing; cf. Maimonides, Mizvat Lo' Ta'aseh 301; De'ot 7:1. See *Halakot Gedolot*, Hakdamah, who lists it separately; cf. Radbaz, *Mezudat David, Ta'amei Mizvot*, Mizvah 135. Both the Hinnuk and Maimonides believe that it is also included in the injunction not to utter a false report (Exod. 23:1). See *Ketubot* 46b and *Makkot* 23a for talmudic support in both instances.
67. 'Arakin 15b.
68. Mizvah 236. Cf. Maimonides, Hobel U-Mazik 8:10.
69. See Ibid. 8:11; cf. D. Kaufmann, "Jewish Informers in the Middle Ages," In *J. Q. R.* VIII, 1896 (Ktav Publishing House, 1966), including responsa by Rashba and R. Meir of Rothenberg.
70. Mizvah 338.
71. Mizvah 527 based on Deut. 20:10. See Rashi and Nahmanides, ad loc. Cf. D. S. Shapiro, "The Jewish Attitude Towards Peace and War," in *Israel of Tomorrow*, ed. Leo Jung (N. Y. 1946) p. 238-9.
72. Cf. *Sifre*, Deut. 20:1; 21:10; Maimonides, Melakim 5:1.
73. Mizvot 425, 527, 603; Maimonides, ibid.
74. Mizvah 527. Cf. Maimonides, Mizvat 'Aseh 190; Melakim 6:1, 4, 7; cf. commentary of *Lehem Mishneh*, Melakim 6:1.
74a. Mizvah 525; additional scriptural sources cited are Deut. 3:22; 7:21.
75. Mizvah 262; cf. Maimonides, Mizvat Lo' Ta'aseh 30.
76. Ibid. Cf. Mizvah 188.
77. Mizvah 427.
78. Mizvah 111.
79. Mizvah 262.
80. Cf. Rashi and Ibn Ezra ad loc.
81. For a concise definition of the *ger toshab* see G. F. Moore, *Judaism* (Cambridge 1932), I, p. 339ff.
82. Mizvah 347. Cf. *'Abodah Zarah* 64b; Maimonides, 'Issurei Bi'ah 14:7.
83. Mizvah 14; cf. *Keritot* 9a.
84. Cf. Maimonides, Melakim 8:10; 'Abodah Zarah 10:6; Ma'kalot 'Asurot 11:7.
85. See Tosefta' *'Abodah Zarah* IX, 4; *Sanhedrin* 56a; *Hagigah* 11b; *Midrash, Genesis Rabbah* 16:9, 24:5; Maimonides, Melakim 9:1; Nahmanides, *Perush ha-Torah*, Gen. 34:13. Additional prohibitions, such as eating blood of a living animal, mating animals of different species, castration, sorcery and grafting trees of different kinds, are listed by some of the Sages. See *Sanhedrin* 56b.
86. Mizvah 417.
87. Mizvah 416.

88. Ibid. This is already noted in the Talmud. See Tosefta *'Abodah Zarah* IX, 4 and in *Sanhedrin* 57b. The Rabbis, furthermore, distinguish between the basic "seven Noahian commandments which were commanded them and for which they may incur punishment," and thirty other commandments which "they took upon themselves." See *Hullin* 92a; *Sanhedrin* 57a.

89. Among prohibited sexual perversions the Hinnuk includes homosexuality and unnatural acts with an animal. See Mizvah 209; cf. Maimonides, Issurei Bi'ah 14:18. Forbidden relations include a married woman, his mother, his father's wife and his sister from the same mother. See Mizvot 35, 212, 416.

90. For the Hinnuk's discussion of the legal distinctions, see Mizvot 26, 35, 190, 191, 192, 416, 452; cf. Tosefta *'Abodah Zarah* IX, 4; *Sanhedrin* 57b; Maimonides, Melakim, chapters 9-10.

91. See *Yoma* 67b, and *Sanhedrin* 56b.

92. Melakim 8:11. The Hebrew rendition of the last sentence in this passage in the Vilna and Rome editions of the Mishneh Torah concludes with the words "*nor* of their wise men." אבל אם עשאן מפני הכרע הדעת אין

זה גר תושב ואינו מחסידי אומות העולם ולא מחכמיהם.

The Venice edition, however, reads אלא מחכמיהם, "but he is of their wise men." The latter reading is obviously the more likely one. See *Tosafot Yom Tob* on M. *Abot* III, 14, who quotes this passage and, apparently on simply logical grounds, emends the reading to אלא מחכמיהם. Cf. also I, Epstein, *The Faith of Judaism*, (London, 1960) p. 43, n. 20, who cites the *Responsa* of Rabbi Moses Alashkar (R.17), and the *Mishnat Rabbi Eliezer* (ed. Enelow, p. 121) in support of the latter reading.

93. Cf. E. Berkovits, *God, Man and History* (N. Y. 1965) p. 183, n. 4.

94. In order for the Noahian commandments to be binding upon mankind, they had again to be divinely ordained on Sinai. See *Sanhedrin* 59a, where the following principle is enunciated with regard to these and other laws ordained in the Torah before the revelation at Sinai: "Every law that was enjoined upon the children of Noah and was repeated at Sinai is meant to apply to both (Israelites and non-Israelites). If it was enjoined upon the children of Noah and it was not repeated at Sinai it is meant to apply only to Israelites and not to the children of Noah (non-Israelites)." For the significance of the fact that these laws were encompassed again under the divine command at Sinai see Maimonides' *Perush ha-Mishnayot*, Hullin 7:6.

95. Cf. Tosefta, *Sanhedrin* XIII, 2; *Sanhedrin* 105a; and Rashi, ad loc; Maimonides, *Perush ha-Mishnayot, Sanhedrin* X, 2; Teshubah, 3:5; Melakim 8:11. The Talmud further asserts that a gentile who occupies himself with the Law is the equal of Israel's high priest. See *Sanhedrin* 59a, where this general statement of R. Meir is taken to refer to the Noahian laws.

R. Meir bases his view on the verse, "Ye shall therefore keep My statutes and Mine ordinances, which if a man do, he shall live by them" (Lev. 18:5); Scripture does not state priests, levites or Israelites, but any man. Cf. *Sifra*, ibid; *'Abodah Zarah* 3a; *Baba' Kamma'* 38a.

96. Mizvot 93, 94. Cf. Maimonides, 'Abodah Zarah, chapter X.

97. Cf. *'Abodah Zarah* 20a; Maimonides, op. cit. 10:4; *Sefer ha-Mizvot*, Mizvat Lo' Ta'aseh 51. For a discussion of the prohibition as applicable to all aliens, see commentaries *Minhat Hinnuk* and *Mishneh le-Melek* on the *Sefer ha-Hinnuk*, ibid., and J. Ruzanis, *Derek Mizvoteka*, Part II, p. 67.

98. See Maimonides, op. cit. 10:6; cf. Rabad, ibid.

99. See Mizvah 94. Cf. *'Abodah Zarah* 64b; *Pesahim* 21b; *Sifra*, Lev. 25:35. Ibn Ezra stipulates additional requisites for the *ger toshab* which include abstaining from work on the Sabbath and on Yom Kippur, and refraining from prohibited sexual relations and from eating blood. See *Perush ha-Torah* Exod. 20:8; cf. ibid. 22:20; *Keritot* 9a; Jer. *Yebamot* 8:1. See note 139 regarding observance of the Sabbath.

100. See Maimonides, Melakim 10:12. The institution of *ger toshab* was legally existent in the Holy Land, under conditions of Jewish independence and statehood, when the Jubilee was in force. See *'Arakin* 29a; Maimonides, Shemitah ve-Yobel 10:9; 'Abodah Zarah 10:6; Issurei Bi'ah 14:8.

101. M. *Baba' Mezia* IX, 12; Ibid. 111b; see Mizvah 230; The Hinnuk notes that Maimonides includes every gentile as being entitled to this right as well. Cf. Mizvat 'Aseh 200; but see also Sekirut 11:1.

102. Cf. Maimonides, Melakim 10:11, 12. The resident alien was judged in accordance with his own laws, a preferred status afforded him above that of the heathen.

103. Mizvah 216; cf. Maimonides, Matnot 'Aniyim 1:9.

104. M. *Gittin* V, 8; see Mizvah 216.

105. *Gittin* 61a.

106. Melakim 10:12. Cf. 'Abodah Zarah 10:5; 'Abadim 9:8.

107. Cf. *Pesakim* 21a; *Hullin* 114b; *'Abodah Zarah* 20a.

108. Cf. the controversy, cited in the Mishnah, *Yadaim* IV, 7, between the Sadducees and the Pharisees on the master's responsibility for injuries inflicted by his slave, which reflected the opposing Jewish and non-Jewish attitudes toward slavery. Cf. S. Belkin, *Philo and the Oral Law* (Cambridge, 1940) p. 91f.

109. See Mizvah 344.

110. See Mizvot 42, 347.

111. Mizvot 50, 347. Cf. Exod. 21:20; *Mekilta* and Rashi ad loc. Maimonides, 'Abadim 9:8.

112. Mizvah 347. Cf. Ibn Ezra, *Perush ha-Torah*, Lev. 25:46; *Sotah* 3a.

113. Mizvah 211.
114. Mizvah 347; cf. *Yebamot* 48b; Maimonides, Milah 1:6.
115. Mizvah 347; M. *Gittin* IV, 6. Cf. Mizvot 568, 569.
116. Ibid. Cf. *Gittin* 40a.
117. Cf. M. *Abot* II, 7; *Kiddushin* 20a.
118. Mizvah 229. Cf. *Sifre*, Deut. 23:16, 17; *Hullin* 94a; Maimonides, Genebah 1:1; 7:8; *Mekirah* 18:1, 3; *Gezelah ve-'Abedah* 1:2; *De'ot* 2:6; R. Moses of Coucy, *Sefer Mizvot Gadol*, Mizvot Lo' Ta'aseh 155, 170; *Shulhan 'Aruk*, Hoshen Mishpat 228:6.
119. See statement of Rabbi Akiba, *Baba' Kamma'* 113a; cf. Maimonides, *Gezelah ve-'Abedah* 11:3-5. For the example of Simeon ben Shatah, cited by the Sages, see Jer. *Baba' Mezia* 2:5; *Deut. Rabbah* 3:5.
120. M. *Baba' Mezia* V, 6; Ibid. 71a.
121. Mizvah 573.
122. *Sefer Ha-Mizvot,* Mizvat 'Aseh 198; Malveh ve-Loveh 5:1.
123. The Hinnuk is thus inclined because he tends towards Nahmanides' construction of the mizvah. See *Hassagot, Sefer Ha-Mizvot*, Shoresh VI; cf. *Hassagot Ha-Rabad*, Malveh ve-Loveh 5:1. The differing views of Maimonides and Nahmanides turn on an understanding of the *Sifre*, Deut. 23:21; see also Rashi, ibid.
124. Cf. Maimonides, *Perush Ha-Mishnayot, Baba' Kamma'* IV, 3. Cf. *Makkot* 24a.
125. *Baba' Kamma'* 113a; cf. Maimonides, Melakim, 10:12.
126. M. *Baba' Kamma'* IV, 3; cf. ibid. 38a.
127. Nizkei Mamon 8:5; Cf. Rabad, ad loc. who differs with Maimonides, and *Migdal 'Oz* who cites the Jerusalem Talmud, *Baba' Kamma'* 4:3 in support of Maimonides.
128. Cf. Maimonides, *Perush ha-Mishnayot, Baba' Kamma'* IV:3.
129. See Tosafot, *'Abodah Zarah* 2a, and also 57b, citing the Tosafists in the name of Rashi, who quotes the Gaonic Responsa; cf. *Shulhan 'Aruk*, Yoreh De'ah 148:12.
130. *Shitah Mekubezet, Baba' Kamma'* 38a, 113a; quoting the Me'iri. See Me'iri, *Baba' Kamma'* 37b. See also *Tiferet Yisra'el*, Commentary on M. *'Abodah Zarah* I, 1. Cf. Rabbi B. H. Epstein, *Torah Temimah*, Lev. 25:14, n. 83; Rabbi J. E. Henkin, *Hadarom*, Vol. X, 5719, p. 8.
131. Mizvot 35, 416, 211.
132. Cf. Nahmanides, *Perush ha-Torah*, Deut. 23:18, basing himself upon a statement in the *Sifre*, ad loc.
133. Mizvah 209. However, see Ibn Ezra, *Perush Ha-Torah*, Lev. 20:1.
134. Cf. Rashi and Nahmanides, ad loc.
135. See Mizvah 35, where the Hinnuk notes the difference between Jew and non-Jew with regard to the concept of marriage. Cf. *Sanhedrin* 57b; Maimonides, Melakim 9:7. See also Mizvah 566 on the conduct of Jewish soldiers in military camp in view of Israel's distinctive spiritual status.

136. M. *Abot* III, 14.

137. See commentaries of *Tosafot Yom Tob* and *Tiferet Yisra'el,* ad loc.
Tosafot Yom Tob draws attention to the fact that Rabbi Akiba chose as
proof-text for his assertion that all men are beloved of God, not any of
the verses that occur previously in Scripture, but the verse, "For in the
image of God made He man" (Gen. 9:6), which appears significantly in
connection with the laws given by God to Noah and his descendants.

138. See Mizvah 14. Cf. Deut. 14:21. "Ye shall not eat of anything that dieth
of itself; thou mayest give it unto the stranger that is within thy gates,
that he may eat of it; or thou mayest sell it unto a foreigner; for thou art
a holy people unto the Lord thy God." Reference is to the *ger toshab*
and the non-resident gentile, both of whom are not forbidden to eat
nebelah, the flesh of animals not properly slaughtered according to Jewish
law. See *Sifre* and Rashi, ad loc.

139. Cf. *Sanhedrin* 58b; Maimonides, Melakim 10:9. An exception is the
ger toshab for whom the Sabbath is to be a day of rest as well. See Deut.
5:14; Exod. 20:10. Cf. Nahmanides ad loc.; Rashi, Exod. 23:12. Cf.
Mekilta', Exod. 20:10; 23:12; *Yebamot* 48b, Rashi and Tosafot, ad loc.

140. Cf. *Sanhedrin* 59a; Maimonides, ibid., cf. also *'Abodah Zarah* 3a, *Hagigah*
13a; Tosafot, ibid; and particularly commentaries of Maharsha' and
Me'iri ad loc.

141. Cf. Maimonides, ibid; see especially the commentary of Radbaz, ad loc.

142. See Mizvah 416.

NOTES TO CHAPTER EIGHT

MAN'S SPIRITUAL DIMENSION

1. Cf. M. *Yoma* VIII, 9. Jer., *Shekalim* III, 2. Cf. Maimonides, *Moreh
Nebukim,* Part III, end of chapter 35. Maimonides indicates the nature
of his fourteen classes of commandments according to this division and
notes that commandments between man and God may affect relations
between man and his fellowman. In his *Commentary* on M. *Pe'ah* 1:1,
Maimonides notes that while both classes of commandments are rewarded
in the world to come, the latter also benefit man in this world by establishing better human relations.

2. See Nahmanides, *Perush ha-Torah,* Exod. 20:12, 13: "Five are in honor
of God, and five are for the benefit of man."

3. See *Kiddushin* 30b.

4. Mizvah 33. Saadiah, in an interesting parallel, posits the relationship of
man and God on the basis of a grateful recognition by man of his creation as a divine "act of bounty and grace." See *'Emunot ve-De'ot,* III,
Exordium.

5. Mizvah 432.
6. Mizvah 418.
7. Ibid., and Mizvah 331; cf. Mizvah 95. See Maimonides *Sefer ha-Mizvot*, Mizvat 'Aseh 3; Yesodei ha-Torah 2:1; Teshubah 10:2-4. Cf. *Sotah* 31a; Rashi ad loc; *Sifre*, Deut. 6:5.
8. Mizvah 95.
9. Ibid. Cf. M. *Abot* I, 3. See *'Abodah Zarah* 19a. In commenting on the verse, "Happy is the man that feareth the Lord, that delighteth greatly in His commandments" (Ps. 112:1), R. Eliezer emphasizes, "in His commandments, and not in the reward for His commandments." Cf. *Sotah* 22b for the distinction that the Talmud draws between "the Pharisee from fear" and "the Pharisee from love"; see Rashi and Tosafot, ibid. The religious motive thus extolled is often described by the Rabbis as doing the mizvah "for its own sake," (*lishmah*) or "for the sake of heaven" (*le-shem shamaim*); cf. M. *Abot* II, 12; *Sifre*, Deut. 32:2.
10. See M. *Abot* III, 7; *Berakot* 35a; *Sanhedrin* 39a; *Sifra*, Lev. 25:23. See *Mishneh Torah*, Rozeah 1:4, wherein Maimonides records the law that the Court may not accept ransom for the life of a murderer (Num. 35:31), asserting that the reason for it is that, in the final account, human life is "the possession (*kinyan*) of God." Cf. also S. Belkin, *In His Image* (Abelard-Schuman, 1960) p. 32f.
11. Mizvah 18. Cf. Tur, *Yoreh De'ah* 247. A man is to regard his wealth as "a trust fund to be used in accordance with the will of the depositor, and His will is that he should distribute a portion of it to the poor."
12. Mizvah 330; cf. Mizvah 357.
13. *Berakot* 35a. The Talmud adds, "Whoever benefits from this world without a blessing has committed a sacrilege." Cf. Maimonides, Berakot 1:2.
14. Mizvah 430.
15. Ibid.
16. *Yebamot* 64a.
17. Mizvah 430.
18. Mizvah 25.
19. Mizvah 417.
20. Mizvah 26.
21. See *Sifre*, Deut. 15:22; cf. *Mekilta*, Exod. 12:6.
22. See Mizvot 249, 255.
23. See Mizvah 510.
24. Mizvot 5-23.
25. Mizvah 21. Cf. Mizvah 603. This view is also held by Nahmanides; see op. cit., Exod. 20:2.
26. *Moreh Nebukim* III, 39.
27. Mizvah 31.
28. Mizvah 24.

29. Mizvah 32. Cf. Maimonides, *Moreh Nebukim* II, 31; III, 32, 41, 43. Cf. Nahmanides, op. cit., Exod. 20:8; 34:21. However, note the opinion of Nahmanides in his commentary to Deut. 5:15.
30. Mizvah 298.
31. See Exod. 23:11, "that the poor of thy people may eat."
32. See Mizvot 84, 477. Maimonides views *Shemitah* as a means of improving the land and increasing its yield; see *Moreh Nebukim* III, 39.
33. Mizvah 84.
34. Ibid.
35. Ibid. cf. Lev. 25:20, 21; see also Mizvah 477.
36. See Rashi ad loc.
37. Cf. Nahmanides, op. cit., Lev. 25:2. See Mizvah 330, where the Hinnuk also refers to a tradition regarding mystical allusions in the years of *Shemitah* and the Jubilee; cf. Ibn Ezra, ibid.
38. See M. *Sotah* VII, 8.
39. Mizvah 612.
40. Mizvah 612. See also Mizvah 489, where the Hinnuk gives an additional reason. At the end of the *Shemitah* year, when all manner of lordship had been abrogated, *Hakhel* was to demonstrate that all the people, even the women and children, who were then free of subservience to other masters, had assembled before God to acknowledge His sovereignty and to proclaim their fealty to Him.
41. Cf. Exod. 34:27, "For on the condition of these words have I made a covenant with thee and with Israel."
42. Cf. Deut. 12:1.
43. See *Kohelet Rabbah* 1:2; *Sefer Yera'im* 289; *Semag* 230.
44. Reference to what may have been one of the last assemblies of *Hakhel* in the Second Jewish Commonwealth is to be found in the account of the Mishnah, *Sotah* VII, 8, of the reading by King Agrippa in the year 41 C.E. Cf. M. L. Margolis and A. Marx, *A History of the Jewish People*, (Phila. 1938) p. 189. Josephus records the assembly of *Hakhel* in his *Antiquities of the Jews*, Book IV, chapt. 8. Contrary to the Mishnah, which speaks of the reading by the King, he states that it was done by the High Priest, probably reflecting the circumstances of his own day.
45. Hagigah 3:6.
45a. Cf. *Gittin* 36a; Tosafot *'Arakhin* 32b; Maimonides, Shemitah ve-Yobel 4:25; *Kesef Mishneh*, ad loc. For a discussion of *Hakhel* as a historical institution in Jewish life and the considerations for its revival, see "A Revival of the Ancient Assembly of Hakhel" by this writer in *Tradition*, (Fall 1959) Vol. II, 1. Cf. "Zeker le-Mikdash," in *Hakhel*, ed. by B. Rabinowitz-Teumim, (Jerusalem 1945); S. K. Mirsky, *Hakhel*, a monograph pub. by Talpiot (Yeshiva University, New York, 1952).
46. Mizvah 324.

47. Mizvah 422.
48. Ibid.
49. Mizvah 423. Cf. Nahmanides, op. cit., Exod. 13:16.
50. Mizvah 386, citing Num. 15:39. See Rashi, *Menahot* 43b, who points out that the word *zizit* has the numerical value of 600. Taken together with the 8 threads and the 5 knots required on the *zizit* the total is 613, denoting the *Taryag Mizvot*. Cf. Rashi, Num. 15:39.
51. Ibid.
52. *Menahot* 43b; *Midrash Tanhuma*, Parashat Shelah, Perek 15.
53. The sources cited by the Hinnuk in order to establish this mystical sequence are: Exod. 24:10; Ezekiel 1:26; *Pirkei de-Rabbi Eliezer* III; *Niddah* 25b; *Menahot* 39a, 43b.
54. Mizvah 325; see *Sukkah* 11b.
55. Mizvah 324.
56. Ibid. cf. *Sukkah* 37b.
57. Cf. Nahmanides, op. cit., Lev. 23:40. See Midrash, *Leviticus Rabbah* 30:14 for another symbolical meaning ascribed to the cluster of the four species, also cited by the Hinnuk.
58. Cf. Mizvot 5-17, 19-21, 89, 90, 297-301, 487.
59. Mizvah 324.

NOTES TO CHAPTER NINE

THE SERVICE OF GOD

1. Mizvah 95.
2. Ibid.
3. Ibid.
4. Ibid. Cf. M. *Zebahim* XIV, 8; Maimonides, Beit ha-Behirah 1:3.
5. In accord with rabbinic tradition, the Hinnuk speaks of the *Beit ha-Mikdash* as being "at the very center of the world" (Mizvah 95). Cf. *Midrash Tanhuma*, Parashat Kedoshim 10, "The Land of Israel is in the center of the world, Jerusalem in the center of the Land of Israel, and the *Beit ha-Mikdash* in the center of Jerusalem." Cf. Judah Halevi, *Kuzari* II, 20. However, cf. *Genesis Rabbah* 39:24; Rashi, *Perush ha-Torah*, Gen. 12:9.
6. Cf. M. *Kelim* I, 6, 8. See Mizvot 568, 569.
7. Mizvot 247, 360, 473.
8. Mizvah 360.
9. See Mizvah 254.
10. Mizvah 98. Cf. Maimonides, *Moreh Nebukim* III, 45.
11. Mizvah 103; cf. Mizvot 110, 108.

12. Mizvah 99.

13. Mizvah 388. Maimonides adds that the guards also served to prevent those who were unclean, or otherwise unauthorized, from entering the Sanctuary. See *Moreh Nebukim* III, 45. Cf. M. *Middot* I, 2.

14. *Sifra'*, Lev. 19:30. Cf. Maimonides, Beit ha-Behirah, 6:16.

15. Mizvah 95. Cf. Mizvah 254.

16. M. *Megillah* III, 3.

17. *Sifra*, Lev. 19:30.

18. Mizvah 565; see Maimonides, *Sefer ha-Mizvot*, Mizvat Lo' Ta'aseh 78; cf. *Perush ha-Mishnayot*, Kelim I, 8. The Hinnuk notes the ascending degrees of sanctity of the camp of the Levites and the camp of the *Shekinah*. See *Pesahim* 68a, based on Deut. 23:11; cf. Rashi, Num. 5:2 for the three camps designated about the Sanctuary, the two aforementioned and the camp of the Israelites.

19. Cf. Mizvot 184, 362, 363. On the differences of opinion regarding the present status of the prohibition, and the eternal sanctity of the Temple area, see Maimonides, Beit ha-Behirah 6:16 and *Hassagot ha-Rabad* ad loc. Cf. Tosafot, *Yebamot* 82b; *Semag*, Mizvat 'Aseh 163. For a full discussion of this question, see Rabbi A. I. Kook, *Mishpat Kohen*, Jerusalem, 1937, Responsum 96.

20. Ibid. See A. I. Kook, op. cit., who understands Maimonides to mean that, since this was once the abode of the *Shekinah*, its glory and holiness are never removed. In support of this view he cites the statement in the Talmud, *Yoma* 21b, that the *Shekinah* no longer dwelt in the Second Temple. In his opinion, moreover, Rabad does not question the ruling that the prohibition is binding at this time. He only contends that it is not subject to the penalty of extirpation (*karet*). Cf. Kuzari II, 23; III, 1, 11; V, 22, 23. Halevi distinguishes between the visible and the invisible *Shekinah*, the latter still abiding with Israel, especially in the Holy Land.

21. Mizvah 119. On the Hinnuk's rationale for the sacrifices, see Mizvah 95; cf. Mizvot 116, 117, 124, 144.

22. Mizvah 95.

23. *Moreh Nebukim* III, 32. Cf. Ibid., 46. For midrashic support of Maimonides' view, see *Leviticus Rabbah* 22:5, based on Lev. 17:1-7. Cf. *Mekilta*, Exod. 12:21; see *Torah Temimah*, ibid., n. 188.

24. See *Moreh Nebukim*, ibid. "I know that you will at first thought reject this idea and find it strange. You will put the following question to me in your heart: How can we suppose that divine commandments, prohibitions and important acts, which are precisely set forth and for which certain seasons are fixed, should not have been commanded for their own sake?" However, see Maimonides' statement at the end of chapter 36, where he evidently suggests a positive role for sacrifices, to facilitate repentance. See also Meilah 8:8.

A PHILOSOPHY OF MIZVOT

25. *Perush ha-Torah*, Lev. 1:9.
26. For a reconciliation of the opposing views of Maimonides and Nahmanides, see R. Meir Simha Cohen of Dvinsk, *Sefer Meshek Hokmah*, at the beginning of his commentary on Leviticus, citing the commentary of Ralbag to Kings.
27. Op. cit., Lev. 1:9.
28. Mizvah 95. In support of his thesis he cites the Mishnah, *Sotah* II, 1, which suggests the following reason for the fact that the offering brought for a suspected adulteress consisted of coarse barley meal: "Just as her deed was the deed of cattle, her offering is the food of cattle." Several other statements by the Sages reflect a similar attitude. See *Sotah* 3a, "No man sins unless the spirit of insanity has entered into him." Cf. *Niddah* 31b, *'Arakin* 16b, *Leviticus Rabbah* 16.
29. Mizvah 132; cf. Maimonides, Yesodei ha-Torah 3:10, 4:2; *Kuzari* II, 26.
30. Ibid. cf. Maimonides, *Moreh Nebukim* II, 29; *Perush ha-Mishnayot*, *Abot* V, 6; *Shemonah Perakim* VIII. Maimonides ascribes this view to the Rabbis. Cf. *Genesis Rabbah* 5; *'Abodah Zarah* 54b, "The world follows its regular course."
31. Mizvah 401. Cf. Mizvah 105.
32. Mizvot 389, 394, 509. Cf. *Ta'anit* 27a; Maimonides, Kelei ha-Mikdash 4:3.
33. Mizvot 151, 152, 184, 263, 265, 275, 277, 278.
34. Mizvot 280, 378, 396. Cf. *Baba Kamma* 110a for the twenty-four priestly dues.
35. Mizvot 107, 136, 266, 270, 272.
36. Mizvah 394. See Deut. 18:7; *'Arakin* 11a.
37. Mizvah 450. See Deut. 33:10.
38. Mizvot 395, 408, 504. See Num. 18:24; 35:2-8; Deut. 14:29; 18:1, 2; Maimonides, *Moreh Nebukim* III, 39.
39. Mizvah 505, See Deut. 18:1; *Sifre*, ibid.
40. Mizvah 509. See M. *Ta'anit* IV, 1-3; Maimonides, Kelei ha-Mikdash 6:1-7.
41. The Talmud also refers to certain prayers recited by the priests. Cf. M. *Tamid* V, 1; *Berakot* 11b.
42. Mizvot 88, 95.
43. Mizvah 95. It is Maimonides' expressed opinion, quite evidently in line with his general view of sacrifices, that "supplications, prayers and similar modes of worship," rather than sacrifices, are the primary object of the Temple service. See *Moreh Nebukim* III, 32.
44. M. *Tamid* IV, 3; V, 1; cf. *Yoma* VII, 1. See Rashi, *Yoma* 68b, who states, "A synagogue was adjacent to the Temple Court."
45. M. *Ta'anit* IV, 1-3; see Maimonides, *Perush ha-Mishnayot*, ad loc.

46. Cf. M. *Bikkurim* III, 6; I Sam. 1:12; I Kings 8:15-54; Isaiah 56:7.
47. Mizvah 433.
48. On this point the Hinnuk quotes Maimonides; see Mizvat 'Aseh 5. The Sages specifically cite study of the law as having been implied by the injunction, "to serve him." See *Sifre*, Deut. 11:13. Even the normal activities of life, when motivated by higher purpose, can be utilized as means to serve God. See De'ot. 3:3; cf. M. *Abot* II, 12.
49. *Sifre*, Deut. 11:13; *Ta'anit* 2a.
50. Cf. *Sifre*, Deut. 3:24. See *Rosh Hashanah* 17b for the tradition that God taught Moses how to pray. "God wrapped Himself in a *tallit* and taught Moses the order of the prayers."
51. Mizvah 433.
52. Ibid.
53. *Berakot* 31a; cf. *Sanhedrin* 22a; M. *Abot* II, 13.
54. Mizvah 433. See M. *Berakot* II, 1; 30b, 31a. Cf. Maimonides, Keriat Shema' 2:1, Tefillah 4:15, 16.
55. *Berakot* 6a.
56. Mizvah 433. The Sages derive this from the verse, "But as for me, I direct my prayer unto Thee, O Lord, in a time of favor" (Psalms 69:14), which they expound as follows: "When is it a time of favor? In the time that the congregation is in worship." See *Berakot* 8a; cf. ibid., 21b. Cf. also Maimonides, Tefillah 8:1; *Kuzari* III, 19.
57. Mizvah 433.
58. Tefillah 1:1. "To pray daily is an affirmative duty, as it is said, 'And ye shall serve the Lord your God' " (Exod. 23:25).
59. *Hassagot Ramban, Sefer ha-Mizvot*, Mizvat 'Aseh 5.
60. Maimonides and the Hinnuk likewise consider it a duty to offer up supplications and to sound trumpets over every calamity that befalls the community, As Maimonides points out, this mizvah is of the essence of repentance, in that it is prayer invoked in the realization that misfortune has befallen them because of their iniquities. See Ta'aniot 1:1, 2. Cf. Mizvat 'Aseh 59; *Moreh Nebukim* III, 36. See Mizvah 384.
61. See Jer. *Berakot* IV, 1, for prayer at the three changing intervals of the day. Cf. Mizvah 606, "Prayer and supplications before God, blessed be He, must be recited with great care."
62. Mizvah 433. Cf. Maimonides, Tefillah 1:4; *Berakot* 33a; *Megillah* 17b. A nineteenth benediction against heretics was subsequently added to the *Shemoneh Esreh* under the authorization of Rabban Gamliel and his *Beit Din* at Jabneh; see *Berakot* 28b. For an analysis of the structure of the Eighteen Benedictions, see *Megillah* 17b, 18a.
63. Mizvah 433; see Maimonides, Tefillah 1:5-8. The Talmud, *Berakot* 26b, cites an opinion that the three daily prayers were instituted by the patriarchs Abraham, Isaac and Jacob.

64. Mizvah 262.
65. *Berakot* 63a.
66. M. *Abot* II, 12. See Maimonides' interpretation of this statement, as well as the verse in Proverbs, in *Shemonah Perakim* V; De'ot 3:3.
67. Hakdamah. He reiterates this in his exposition of these commandments. See Mizvot 25, 26, 417, 418, 432, 387. Cf. *Hayye 'Adam*, Hilkot Berakot u-Tefillot 1:5; *Mishnah Berurah*, Bi'ur Halakah, 'Orah Hayyim I, 1.
68. A parallel listing of "mizvot of the heart," for which a man stands under continuous obligation in respect of his duty to serve God, was already made by Bahya Ibn Pakuda. In the Introduction to his ethical treatise, *Hobot ha-Lebabot*, Bahya writes: "I found that this class of duties is in force continuously throughout our lives without intermission, and that we have no excuse for neglecting them. This applies to such duties as: To confess the unity of God with all our heart; To render Him service inwardly; To revere Him; To love Him; To yearn to fulfill the precepts obligatory upon us, as Scripture declares, 'O that my ways were directed to observe Thy statutes' (Ps. 119:5); To trust in Him and surrender ourselves to Him, as it is said, 'Trust in Him at all times, ye people; pour out your heart before Him' (Ps. 62:9); To remove hatred and jealousy from our hearts; To abstain from the superfluities of this world which disturb and hinder us in the service of God. For all these are obligatory at all seasons, in all places, every hour, every moment, and under all circumstances, as long as we have life and reason."
69. Mizvah 387. See *Berakot* 12b; Maimonides, Mizvat Lo' Ta'aseh 47; Abodah Zarah 2:3.
70. Cf. *Sifra*, Lev. 18:3; *Sifre*, Deut. 12:30.
71. Mizvah 262; cf. Maimonides, Mizvat Lo' Ta'aseh 30.
72. Mizvah 489. The Hinnuk believes the fostering of this awareness to have been the intent of the commandment to appear before the Lord in the Sanctuary in Jerusalem on the three pilgrimage Festivals.
73. Mizvah 418.
74. Cf. *Sifre*, ibid. Cf. *Pirkei Abot*, Kinyan Torah VI, 1.
75. Hakdamah. Cf. Maimonides, *Moreh Nebukim* III, 36.
76. Mizvah 419. Cf. Maimonides, Mizvat 'Aseh 11; Talmud Torah 1:1. While the obligation to impart instruction in the Law is primarily that of the father, since the injunction reads, "And thou shalt teach them diligently unto thy children" (Deut. 6:7), the duty nevertheless devolves upon others as well inasmuch as a man's disciples are also called his children. Cf. *Sifre*, ibid. See also Maimonides, ibid., 1:2, "A duty rests on every scholar in Israel to teach all disciples who seek instruction from him."
77. Ibid. Cf. Maimonides, op. cit., 1:8, 10.
78. Cf. Maimonides, Teshubah 9:1, 2.

79. Mizvah 376.
80. Mizvot 374, 376. See Chapter VI for further discussion of the Hinnuk's view of the Nazirite.
81. See *Shemonah Perakim* IV. Cf. De'ot 3:1. For Bahya's views on abstinence see *Hobot ha-Lebabot* IX, 3. The Torah way, Bahya maintains, is to be active in the world, to provide for human needs and to benefit mankind, while being separate from the world inwardly.
82. See *Nedarim* 10a, *Nazir* 19a. The Sages conclude, "If one who has only denied himself the enjoyment of wine is called a sinner, how much more one who deprives himself of everything."
83. Jer. *Nedarim* IX, 1.
84. Mizvah 488.
85. Ibid. Cf. Mizvah 262.
86. Mizvah 529.
87. Mizvah 418.
88. *Sifre*, ibid. Cf. Maimonides, Teshubah 10:2.
89. Mizvah 88.

NOTES TO CHAPTER TEN

THE DIVINE IMPERATIVE

1. Mizvah 87. For the Hinnuk's view of retribution as a principle of belief, see chapter IV.
2. M. *Sotah* I, 7. See ibid. 8b for the discussion in the Talmud on the continuation of judgments similar to the four modes of execution through divine intervention, even though actual execution by a temporal court had been suspended when the Sanhedrin ceased to function.
3. Mizvah 171; cf. Mizvah 173.
4. See *Sifre*, Deut. 24:9; cf. Rashi and Ibn Ezra, ibid. Nahmanides, ibid., understands this scriptural verse as a prohibition against slander, to be included among the *Taryag Mizvot*. He does not, however, list it as a separate mizvah in his *Hassagot*. The Hinnuk includes it under the prohibition against talebearing. See Mizvah 243; cf. Maimonides, *Sefer ha-Mizvot*, Mizvat Lo' Ta'aseh 301. In a word-play the Talmud equates *mezora'*, a leper, with *mozi' shem ra'*, a slanderer. See *Arakin* 15b.
5. Mizvah 171.
6. Ibid.
7. This statement is made apropos of the destruction visited upon the inhabitants of the city of Sodom. See *Genesis Rabbah* 51:5.
8. Mizvah 171.
9. Cf. Jer. *Hagigah* II, 1.

10. Cf. *Hagigah* 5a. See *Sotah* 3b, "Before Israel sinned the *Shekinah* abode with each individual, as it is said, 'For the Lord, thy God, walketh in the midst of thy camp.' When they sinned, the *Shekinah* departed from them, as it is said, 'That He see no unseemly thing in thee and turn away from thee' " (Deut. 23:15).

11. Mizvah 171.

12. *Moreh Nebukim* III, 51.

13. Mizvah 546. Cf. Mizvah 62.

14. Ibid.

15. See *Shabbat* 32a.

16. Mizvah 169. Cf. Maimonides, *Moreh Nebukim* III, 36; Ta'aniot 1:1-3, 9.

17. Mizvah 30. It is noteworthy that the Rabbis in the Talmud, taking the *shem ha-meforash*, the ineffable name of God, as denoting God's attribute of mercy, view Scripture's repetition of the Tetragrammaton among the thirteen divine attributes (Exod. 34:6) as signifying that God is merciful to man before he sins and that He likewise extends His mercy to him after he sins if he has repented. See *Rosh Hashanah* 17b; Rashi and Tosafot ad loc.

18. Mizvah 594.

19. Mizvah 364.

20. See *Sefer ha-Mizvot*, Mizvat 'Aseh 73; Teshubah 1:1. Cf. Nahmanides, *Perush ha-Torah*, Deut. 30:11.

21. Mizvah 364. See Maimonides, Teshubah 2:2.

22. See Mizvah 75. Cf. *Sanhedrin* 25a, *Yoma* 86b, *Kiddushin* 39b; Maimonides, Teshubah 2:1; 'Edut 12:9.

23. M. *Yoma* VIII, 9.

24. Mizvah 364. See Maimonides, Teshubah 2:9.

25. See Rashi, Exod. 31:18, 33:11.

26. Cf. Maimonides' reference to Rosh Hashanah as "a preparation for, and an introduction to, the day of the Fast." *Moreh Nebukim* III, 43.

27. Mizvah 311; see also Mizvah 405. Cf. *Rosh Hashanah* 26b; Maimonides, Teshubah 3:4. For another meaning of the blowing of the *shofar* as a reminder of the binding of Isaac, see Mizvah 331.

28. Ibid. Cf. *Abodah Zarah* 4a; M. *Rosh Hashanah* I, 2; ibid. 18a; Maimonides, Teshubah 3:3; *Moreh Nebukim* III, 36.

29. Mizvah 185; cf. *Yoma* VIII, 1, 9.

30. Ibid. Cf. Rashi, *Yoma* 36b.

31. See Hinnuk's Hakdamah, where he implies a renewal of the scapegoat ritual on Yom Kippur (Lev. 16:10) in Messianic days to cleanse the people of the dross of sin which may yet remain.

32. Cf. *Shebuot* 13a; Maimonides, Teshubah 1:1, 3, 4. See especially the statement of R. Yonah b. Abraham of Gerona in his *Sha'arei Teshubah* IV, 17. "Is it not written, 'from all your sins shall ye be clean before

the Lord' (Lev. 16:30) (by means of the Day of Atonement alone, without repentance)? The answer is that 'ye shall be clean before the Lord' is a positive commandment of repentance, that we seek out and search our ways and return to God on the Day of Atonement. And though we have been commanded to do this at all times, the obligation is greater on the Day of Atonement; and the cleanliness referred to is repentance and correction of deeds." Tr. by S. Silverstein, *The Gates of Repentance* (Jerusalem, 1967), p. 375. Cf. also commentary on Lev. 16:30 by R. Obadiah b. Jacob Seforno.

33. Mizvah 364. Cf. M. *Abot* II, 15; *Shabbat* 153a.
34. See M. *Sanhedrin* VI, 2. Cf. Maimonides, Sanhedrin 13:1.
35. See Maimonides' explanation of the case where one is guilty of several transgressions. "Should the court inflict the death penalty upon him for one of these transgressions his confession atones for all, solely by reason of his repentance and not because the one punishment that the court metes out to him can atone for his many sins." *Perush ha-Mishnayot*, Nazir VI, 4. Cf. *Tosafot Yom Tob*, ibid.
36. See *Shabbat* 32a. Cf. Maimonides, Teshubah 2:1. See Mizvah 264 for the Hinnuk's view of *teshubah* as the essential reflective element in the commandment obliging one to mourn for a deceased relative.
37. Mizvah 82.
38. Ibid.
39. See M. *Sanhedrin* VI, 2; ibid. 47a, 78a. Cf. S. R: Hirsch, *The Pentateuch* (London 1959) Gen. 9:6, Vol. I, p. 178.
40. Expressive of this concept is the familiar statement, "He stands bound by the oath on Mount Sinai." See *Nedarim* 8a, *Shebuot* 21b, *Yoma* 73b.
41. Mizvah 491. Cf. Maimonides, Mizvat 'Aseh 176.
42. Mizvah 594.
43. Mizvah 6. Cf. *Ketubot* 86a, *Hullin* 132b. The Hinnuk also invokes this principle with regard to the commandment to honor parents (Mizvah 33). However, see the gloss of *Mishneh le-Melek*, who demurs in this instance on strictly technical grounds.
44. Gerushin 2:20. Cf. *Baba Batra* 48a, Rashi, ibid.
45. Cf. Kinyan Torah, *Abot* VI, 2.
46. See Mizvah 69. The Rabbis venture the opinion that God did not disclose the rewards for the commandments of the Torah, lest people choose to keep the ones that offer greater reward and neglect the others. See *Pesikta Rabbati*, chapt. 23.
47. See *Sotah* 37b. There is also implied here the responsibility that all Israelites bear for one another in the observance of the commandments. The Talmud refers to this as the principle that "all Israelites are guarantors for one another." See *Shebuot* 39a; *Sanhedrin* 27b.
48. See *Zebahim* 106b, *Sanhedrin* 54a, *Yoma* 81a.

49. Mizvah 69.
50. Ibid.
51. Exod. 20:1. Cf. *Mekilta*, ibid., 20:3, "As you have accepted My kingship, so must you accept My decrees." This statement is intended to convey the imperative nature of the laws, that is to say, they are not optional, but mandatory. Cf. C. B. Chavel, *Commentary on the Torah by Nahmanides*, Exod. 20:2, p. 389, citing the interpretation of the *Mekilta* in *Sho'el Umeshib*, Responsum 51.
52. Cf. Rashi, Num. 15:41, based on *Sifre*, ibid.
53. *Shabbat* 88a; cf. Rashi and Tosafot, ad loc.; Cf. also Rashi, Exod. 19:17.
54. *Nezah Yisra'el*, chapt. XI.
55. *Sifra*, ibid.
56. *Sifra*, Lev. 20:26; cf. Rashi, ibid. Cf. Maimonides, *Shemonah Perakim* VI.
57. *Kiddushin* 31a, *Abodah Zorah* 3a, *Baba Kamma* 38a, 87a. See Maimonides, Talmud Torah 1:13.
58. Tosafot, Ri ha-Zaken, in a gloss on *Kiddushin* 31a. Cf., however, the explanation of Tosafot, ibid. For S. R. Hirsch's exposition of this concept of the free-willed decision to submit to Divine legislation as the basis of Judaism, expressed in the statement *na'aseh ve-nishma'*, in contrast with Kant's espousal of moral self-legislation, or the autonomy of the will, as the sole principle of all moral laws and of all duties, see I. Grunfeld, Introduction to *Horeb*, Vol. I, p. lxx-lxxx, cxiv.
59. *Tosefta, Shebuot* 3:5.
60. *'Emunot ve-De'ot* III, 2.
61. *Abodah Zarah* 19a.
62. M. *Abot* I, 3.
63. Teshubah 10:2, 4. Cf. Me'ilah 8:8.

NOTES TO CHAPTER ELEVEN

PERSPECTIVES ON THE MIZVOT

1. Cf. I. Epstein, *The Faith of Judaism*, (Soncino Press, London 1954), Excursus II, p. 372; "The Conception of the Commandments of the Torah in Aaron Halevi's Sefer ha-Hinnuk," in *Essays Presented to J. H. Hertz*, (London 1942), pp. 145-158. Epstein contends that the Hinnuk's main emphasis is upon perfection of humanity, whereas Maimonides' main emphasis is upon perfection of the individual. This distinction would appear to be unwarranted; indeed the emphasis on the part of the Hinnuk may well be in reverse order. See especially Mizvah 95; cf. *Moreh Nebukim* III, 27, 28, 35, 38.

2. Mizvah 166. See chapt. VII.
3. See Mizvah 16.
4. Mizvah 3. See chapt. III.
5. *Moreh Nebukim* III, 48.
6. Ibid., III, 43.
7. Cf. Mizvot 7, 8, 13, 14, 15, 16, 21, 298.
8. This may explain the fact that the Hinnuk advances reasons for the several mizvot for which Maimonides fails to offer any reasons. Thus, for the table and show-bread he cites the reason given by Nahmanides. See Mizvah 97; cf. Nahmanides, Exod. 25:24, 30. In the purification of the leper his reasons for the use of the prescribed objects are along lines intimated by the Sages. See Mizvah 173; cf. the commentaries of Rashi, Ibn Ezra, Rabeinu Bahya, and Nahmanides on Lev. 14:4. Although the Hinnuk refrains from giving a reason for the red heifer, in deference to the expressed sentiment of the Sages, he nevertheless attempts to explain the paradox of its power simultaneously to purify the unclean and to defile the clean by indicating that certain herbs and medicines possess a similar characteristic of producing opposite effects. See Mizvah 397; cf. Saadiah, *'Emunot ve-De'ot*, III, 10.
9. Mizvah 482.
10. Mizvah 431: cf. *Minhat Hinnuk* ad loc.
11. Mizvah 550.
12. Mizvot 553, 554.
13. Mizvot 557, 558; cf. *Shulhan 'Aruk*, 'Eben ha-'Ezer 177:3.
14. *Moreh Nebukim* III, 48.
15. Mizvah 92.
16. Cf. Mizvot 62, 244, 552. Cf. Nahmanides, *Perush ha-Torah*. Lev. 19:19. Cf. Recanati, *Ta'amei ha-Mizvot*, Mizvot 'Aseh, sec. on *basar be-halab*.
17. Mizvah 62.
18. Ibid.
19. Cf. C. B. Chavel, op. cit., p. 86, who suggests that the Hinnuk's statement in Mizvah 30, regarding the greater severity of a vow over an oath, reflects the influence of the Zohar.
20. Mizvah 98; cf. Mizvah 72.
21. Mizvah 324.
22. Mizvah 95. Cf. Bahya ben Asher, op. cit., Parashat Vayikra' 1:9.
23. Mizvah 104; cf. Mizvah 138.
24. Mizvah 598; cf. Nahmanides, op. cit., Genesis 38:8.
25. Ibid.
26. Mizvah 330; cf. Mizvah 84.
27. For a similar view on the interaction of psychic and somatic states, held by certain of the exegetes, see Abrabanel, *Perush*, Gen. 32:25-32; Malbim, *Perush ha-Torah ve-ha-Mizvah*, Gen. 32:33. See chapt. V.

28. Cf. G. Scholem, *Major Trends in Jewish Mysticism.* (Schocken Books, New York 1946) p. 29-30.

29. Hakdamah to Ta'amei ha-Mizvot, in *Sefer Likutei Torah ve-Ta'amei ha-Mizvot,* end of Parshat Bereshit. (Pub. by Research Center of Kabbalah, Jerusalem 1970) Part XII, p. 36.

30. The mystical concept of mizvot is described in a more contemporary work, entitled *Nefesh ha-Hayyim,* by R. Hayyim of Volozhin, disciple of the Gaon of Vilna. R. Hayyim, who attained renown as expositor of Jewish mysticism, formulated a neo-kabbalistic system, which he developed from the Zohar and Lurianic Kabbalah. In discoursing upon the central position of Torah in the world structure as conceived by the Kabbalah, R. Hayyim traces the profound, mystical force of the mizvot. See *Nefesh ha-Hayyim* I, 2, 3, 6, 7, 22.

31. From the time of the kabbalistic school of Gerona, early in the 13th century, kabbalistic scholars already embarked upon mystical interpretations of the mizvot, among the first being Ezra ben Solomon and Jacob ben Sheshet. See G. Scholem, op. cit., p. 355, n. 28.

32. Among the important works of this school of thought, where the Hinnuk's influence is evident, is the *Ta'amei ha-Mizvot,* a classic work on mizvot written by Menahem Recanati, a Kabbalist of the fourteenth century, and *Mezudat David,* a comprehensive exposition of the mizvot, written by David Ibn Zimra, in the sixteenth century.

33. See Mizvot 84, 477.

34. Exod. 23:11, 12. Cf. *Mekilta,* ibid. 23:12.

35. See Exod. 20:10. Lev. 25:4. For its halakic implications, see *Sifra,* Lev. 25:4; *Mekilta,* Exod. 23:12; Rashi ad loc. For its conceptual meaning along the lines indicated by the Hinnuk, see Malbim, *Perush Hatorah ve-Hamizvah,* Lev. 25:4.

36. In this regard note the statement of R. Samuel Eidles in the Introduction to his commentary on the Talmud. The author emphasizes the integral relationship between Halakah and Aggadah and indicates his regret in having divided his work into two separate parts when in reality they are one. See Hakdamat Maharsha' to *Hidushei Halakot.*

37. *Perush ha-Torah,* Exod. 20:1.

38. Cf. Nahmanides, *Perush ha-Torah,* Hakdamah.

39. See Mizvah 3; *Gen. Rabbah,* chapts. 77, 78; cf. Nahmanides, op. cit., 32:26; Maimonides, *Perush ha-Mishnayot,* Hullin, VII, 6.

40. See *Sanhedrin* 56b, *Shabbat* 87b, *Horayot* 8b. Cf. Nahmanides, op. cit., Exod. 15:25, who expounds on the significance of the laws given at that time; Rashbam, ibid; Maimonides, *Moreh Nebukim* III, 32.

41. For the occasional use by the Midrash of certain forms of halakic exegesis in its exposition of Scripture, and their adaptation in liturgical

poetry, see A. Mirsky, *Mahzabtan shel zurot ha-Piyut*, (Jerusalem 1968);
"Re'shit ha-Piyut," *'Iyunim*, Hoberet 34.

42. See the Hinnuk's Prologue to Deuteronomy. Cf. *Yebamot* 4a, where the
    Rabbis cite the proximity of the prohibition of wearing wool and linen
    together (*sha'atnez*) to the commandment to make fringes (*zizit*) in the
    corners of a garment (Deut. 22:11, 12) as indication that a mandatory
    precept overrides a prohibitive precept. R. Eleazar concludes that *semukim*
    is a principle of the Torah. See the ensuing discussion in the Talmud as
    to whether the principle applies throughout Scripture or only in Deuter-
    onomy, and the additional cases in point cited by the Rabbis. Cf. *Ta'anit*
    26b for the law forbidding one who is intoxicated from bestowing the
    priestly blessing. The law is derived from the proximity in Scripture of
    the priestly blessing to the chapter concerning the Nazirite (Num.
    6:1-27). In this latter instance the analogy is an *'asmakta'* of a rabbinic
    nature only. Cf. Me'iri's discussion of the halakic force of analogy in
    Scripture, ibid. For further references see chapter III, n. 8.
43. See *Rosh Hashanah* 32a; Rashi, ibid.
44. See *Megillah* 17b.
45. See *Kiddushin* 20a; Rashi, Lev. 26:1.
46. See *Sifre*, Deut., 21:18; *Tanhuma*, Parshat Ki Teze', par. 1; Rashi, ibid.
    21:11, 18, 22; cf. *Sanhedrin* 68b, 71b, 72a. Cf. *Sotah* 2a for the con-
    nection noted by the Sages between the laws of Sotah and Nazir, based
    upon the contiguity of texts in Scripture. See Num. 5:11-6:21; Rashi,
    ibid. 6:2. See also *Kiddushin* 20a for their interpretation of the sequence
    of laws in Leviticus 25; cf. Rashi, Lev. 26:1.
47. See *Tanhuma*, ad loc.; Rashi, ibid, 22.8.
48. *Sifra*, Lev. 19:11.
49. *Sifra*, Lev. 23:3.
50. *Hullin* 78b; *Bekorot* 45b.
51. The Halakah follows the view of the Rabbis. See Rashi, Lev. 22:26;
    Maimonides, Shehitah 12:11; *Shulhan 'Aruk*, Yoreh De'ah 16:2.
52. *Perush ha-Torah*, Deut. 22:6.
53. Mizvot 294, 545.
54. *Moreh Nebukim* III, 48.
55. *Perush ha-Torah*, Exod. 21:2.
56. Ibid. Lev. 19:18.
57. *Perush ha-Torah*, Lev. 19:17.
58. Part III, 48.
59. Exod. 23:19; 34:26.
60. For a similar association between the Festivals and the prohibition, based
    upon the confluence of verses, but resulting in a different conclusion, see
    Rashbam, *Perush ha-Torah*, Exod. 23:19.

61. *Perush ha-Torah*, Lev. 19:26, 28; cf. Rashi, ibid. 19:28.

62. *Moreh Nebukim*, III, 37; cf. *Sefer ha-Mizvot*, Mizvat Lo' Ta'aseh 44; 'Abodah Zarah 12:1, 7.

63. *Bet Yosef*, Yoreh De'ah 181.

64. *Moreh Nebukim* III, 46.

65. See *Yebamot* 4a; Rashi ad loc. Cf. Maimonides, Yibum ve-Halizah 2:14; 'Ishut 25:12.

66. Cf. M. *Yebamot* III, 7; *Yebamot* 87b; Rashi ad loc.; Tosafot, *Yebamot* 2a, 17b.

67. Cf. *Gittin* 59b. See *Meshek Hokmah*, Parshat Noah, for applications of this principle, including a woman's exemption from the mizvah of procreation, by reason of the Torah's concern that the precept may conceivably confront her with unreasonable demands, or impose conditions contrary to her nature.

68. See *Sotah* 46a for the explanation given by R. Johanan ben Saul for the commandment requiring that a heifer's neck be broken in an uncultivated valley in expiation of an untraced murder (Deut. 21:4). "Let something which did not produce fruit have its neck broken in a place which is not fertile and atone for one who was not allowed to produce fruit." A tentative presumption by the Talmud is that, given the reason advanced by R. Johanan ben Saul, the commandment as specified would be limited in its application to the case of one who was capable of having children. Apparently, the Rabbis here accepted the reason as halakically valid, even though the basic intent was plainly to develop a moral lesson.

69. *Baba Mezia* 115a; cf. Tosafot, *Sotah* 14a. See Maimonides, Malveh ve-Loveh 3:1, *Lehem Mishneh*, ad loc.; 'Issurei Bi'ah 12:1, *Kesef Mishneh*, ad loc. Both commentaries infer that Maimonides may, in fact, be following the opinion of R. Simeon.

70. Cf. S. R. Hirsch, *The Pentateuch*, commentary on Deut. 24:17, trans. by I. Levy (London, 1962).

71. This mode of exposition of the mizvot, based upon a broader development of their interrelationships and a more intensive analysis of their inherent halakic principles, was carried forward toward the formulation of a philosophy of Jewish laws by R. Samson Raphael Hirsch, in his *Horeb* and his commentary on the Pentateuch. See the Introduction by I. Grunfeld to *Horeb*, Vol. 1 (London 1962). For a contemporary study of halakic concepts in the formulation of a philosophy of Jewish laws, see Dr. Samuel Belkin's *In His Image: The Jewish Philosophy of Man* (New York, 1960); "The Philosophy of Purpose," in *Studies in Torah Judaism*, ed. L. D. Stitskin (Yeshiva University, Ktav Publishing House, 1969); and Dr. Joseph B. Soloveitchik's " 'Ish Ha-Halakah," in *Talpiot*, Vol. 1, nos. 3-4, ed. S. K. Mirsky (New York, 1944).

NOTES TO CHAPTER TWELVE

THE CONTINUING QUEST

1. On this aspect, see Eliezer Goldman, "Ha-mizvah ke-natun yesodi shel ha-dat," in *Ta'amei ha-Mizvot be-Yameinu* (Jerusalem, 1960).
2. For a similar application of the verse, see Jacob Zvi Mecklenburg, *Ha-Ketab ve-ha-Kabbalah*, Deut. 29:28. Mecklenburg cites Maimonides' interpretation as follows: כתב רב״ח שמעתי בשם הרמב״ם ז״ל פירוש פסוק זה, הנסתרות לה׳ א׳ סודות התורה הנסתרות וטעמי המצות להש״י הם, ואם לא יזכה אדם שיקח שמץ מנהם בידיעת שרש המצוה בענין גופני, אין לו להמנע מזה שהרי הנגלות לנו ולבנינו לעשות.

   See Ralbag's explanation of the verse in a similar vein, also cited there. Cf. ibid. 29:18.
3. This is essentially the central thesis of Judah Halevi's work. See *Kuzari* I, 98, "The theory I had formed, and the opinion of what I saw in my dream thou now confirmest, namely, that man can only merit divine influence by acting according to God's commands."
4. Cf. Malbim's commentary on Psalms 119:86, "All Thy commandments are faith." Malbim explains this to mean, "The foundation of the mizvot is belief in God who commands, and in His commandments."

   כל מצותיך אמונה, שצריך להאמין, וזה יסוד המצות שיאמין במצוה ובמצותיו.
5. Cf. Mizvot 73, 159.
6. See Mizvah 73. Cf. *Sefer ha-Mizvot*, Mizvat Lo' Ta'aseh 365, at end. Expressing a similar fear, Maimonides asserts that God concealed the reasons of most of the commandments in the Torah "because the people would not comprehend them."
7. See Hakdamah to *Sefer ha-Hinnuk*.
8. Mizvah 117. For further discussion, see chapter V.
9. See Epilogue to Leviticus; cf. Mizvot 175, 440. Cf. *Midrash, Song of Songs* 1:17.
10. *Moreh Nebukim*, chapters 26-49. Cf. *Berakot* 63a, M. *Abot* II, 17. Regarding the reasons advanced by Maimonides, Ritba states, "He proposed them not because he believed them to be the essential reasons for the commandments, but because he wished to give at least a partial reason, in order that even the common people would know how to refute the sceptic with some intelligent answer." *Sefer ha-Zikaron*, Parshat Vayikra'.
11. *Kuzari* II, 26.
11a. Cf. Shabbat 88a.
12. See *Midrash Tanhuma*, Parshat Shelah 16; cf. *Numbers Rabbah* 17:7. The Midrash cites examples to show how the mizvot affect a man's daily activities. For a discussion of the role of Halakah in imparting new meaning to natural phenomena, see R. Joseph B. Soloveitchik, " 'Ish ha-Halakah" op. cit.

13. Heinemann classifies the expositors of *ta'amei ha-mizvot* on a purely subjective basis, into three groups: אנשי מעשה, אנשי רוח, אנשי רגש
See *Ta'amei ha-Mizvot*, volume I, p. 138-139. While this classification is valid in a limited sense, it fails to give due weight to the impact of the cultural forces and the philosophic concerns of each age.

14. Cf. *Gittin* 6b, *Erubin* 13b, *Hagigah* 3b.

15. See Mizvah 95.

16. *Mekilta* 20:8; cf. Rashi, ad loc. The *Mekilta's* citation of self-contradictory statements found elsewhere in Scripture would seem to intimate that this rabbinic dictum has a broader conceptual meaning, going beyond the immediate problem of an apparent scriptural discrepancy.

17. Cf. Mecklenburg, *Ha-Ketab ve-ha-Kabbalah*, Deut. 29:28, who cites Ralbag for a similar view, as follows: ובכלל הנה ג"כ מה שזכרה תורה
תועלת מצוה אפשר שיהיה בה אצלו הש"י תועלת אחר ... כש"כ במה
שלא נזכר בתורה התועלת אבל עמדנו עליו על דרך החקירה והעיון, והבן
זה השרש כי הוא מגדולי השרשים התוריים לשמור חכמת התורה.

18. Mizvah 545, citing *Numbers Rabbah* 19:4 relevant to a discussion on fathoming the reason for the mysterious law of the red heifer.

19. It is noteworthy in this connection that Rashi, notwithstanding his fundamentalist position, evidently accepted the view that the reasons for the Torah laws would ultimately be revealed by God. In his commentary on the verse, "For thy love is better than wine" (*Song of Songs* 1:2), Rashi follows the Midrash in taking wine to be symbolic of the Torah, and asserts, "God gave Israel the Torah . . . and promised to appear to them again to reveal the secret of its reasons and its hidden mysteries."

20. Mizvah 95. ידוע הדבר ומפורסם ביניגו העם מקבלי המצות כי שבעים
פנים לתורה.
See *'Otiot de Rabbi Akiba; Numbers Rabbah* 13:15.

NOTES TO EXCURSUS

THE SEFER HA-HINNUK

1. On the question of authorship, see D. Rosin, "Ein Compendium der Judischen Gesetzeskunde," in *Judisch-Theologisches Seminar* (Breslau, Jahresbericht 1871); C. B. Chavel, Sefer ha-Hinnuk (Jerusalem, 1956) p. 5-7, and Supplement, ibid.; Kuntres Hagahot in *Sefer ha-Hashlamah le-Minhat Hinnuk ha-Shalem*, op. cit., vol. II, p. 133.

2. Epilogue to Leviticus. קראתי שם הספר חינוך

3. Hakdamah. איש יהודי מבית לוי ברצלוני
Cf. also Mizvah 394.

4. ספר החינוך שחיבר הרב רבי אהרן זלה"ה

5. A possible assumption is that it is based upon a pointed reference in Mizvah 95 to Num. 8:21 containing the name of Aaron, the high priest.

In the second edition, printed in Venice in 1600, a marginal note calls attention to this reference and states that the author here hints at his name being Aaron. This marginal note found its way into the text in later editions. It is also suggested that the author's reference to Mal. 2:5 in his Iggeret may be an oblique allusion to his name, since in an old Midrash (*Sifra*, Shemini, ed. Weiss, I, 45d) this verse is referred to Aaron. See S. Kook, *Kiryat Sefer*, Shanah 17, Hoberet I, (Nissan 1940), p. 83.

6. *Shalshelet ha-Kabbalah*, p. 44.

7. Cf. Rama', Yoreh De'ah 61:21; and Shak, Yoreh De'ah 157:1, note 10, and Hoshen Mishpat 388:2, note 22. Cf. S. M. Hanes, *Toledot ha-Poskim*, p. 130b.

8. *Shem Ha-Gedolim*, (ed. Ben Jacob, Vilna, 1853) Ma'areket Gedolim I, p. 132. Azulai notes that, whereas Rabbi Aaron ha-Levi is known to have been a disciple of Nahmanides, the author of the *Sefer ha-Hinnuk* refers to Nahmanides as to one deceased, while often referring to his teacher as to one yet living. It must be admitted, however, that this is of little consequence, since the term ז"ל may well be the interpolation of a copyist after the death of Nahmanides. It is also suggested that the different references may indicate separate periods in the course of writing the Hinnuk, namely, before and after the death of Nahmanides. See notes, ibid.

9. For citations, see D. Rosin, op. cit., pp. 132-134. In a discussion of the law of inheritance (Mizvah 400) the Hinnuk cites an opinion, ascribed by him to his teacher, which is identical with a decision rendered by Rabbi Solomon ben Adret in a similar case (Responsa, 704). In a monograph on the *Sefer ha-Zikkaron* of the Ritba (Jerusalem, 1956), p. 77-79, K. Kahane cites this very responsum by Rabbi Solomon ben Adret and draws attention to another responsum in manuscript by Rabbi Aaron ha-Levi wherein he sharply disputes the Rashba's decision in this case. In the opinion of Kahane the fact that the *Sefer ha-Hinnuk* agrees with the Rashba in this disputed decision is proof that the Sefer ha-Hinnuk could not have been written by Rabbi Aaron ha-Levi of Barcelona.

10. He meticulously traces his ancestry to Rabbi Zerahiah ha-Levi of Gerona, a famed scholar of the 12th century. Moreover the intense controversy between Rashba and Rabbi Aaron ha-Levi and, in particular, Rashba's characterization of the latter are completely at variance with the benign and humble character of the author as reflected in the *Sefer ha-Hinnuk*. See Hakdamah of Rashba to *Mishmeret ha-Bayit*; cf. Hinnuk's Hakdamah and Epilogue to Leviticus.

11. It has been proposed by D. Rosin, op. cit., p. 88, that the author, though not the celebrated Rabbi Aaron ha-Levi, was probably another scholar, also of Barcelona, named Aaron ha-Levi. While Rosin's proposal preserves the tradition as to the name of the author, it is nevertheless sub-

ject to the question raised above regarding the reliability of the tradition itself. We have only the information supplied by the author, namely, that he was a Levite and a native of Barcelona. Indeed, S. Kook suggests that this very allusion in the Hakdamah to איש יהודי מבית לוי ברצלוני may have been a hint by the author that his name is Mordecai, as in Megillat Esther 2:5. See op. cit., p. 83, n. 6.

Rabbi David ben Zimra, a Palestinian scholar of the 16th century, in whose time there appeared the first printed edition of the *Sefer ha-Hinnuk*, quotes it in his own work and gives the author's name, en passant, as Rabbi Baruk. See Ta'amei ha-Mizvot, *Mezudat David*, (Zalkawa, 1862), Mizvah 206, p. 39, וכן ר' ברוך בעל החינוך האריך הרבה

However, we have no knowledge of a scholar bearing the name of Baruk, a Levite of Barcelona, in any of the other sources, and the name, appearing only once in this work, though the *Sefer ha-Hinnuk* is frequently and extensively quoted in it, could conceivably have been an erroneous transcription or interpolation.

12. The decision of the Rashba, cited above, is offered as proof by Chavel, *Kuntres Hagahot*, in op. cit., p. 133, that the author of the *Sefer ha-Hinnuk* was a disciple of the Rashba.

13. Mizvah 330.

14. See n. 8 above where it is indicated that this presumed difficulty is not a valid concern.

15. Rosin, op. cit., p. 77. Rosin believes the text to be faulty. This is already intimated by Azulai, op. cit., who states "perhaps this is an error by the scribe."

16. Listed in the Codex of Mss. in the Vatican Library by Bartolocci, *Bibliotheca Magna Rabbinica*, Vol. I, p. 90.

17. An early date is also indicated by the fact that the *Sefer ha-Hinnuk* is quoted by Menahem Recanati, an Italian scholar who lived at the end of the 13th and the beginning of the 14th centuries. Recanati refers to the author as being deceased. On folio 122b of the work in manuscript the following statement, which is not found in the printed editions (Constantinople 1544, Basle 1581, Amsterdam 1708), appears: והוא ז"ל בעל החינוך סתר זה ואמר כי הבורא אינו עושה רעה לאדם אלא בהסתרת פנים ואז הוא מונח תחת המקרה... ועל דברי הרב ז"ל יש לתמוה מאד. The manuscript is in the British Museum. The above quotation is from the *Catalogue of Hebrew and Samaritan Mss. in the British Museum*, compiled by G. Margoliouth, (Oxford U. Press, 1915), Part III, p. 17, #743, 5.

18. See M. L. Margolis and A. Marx, *A History of the Jewish People* (Philadelphia, 1938), p. 396-97.

19. See Mizvah 298 for reference to a halakic discussion in a commentary of his on the talmudic tractate *Bezah*. Rabbi Aaron ha-Levi wrote commentaries on the Talmud, among them one on *Bezah* which was first

published in Livorno, 1810 and republished (Jerusalem, 1959) in *Sefer Shitat ha-Kadmonim'al Maseket Bezah*. This edition does not include the discussion referred to.

20. A genuine spirit of humility and piety in approaching their holy work was the hallmark of the scholars of that age. See Hakdamah to *Sefer ha-Zikkaron*; Hakdamah to *Midrash Rabbeinu Bahya*; cf. Hakdamah to *Sefer Hobot ha-Lebabot*; Hakdamah to *Sefer Torat ha-Bayit*. The *Sefer ha-Hinnuk* throughout attests eloquently to its author's sincere piety and humility.

21. In respect of the latter, it is indicative that the Hinnuk states that he wrote his treatise expressly for his son and his youthful friends, hence presumably not for scholars. See Hakdamah and Epilogue to Leviticus. The *Sefer ha-Hinnuk* is, to be sure, a serious, systematic work that manifests painstaking research and consummate writing. Such a deferential manner, however, was not uncommon among scholars. Rabbi Menahem ha-Me'iri informs us in the Introduction to his *Bet ha-Behirah* on *Abot* that in Gaonic times, when talmudic learning was widespread, the Gaonim saw no necessity to write books, except to meet specific needs. He cites the example of R. Ahai Gaon, who, it was claimed, wrote his *Sefer ha-She'eltot* for his own son who was not inclined to study, providing him with halakic lessons from the Talmud along with the scriptural reading for the Sabbath in order to facilitate his study. He also cites the case of Saadiah Gaon, who wrote his *Sefer ha-Pikadon* (the *Book of Deposits*) for the benefit of a certain Rabbi who was constantly beset by halakic problems of that nature.

22. The author refers to this in his Hakdamah and in the Epilogue to Leviticus. Cf. the *Letter of Hasdai Crescas to the Congregation of Avignon*, in Ibn Virga's, *Shebet Yehudah*, ed. Wiener, I; p. 128 ff. See Graetz, *History of the Jews*, (Philadelphia, 1894), Volume IV, chapters 4 and 5.

23. An example is the *Sefer ha-Neyar*, an anonymous 13th-century code of Jewish Law, edited by this writer and published by Sura Institute for Research and Yeshiva University (New York, 1960). See the Introduction, especially chapter II, dealing with the author and the history of the manuscripts.

24. A list of sources and comparative citations is provided by D. Rosin, op. cit., chapter IV, p. 70-76.

25. For direct references to Alfasi, see Mizvot 49, 244, 350, 405, 506.

26. Cf. Mizvot 111, 138, 352, 507, 573.

27. Quoted widely, it is referred to directly by name in Mizvot 73 and 163. The Hinnuk used the Hebrew translation by Abraham Ibn Hasdai. See Ch. Heller's Introduction to his critical edition of the *Sefer ha-Mizvot*, op. cit., p. 8. On Ibn Hasdai, see Steinschneider, Cat. Bodl. pp. 1235-40. See also D. Rosin, op. cit., p. 101.

28. Cf. Mizvah 352.
29. Mizvah 545; cf. also Mizvah 148.
30. Cf. Prefatory Letter: "Rabbi Moses Nahman, of blessed memory, the author of a very distinguished book on the reckoning of the commandments." The Hinnuk refers to this work as the "Sefer ha-Mizvot of Ramban," cf. Mizvah 106; and frequently in context simply as "his Sefer ha-Mizvot."
31. Reference is also made to Nahmanides' Hilkot Bekorot (Mizvah 18), to the *Sefer Torat ha-'Adam* (Mizvot 264, 365). There are also quotations from his Novellae on the Talmud; on tractate *Makkot* (Mizvah 339) and on *Mo'ed Katan* (at the end of Mizvah 323). An indirect reference to his *Milhamot*, a treatise in defense of Alfasi, is to be found in Mizvah 325.
32. Cf. Mizvot 4, 27 as examples of this. See also chapter II.
33. Mizvah 573.
34. See Mizvah 153, where the Hinnuk notes that he included several mizvot in accord with the reckoning of Maimonides even though he inclines to the opposing view of Nahmanides. He lists as separate commandments, for example, searching for the prescribed signs in cattle and wild animals (Mizvah 153), in fish (Mizvah 155), in locusts (Mizvah 159), and in birds (Mizvah 470), despite the fact that he agrees with the contention of Nahmanides (Hassagot, *Sefer ha-Mizvot,* Shoresh VI) that these are not to be counted separately, but they fall naturally under the respective commandments enjoining us to abstain from eating them. Cf. also Mizvot 138, 160, 161, 476, 573.
35. The commandment omitted by the Hinnuk, though listed by Maimonides and all other codes, is the prohibition for a common man, one not of the seed of Aaron, to eat the meat of the most hallowed offerings. For Maimonides' discussion of this mizvah, see *Sefer ha-Mizvot*, Mizvat Lo' Ta'aseh 148; *Mishneh Torah*, Ma'aseh ha-Karbanot 11:8.
36. The Hinnuk substitutes for it the commandment, not to offer the Passover sacrifice on a private altar (Mizvah 487). He bases this prohibition upon the scriptural verse, "Thou mayest not sacrifice the Passover offering within any of thy gates" (Deut. 16:5). Such forbidden practice would, according to the Hinnuk, not only violate the general prohibition presently in force against slaughtering hallowed offerings outside of the Sanctuary (Mizvah 186), but it would violate this specific prohibition as well. While Maimonides does not mention this commandment, it is however to be found in the *Halakot Gedolot* and in the *Azharot* of Saadiah Gaon. Whether the Hinnuk included it on the basis of a different recension of the *Sefer ha-Mizvot* or because he preferred to follow the *Halakot Gedolot* in this instance is not known.

In drawing attention to this commandment, Judah Rusanis states that it is not included by any of the authorities. See *Derek Mizvoteka*, end of Part IV. See Ch. Heller's critical 'edition of the *Sefer ha-Mizvot*, Foreword, p. 1, n. 1, wherein he notes the oversight. He further quotes from the *Ma'aseh Nissim*, a compilation of questions propounded by Daniel ha-Babli regarding the *Sefer ha-Mizvot* and replies by Abraham ben Maimon, son of Maimonides, from which it appears that Daniel ha-Babli had questioned the inclusion by Maimonides in his *Sefer ha-Mizvot* of this prohibition against offering the Passover sacrifice on a private altar. Abraham ben Maimon is cited as stating that the commandment had never been reckoned by Maimonides but, in all probability, had been included by error in some faulty recensions of Maimonides' works.

37. Mizvah 111. For additional variants see Mizvot 298, 314, 320.
38. Cf., for example, Mizvot 379, 433. For an apparent difference of views between the Hinnuk and Maimonides regarding the day designated for the Festival of Shabuot, see Mizvot 308, 309, and *Hilkot Temidim Umusafim* 8:1; cf. *Minhat Hinnuk*, ibid; S. Goren, *Torat ha-Mo'adim* (Tel Aviv, 1964), p. 362.
39. Cf. Hakdamah and Mizvah 24. On the Jerusalem Talmud see Mizvot 77, 114, 426.
40. See Hakdamah in reference to the *Sifra*, *Sifre*, *Tosefta*, and *Mekilta*. For the latter see Mizvah 155. See also Mizvah 357 for a quotation from the Haggadah of Passover.
41. Mizvot 4, 150.
42. Mizvah 421.
43. Mizvah 330.
44. For a direct reference see Mizvot 62, 208, 283, 329, 350, 421.
45. Mizvah 350.
46. Mizvot 236, 264, 507, 560.
47. Mizvot 111, 228.
48. Some have been found to coincide with passages in the works of Rabbi Solomon ben Adret and Rabbi Asher ben Yehiel. See D. Rosin op. cit., pp. 75-76, 111-128, 132-134. For the Hinnuk's references to kabbalistic sources, see chapter XI.

For a listing of the manuscripts and the printed editions of the *Sefer ha-Hinnuk* see D. Rosin, op. cit. See also C. B. Chavel, M. Leiter, Y. Rubinstein, in *Sefer ha-Hashlamah le-Minhat Hinnuk ha-Shalem* (New York, 1952).

INDEX OF MIZVOT CITED
FROM THE SEFER HA-HINNUK

The mizvot are listed in column 1 in their biblical order as they appear in the standard editions of the *Sefer ha-Hinnuk*. Column 2 contains the number of the mizvah in Maimonides' *Sefer ha-Mizvot*, where the positive and negative commandments are given separately, and herein designated as *p.* and *n.* respectively. Column 3 indicates the biblical source for the commandment. The page numbers in bold type in column 4 signify that the mizvah, in addition to being cited, is quoted as well.

Hin-nuk	Ram-bam	Genesis	Page	Hin-nuk	Ram-bam	Exodus	Page
1	p.212	1:28	110	21	p.157	13:8	62, **137**, 171
2	p.215	17:10	128	24	n.321	16:29	138
3	n.183	32:33	**43, 46,** 171	25	p.1	20:2	48, **49,** 51, **54,**
		Exodus					55, **56, 58, 136,**
5	p.55	12:6	**137**				153
6	p.56	12:8	**137, 165**	26	n.1	20:3	71, **136,** 153
7	n.125	12:9	**137,** 171	30	n.62	20:7	**161**
8	n.117	12:10	**137,** 171	31	p.155	20:8	**137**
9	p.156	12:15	**137**	32	n.320	20:10	**138**
10	p.158	12:18	**137**	33	p.210	20:12	**114-115, 133,**
11	n.201	12:19	**137**				**219 n.72**
12	n.198	12:20	**137**	35	n.347	20:13	111, 130
13	n.128	12:43	**40, 41, 137,** 171	38	n.265	20:14	95
14	n.126	12:45	**41, 137,** 171	42	p.232	21:2	**39, 117,** 128
15	n.123	12:46	**137,** 171	43	p.233	21:8	118
16	n.122	12:46	**88, 89, 113-114,**	49	p.236	21:18	**103**
			137, 170, 171	62	n.310	22:17	**173**
17	n.127	12:48	41, **137**	63	n.252	22:20	**120**
18	p.79	13:2	**135, 137**	64	n.253	22:20	120
19	n.197	13:3	**137**	65	n.256	22:21	119, 120
20	n.200	13:7	**137**	66	p.197	22:24	**92, 97**

INDEX OF REFERENCES

The index is to passages quoted from the works listed.

BIBLE

MISHNAH

TOSEFTA

MIDRASH

JERUSALEM TALMUD

BABYLONIAN TALMUD

ARISTOTLE
Greek philosopher
Fourth century B.C.E.

PHILO JUDAEUS
Jewish philosopher
c. 20 B.C.E.—50 C.E.

POST-TALMUDIC AUTHORS

ABRABANEL, ISAAC
Fifteenth century biblical exegete, philosopher

ABRAHAM IBN EZRA
Twelfth century biblical exegete, philosopher

MALBIM
Meir Loeb ben Jehiel Michael
Nineteenth century biblical exegete

INDEX OF SUBJECTS